Intellectual Prope
Knowledge

MW01132293

After colonization, indigenous people faced an extractive property rights regime for both their land and knowledge. This book outlines that regime, and how the symbolic function of international intellectual property continues today to assist states to enclose indigenous people's knowledge. Drawing on more than 200 interviews, Peter Drahos examines the response of indigenous people to the colonizer's non-developmental property rights. The case studies reveal how they have adapted to the state's extractive order through a process of regulatory bricolage. In order to create a new developmental future for themselves, indigenous developmental networks have been forged – high-trust networks that include partnerships with science. *Intellectual Property, Indigenous People and their Knowledge* argues for a developmental intellectual property order for indigenous people based on a combination of simple rules, principles and a process of regulatory convening.

PETER DRAHOS is a professor at the Australian National University and holds a Chair in Intellectual Property at Queen Mary, University of London. He is a member of the Australian Academy of Social Sciences.

Cambridge Intellectual Property and Information Law

As its economic potential has rapidly expanded, intellectual property has become a subject of front-rank legal importance. *Cambridge Intellectual Property and Information Law* is a series of monograph studies of major current issues in intellectual property. Each volume contains a mix of international, European, comparative and national law, making this a highly significant series for practitioners, judges and academic researchers in many countries.

Series editors
Lionel Bently
Herchel Smith Professor of Intellectual Property Law,
University of Cambridge

William R. Cornish
Emeritus Herchel Smith Professor of Intellectual Property Law,
University of Cambridge

Advisory editors
François Dessemontet, Professor of Law, University of Lausanne
Paul Goldstein, Professor of Law, Stanford University
The Rt Hon. Sir Robin Jacob, Hugh Laddie Professor of Intellectual Property, University College, London

A list of books in the series can be found at the end of this volume.

Intellectual Property, Indigenous People and their Knowledge

Peter Drahos

CAMBRIDGE
UNIVERSITY PRESS

CAMBRIDGE
UNIVERSITY PRESS

University Printing House, Cambridge CB2 8BS, United Kingdom

One Liberty Plaza, 20th Floor, New York, NY 10006, USA

477 Williamstown Road, Port Melbourne, VIC 3207, Australia

314-321, 3rd Floor, Plot 3, Splendor Forum, Jasola District Centre, New Delhi - 110025, India

79 Anson Road, #06-04/06, Singapore 079906

Cambridge University Press is part of the University of Cambridge.

It furthers the University's mission by disseminating knowledge in the pursuit of education, learning and research at the highest international levels of excellence.

www.cambridge.org
Information on this title: www.cambridge.org/9781107686946

First published 2014
First paperback edition 2020

A catalogue record for this publication is available from the British Library

Library of Congress Cataloging in Publication data
Drahos, Peter, 1955- author.
Intellectual property, indigenous people and their knowledge / Peter Drahos.
    pages cm. – (Cambridge intellectual property and information law)
ISBN 978-1-107-05533-9 (Hardback)
1. Intellectual property.   2. Indigenous peoples–Legal status, laws, etc.
3. Traditional ecological knowledge.   I. Title.
K1401.5.D73 2014
346.04′8089–dc23   2013045303

ISBN 978-1-107-05533-9 Hardback
ISBN 978-1-107-68694-6 Paperback

For My Children,
Nikolai and Madeleine

Contents

Preface

We were sitting outside of a pub in Cooktown. Located in Queensland's far north, it is one of those places where a river meets the sea, offering the calmness of refuge from ocean storms. The place was named after Captain Cook, the explorer who filled in the bits of the Australian continent still missing from the maps drawn by European cartographers. Cook spent seven weeks there repairing his damaged ship. We had spent the day speaking to indigenous people about the possibilities for them in the bush food business. Tropical heat makes market gardening seem like too much hard work, but it does make the beer taste good. Squawking seagulls drifted in, keeping a sharp eye for the chance to steal a chip. 'Do you know what indigenous people around here call whitefellas?' asked one of the people who had arranged the meetings for us. Knowing I wouldn't know, he went on to answer the question. 'Seagulls.' 'Why?' I asked. 'Well,' he said, 'they fly in, create a lot of noise, make a mess and then fly out.' We flew out of Cooktown the next day.

After the visit to Cooktown I tried to make sure we didn't hire white four-wheel-drive vehicles. It proved surprisingly difficult. Flying in Qantas' white planes took on a different meaning.

We were in Cooktown as part of a project funded by the Australian Research Council. I was doing the project with my then colleague at RegNet, Luigi Palombi. We had become interested in examining the economic uses that indigenous people might make of their knowledge using intellectual property rights. Initially, establishing contact with indigenous groups proved difficult. Our first real break came when a member of a group we had been trying to see for weeks drove into Broome and got a flat tyre. We received a phone call asking if we wanted to meet with him. Tumbling out of our caravan we rushed to see him and that led to an invitation to visit his community. Over the course of the three years of the project we became smarter about finding ways to make contact with indigenous groups and things got progressively easier. Luigi and I have more than fifty years of experience in intellectual property issues between us. Perhaps word got about that we were useful seagulls. My lasting

ˉenous people we met was their basic kind-
˳ething remarkable given the horrors of

for his company on the road, as well as for the
ut this project. There is not the space to thank
, for conversations which acted as lightning strikes
˳y, I thank David Claudie, Nick Smith, Miranda
and Richard Jefferson. I owe special thanks to Susy
˳ we co-edited in 2011 a special issue of the journal
ell as a book published by ANU E Press in 2012 on the
˳nous knowledge and intellectual property. She has made a
˳oution to this field of research both through her publications
work with New Zealand's Waitangi Tribunal. Despite her many
˳itments, she found the time to read and comment on all the
˳pters, helping me to rethink my ideas and arguments. Finally,
ı thank my wife Julie Ayling who, amidst her own research in the fields
of organized crime and transnational environmental crime, found the
time to extend the patient support I needed to finish the book.

Abbreviations

Berne Convention	Berne Convention for the Protection of Literary and Artistic Works (1886, as revised)
CBD	Convention on Biological Diversity of 1992
Convention 169	Convention Concerning Indigenous and Tribal Peoples in Independent Countries (No. 169) (1989)
DCE	Convention on the Diversity of Cultural Expressions (2005)
FLO	Fairtrade Labelling Organizations International
GIs	Geographical Indications
ICH	Convention for the Safeguarding of the Intangible Cultural Heritage (2003)
IGC	Intergovernmental Committee on Intellectual Property and Genetic Resources, Traditional Knowledge and Folklore
ILO	International Labour Organization
IPC	International Patent Classification
Jarlmadangah Community	Jarlmadangah Burru Aboriginal Community
MA	Millennium Ecosystem Assessment
Nagoya Protocol	Nagoya Protocol on Access to Genetic Resources and the Fair and Equitable Sharing of Benefits Arising from their Utilization to the Convention on Biological Diversity (2010)
NCI	National Cancer Institute
NGOs	Non-governmental organizations
NIAAA	National Indigenous Arts Advocacy Association
NRSC	Natural Resources Stewardship Circle
PGR Treaty	International Treaty on Plant Genetic Resources for Food and Agriculture (2001)
The Code	Queensland Biotechnology Code of Ethics
TK	Traditional Knowledge

TKDL	Traditional Knowledge Digital Library
TRIPS Agreement	Agreement on Trade-Related Aspects of Intellectual Property Rights (1994)
UNDRIP	UN Declaration on the Rights of Indigenous Peoples
UNESCO	United Nations Educational, Scientific and Cultural Organization
UNFCCC	United Nations Framework Convention on Climate Change
WHC	World Heritage Convention (1972)
WIPO	World Intellectual Property Organization
WTO	World Trade Organization

1   The non-developmental state

1.1.   Extractive property

Economically successful states can be non-developmental for indigenous people. It may be that the state is always non-developmental for indigenous people. The pages of this book offer some reasons for formulating this strong claim, but they do not contain the data needed to test it. One would have to examine the history of many states. My case studies are mainly based on fieldwork carried out in Australia between 2008 and 2011, although I do draw on the literature that examines the experience of indigenous groups with state property orders in other countries, such as Canada and India. The case studies reveal a property order that remains extractive for Aboriginal and Torres Strait Islander people, albeit one that is masked by the complexity of property law.

But it is also a time of opportunity for Australia's indigenous people. As we will see in Chapter 4, the symbolic recognition of the value of their knowledge has never been greater. They have also regained some or most of the incidences of ownership over more of their land than at any other time in the history of colonization. The percentage of land in Australia owned or controlled by indigenous people is 16 per cent, with 98 per cent of this land being in very remote locations.[1] If they can overcome the danger of symbolic regulation that follows symbolic recognition, they may yet be able to find a better future for themselves. They are, the cases studies suggest, dealing with the effects of the state's extractive property order on their knowledge systems through a combination of secrecy and the formation of indigenous developmental networks.

As we will see, under extractive intellectual property systems indigenous people tend to end up in an economic no-man's-land. They face the problem of asset transfer under the public domains of intellectual

---

[1] Steering Committee for the Review of Government Service Provision, *Overcoming Indigenous Disadvantage: Key Indicators 2011* (Canberra: Productivity Commission, 2011), 56.

property systems, and they often fail to achieve ownership of an asset because they do not have the capacity to transform the asset in a way that is required under the rules of the system (for example, the inventive step requirement as applied to biotechnology inventions). One approach to this problem is to develop a sui generis system for indigenous knowledge. Within the World Intellectual Property Organization (WIPO) many states support the creation of such sui generis standards (see chapter 4). I argue that sui generis systems pose Weberian dangers of bureaucracy for indigenous people. Instead it might be better to contemplate adjustments to current intellectual property systems based on a combination of simple rules, principles and a system of regulatory convening (see chapter 5).

Returning to my opening claim, Australia, Canada, New Zealand and the United States are examples of prosperous states, but all four have living within their borders indigenous people that do poorly on socio-economic measures. For example, the United Nations Special Rapporteur in 2004 drew attention to the 'human development gaps' existing for indigenous people in Canada in areas such as health care, housing and education.[2] Australia has a long history of underdevelopment of its indigenous people. Faced by continuing poor outcomes on matters as basic as the mortality rates for indigenous children, the Australian federal and state governments in 2008 launched a long-term initiative called 'Closing the Gap'.[3] In New Zealand, socio-economic measures also paint a picture of disadvantage for indigenous people. So, for example, rates of suicide and incarceration amongst indigenous people remain disturbingly high.[4] In the United States, the census data for 2010 shows that approximately 28 per cent of American Indians and Alaska Natives were living in poverty compared to 15 per cent of people for the nation as a whole.[5]

The economic and social problems of indigenous people are not confined to these four states. A UN special report on the position of indigenous people in Asia offers the following bleak summary:

[2] See UN Commission on Human Rights, *Report of the Special Rapporteur on the situation of human rights and fundamental freedoms of indigenous people*, Rodolfo Stavenhagen, Mission to Canada, E/CN.4/2005/88/Add.3, 2 December 2004, available at http://daccess-dds-ny.un.org/doc/UNDOC/GEN/G05/100/26/PDF/G0510026.pdf?OpenElement.
[3] See www.coag.gov.au/closing_the_gap_in_indigenous_disadvantage.
[4] For the details see UN Human Rights Council, *Report of the Special Rapporteur on the rights of indigenous peoples, James Anaya. The Situation of Maori people in New Zealand*, A/HRC/18/35Add.4, 31 May 2011 available at www.ohchr.org/Documents/Issues/IPeoples/SR/A-HRC-18-35-Add4_en.pdf.
[5] Taken from the US Census Bureau, www.census.gov/newsroom/releases/archives/facts_for_features_special_editions/cb11-ff22.html.

Indigenous peoples in Asia are among the most discriminated against, socially and economically marginalized, and politically subordinated parts of the society in the countries where they live. … They are victims of serious human rights violations as a consequence of the dispossession of their lands and natural resources, widespread violence and repression, and assimilation.[6]

The evidence points to a globally persistent pattern of indigenous peoples' disadvantage that occurs in both developed and developing countries. This persistence in developed countries is striking because, on indices of institutional integrity relating to matters such as rule of law and control of corruption, Australia, Canada, New Zealand and the United States do very well.[7] What might explain the seemingly intractable problem of indigenous peoples' underdevelopment in rich states?

One influential idea within economic history is that it is institutions that set a country upon the path to rags or riches.[8] Private property rights are generally the heroes in this story. Institutions that provide individuals with the opportunity to make secure investment decisions at the micro level lead to the macro success of a country. However, institutions can also play the role of villain. Some institutional arrangements concentrate power in the hands of an elite few and allow this elite to prey on the economic efforts of the larger population. Termed 'extractive institutions' by Acemoglu et al., they generally reduce the growth prospects of a country.[9]

Acemoglu et al. use the distinction between secure property institutions and extractive institutions as part of a larger analysis aimed at explaining why the countries that were formerly linked to the flourishing economies of the Aztecs, Incas and Mughals experienced a decline in economic prosperity while countries that began as colonies (Australia, Canada, New Zealand and the United States) became much richer. The critical factor in explaining why these colonies prospered lies not in their

---

[6] UN Human Rights Council, *Report of the Special Rapporteur on the situation of human rights and fundamental freedoms of indigenous people, Rodolfo Stavenhagen, General considerations on the situation of human rights and fundamental freedoms of indigenous peoples in Asia*, A/HRC/6/15/Add.3, 1 November 2007, 4, available at http://daccess-dds-ny.un.org/doc/UNDOC/GEN/G07/148/22/PDF/G0714822.pdf?OpenElement.

[7] Results of various indices for these countries can be found at Transparency International's website at www.transparency.org as well as at the Worldwide Governance Indicators Project at http://info.worldbank.org/governance/wgi/index.asp.

[8] For examples of this line of argument see D. C. North and R. T. Thomas, *The Rise of the Western World* (London: Cambridge University Press, 1973); D.C. North, *Institutions, Institutional Change and Economic Performance* (Cambridge University Press, 1990).

[9] D. Acemoglu, S. Johnson and J. A. Robinson, 'Reversal of Fortune: Geography and Institutions in the Making of the Modern World Income Distribution', *Quarterly Journal of Economics*, 117 (2002), 1235.

geographical endowments but rather in their institutional inheritance. When colonists created property rules that were broadly enfranchising of individual productivity they set a colony upon a long-run growth path. Where they established extractive institutions, as did the Spanish and Portuguese in the Americas, they created the conditions for long-term decline. The choice between establishing productive property rights and extractive ones was heavily affected by population density and whether or not Europeans decided to settle in the colony in large numbers.[10] In places where Europeans became populous, they were more likely to end up with property arrangements that were less discriminatory as amongst themselves than if they were an elite minority seeking to subjugate an indigenous population.

In the colonies that became rich, the colonists progressively created an autonomous legal system. Such a system is characterized by a formal independence from politics and a commitment to rules as tools of governance, accountability and procedure.[11] A property order embedded in autonomous law meets the economist's ideal of well-defined and secure property rights. However, as we will see in the case of Australia, autonomous law's promise of secure property institutions for the colonists has not been extended to indigenous people. Instead indigenous people have had to adapt to an extractive property order that has institutionalized insecurity for their assets. This basic line of argument occupies the first four chapters of the book. The central challenge for indigenous people is to find ways in which to overcome the disadvantages of a property order of the state that is largely non-developmental for them in terms of economic opportunities.

For present purposes, the concept of an extractive property order refers to property systems in which the systems allow one group (the extractor group) to obtain control of assets belonging to a second group without the extractor group obtaining consent and offering proper compensation for the asset transfer. The second group is made worse off and the extractor group is made better off. An extractive property system can also contain rules that prevent a particular group from gaining ownership of assets. Over the course of history indigenous people, women and religious groups have had their property rights restricted by extractor groups. Extractive property systems exclude particular groups from participation in economic life because they cut groups off from the ownership of productive assets.

[10] *Ibid.*, 1231.
[11] P. Nonet and P. Selznick, *Law and Society in Transition: Toward Responsive Law* (New York: Harper & Row, 1978), 54.

Systems rather than institutions are the focus in the extractive property concept. Institutions are sometimes linked to the rules or constraints, both formal and informal, that shape human interaction.[12] One could substitute institutions for systems in the concept of an extractive property order without changing the concept too much, but the term systems does a better job of capturing the integrated complexity of property rules. The systems complexity of modern intellectual property aids extractor groups. Pharmaceutical companies, for example, use the complexity of the patent system to extract massive rents from assets that rightly belong in the public domain and should be the subject of competitive rather than monopoly pricing.[13] The use of systems also draws attention to the fact that alongside rules there are other components, such as actors and values, in a given property system that contribute to its extractive function. The effects of the patent system, for example, do not just depend on its many rules, but on the behaviour of patent offices and patent attorneys.

The case studies and examples presented in the chapters that follow focus on indigenous knowledge assets and the use of intellectual property rights by indigenous people in economic enterprises of their own making. Assets are resources that can be used to generate a flow of income.[14] They can be divided into tangible assets such as real property and intangible assets such as reputation and knowledge. The claim that the property orders of states have been extractive for indigenous people is easy to understand and illustrate using the case of land. Many indigenous groups around the world have lost ownership of their traditional lands and territories to states, a fact recognized by states in the sixth opening paragraph of the United Nations Declaration on the Rights of Indigenous Peoples: 'indigenous peoples have suffered from historic injustices as a result of, inter alia, their colonization and dispossession of their lands, territories and resources'.

How are intellectual property systems extractive when it comes to indigenous peoples' knowledge assets? There are examples in Australia where indigenous people have used copyright to protect their artistic works.[15] These cases suggest that intellectual property systems might

---

[12] D. C. North, *Institutions, Institutional Change and Economic Performance* (Cambridge University Press, 1990), 5.

[13] See Federal Trade Commission, 'Pay-for-delay: How drug company pay-offs cost consumers billions', An FTC Staff Study (Washington, DC, January 2010).

[14] R. Cooter and T. Ulen, *Law and Economics*, 3rd edn. (Reading, MA: Addison Wesley Longman, 2000), 39.

[15] For a critical discussion see K. Bowery, 'Indigenous Culture, Knowledge and Intellectual Property: The Need for a New Category of Rights?' in K. Bowery,

offer indigenous people some security of property in some contexts. They gain security of property for objects that fit the criteria of commodification to be found in these systems. But as the next section makes clear intellectual property systems continue to have extractive effects for indigenous people.

1.2. Extractive intellectual property

While there are many differences of detail amongst different kinds of intellectual property rights such as copyright, designs, patents, trade marks, plant breeders' rights and so on, from an economic perspective all these rights deal with a free-rider problem. A rational economic agent will not invest in making a film, a design or an invention, or in building up the name of a business, if another economic agent can acquire the benefits of these investments for free by, for example, copying the film or manufacturing the invention without having paid the R&D cost. If society does nothing to address the free-rider problem, not enough resources will be devoted to innovation of various kinds.[16] Intellectual property rights, by creating some form of exclusivity, enable their owners to make a private return on their investment. They enable private rent riding. At the same time the social benefits of innovation are only fully realized if an innovation is widely diffused, the diffusion of life-saving medicines being an obvious example of the importance of diffusion to social gain. The mechanism of diffusion within capitalist systems is primarily the market. Markets deal with the problem of private rent riding through competition. In theory, private rents should be dissipated. In order for diffusion to take place, the owners of intellectual property rights cannot through these rights acquire absolutist power. Instead, all intellectual property rights have rules that in one way or another allow for the possibility of their subject matter of protection being returned to the market, or not being removed from the market in the first place.

The rules of intellectual property can be seen as creating a series of relative public domains in which producers know, for example, that under the rules of the patent system an invention has lost the exclusivity conferred upon it by patent rules. Public domains are best thought of as being relative to an intellectual property system. The claim that

M. Handler and D. Nicol (eds.), *Emerging Challenges in Intellectual Property* (Melbourne: Oxford University Press, 2011), 46.

[16] But there are those who argue that markets will perform better without intellectual property monopolies. See M. Boldrin and D. K. Levine, *Against Intellectual Monopoly* (New York: Cambridge University Press, 2008).

something is in the public domain should be read as saying that, for the purposes of a given system such as copyright or patents, the relevant subject matter in question has lost the degree of exclusivity conferred upon it by the system (or it may not have fallen within the protection of the system in the first place).

The public domains of intellectual property are profoundly important to a basic value that has been important in the common law tradition, the freedom of commerce. One can illustrate this using Hohfeld's theory of rights. Copyright is an example of a system that limits the duration of protection and does not extend protection to ideas. In Hohfeldian terms, my right to reproduce works out of copyright or to write detective novels drawing on the ideas of Dashiell Hammett and Raymond Chandler is a liberty (privilege).[17] The correlative of liberty is 'no-right', i.e. copyright owners have no-rights to prevent the exercise of this liberty. Liberties are foundational to the operation of markets. Everyone has a liberty to use ideas to create works (not a claim-right since this would imply a duty on others not to use the idea) and can compete in doing so. Seen in terms of liberties, it is clear that the public domains of intellectual property are fundamental to the operation of markets and consumer interests. Intellectual property rights are rights that interfere in the freedom of commerce because they create duties of non-interference (rights have correlative duties). If we value freedom of commerce and markets then intellectual property rights cannot assume the form of absolutist monarchs, but have to be weakened in some way so that the liberties upon which markets depend ultimately prevail. It is the combination of liberties and no-rights that allows markets to drive down, for example, the cost of medicines that have fallen out of patent protection or books in which the copyright has expired.

Turning now to the protection of knowledge in indigenous societies in Australia, the first point to make is that knowledge is part of an ancestral place-time cosmology, something discussed in detail in chapter 2. Powerful ancestors have transformed the land into a territorial cosmos in which they remain present as active forces, with various geographical features such as waterholes, rock formations and hills marking their transformative work. The human inhabitants of these territories have to understand, respect and care for these territories (territories become divided into Countries, a basic unit of ownership by individual groups). Senior indigenous people are part of long chains of custody of knowledge

---

[17] In Hohfeld's jural scheme, liberty and privilege are equivalent. See W. N. Hohfeld, 'Some Fundamental Legal Conceptions As Applied In Judicial Reasoning', *Yale Law Journal*, 23 (1913), 16, 36.

about Country and ancestors that they impart in various ways to others in order to ensure that the chain of knowledge continues. These senior people carefully stage and control the release of knowledge. Senior people can also draw on ancestral power through the use of songs, ritual, designs and sacred objects.[18] The concepts that dominate the use of knowledge in this world are duty and permission. Senior people have duties in this ancestral system to ensure that the chain of custody of knowledge is maintained and that the ancestral system is used wisely to help indigenous groups adapt to change. It is also clear from the historical evidence that this system of permissions and duties did not prevent the rise of economically beneficial trading networks across Australia and beyond.[19] Access to knowledge, along with use of things such as songs and designs are generally governed by conditional permission (use for a specific purpose) rather than what the lawyer would call a transfer of legal title. This is not so much a world of resources over which there is 'community title' as a world in which the use of knowledge and resources by individuals is governed by a web of duties and use-permissions steered by knowledgeable people.

One way in which to think about indigenous knowledge in this system is to imagine concentric circles made up of individuals. Those in the innermost circle are the most knowledgeable people (often referred to as elders). They have arrived in the inner circle through a life-long process of initiation. Those individuals who occupy the outer rings are at different stages of their initiation journeys. In those cases where this system still survives indigenous people see themselves as part of unbroken chains of custody of knowledge and accompanying duties that in their minds go back many thousands of years. The primary duties of those in the inner circle are to continue the chain of custody so that those who come after will know what to do to keep their Countries (estates) healthy. Elders have a paramount duty of care to keep Country healthy, a duty that is owed to the ancestors in the chain. It is probably not helpful to think about this system too much in Hohfeldian terms, but if a correlative right is required one can say ancestors and Country have rights to certain services that will keep Country healthy for past, present and future generations. The important point here is that it is this inner circle that has responsibility for the purposive steering of an ancestral system for a

---

[18] I. Keen, 'Ancestors, Magic and Exchange in Yolngu Doctrines: Extensions of the Person in Time and Space', *Journal of the Royal Anthropological Institute*, 12 (2006), 515, 523.
[19] See M. Langton, O. Mazel and L. Palmer, 'The "Spirit" of the Thing: The Boundaries of Aboriginal Economic Relations at Australian Common Law', *Australian Journal of Anthropology*, 17 (2006), 307.

given territory, including responsibility for adapting land tenure systems to changing circumstances.[20] Such inner circles would have stretched across Australia in a networked fashion prior to colonization. Native title in Australia is probably less a bundle of customary rights and more a system of knowledge in which the most knowledgeable have the authority to make decisions for their particular ancestral territory. While one can describe an indigenous knowledge system in terms of rights and correlative duties, it may be better to think simply of duties and conditional permissions as lying at the centre of the system. These conditional permissions may be very strong for some resource uses and appear to function as rights to outsiders. However, if the claim that knowledge is at the centre of the ancestral system is correct then those in the outer concentric circles would likely be given permissions rather than an exclusive right. Ancestral systems made up of primary duties to Countries, along with permissions that confer entitlements of varying strength may help to explain why indigenous groups were able to adapt to the great droughts and ice ages that occurred during their 50,000-year occupation of Australia. For a social system to be able to cope with such large-scale environmental changes, it had to have both the stability of structure and the mechanisms to deal with environmental changes.

If now we overlay ancestral systems with systems of intellectual property rights we can see how extractive transfers of knowledge assets may occur. An image on a rock of an ancestor generated long ago by custodians in the chain of knowledge may continue to remain important in ceremonies, with only the initiated having permission to use the image. Under an ancestral system access to and use of the image remains the subject of restrictions. Under copyright law the image as an artistic work enters a public domain in which there are liberties to use and correlative 'no-rights' to prevent use after a period of life of the author plus seventy years. Indigenous knowledge reported as scientific facts in journals and other publications enters a public domain that may have all sorts of ripple effects for indigenous people's knowledge assets as economic assets. The Northern Territory's Biological Resources Act of 2006, for example, extinguishes knowledge as an indigenous person's knowledge if it is to be found in the public domain.[21]

The patent system provides another example of a possible asset transfer. A plant in an ancestral system may be part of a long chain of custody

---

[20] For examples of the work of this inner circle see P. Sutton, 'The Robustness of Aboriginal Land Tenure Systems: Underlying and Proximate Customary Titles', *Oceania*, 67 (1996), 7, 15–20.

[21] See paragraph 29(2)(b).

in which successive generations of indigenous women pass on knowledge and duties of care for the plant. In this kind of system there is no sharp dividing line between the natural and social world. Instead, there is a territorial cosmos in which the human and non-human members are part of an integrated system. For the purposes of patent law the plant exists in a natural world, its genetic information constituting a discovery, a discovery open to all to use for the purposes of patentable invention. The public domain of the patent system is a deeply chronological one in which protection begins with an event (first filing) and is projected to run into the future based on a calculation a company makes about the cost of renewal versus the benefit of renewal of the patent. While indigenous systems of knowledge vary in the way that they structure secrecy within a group, they probably all share the feature that the entry of knowledge into a group does not entail a loss of control over that knowledge. An open secret in an indigenous group does mean it is open to anyone to use, in stark contrast to the knowledge in a public domain. Some knowledge within an ancestral system may over time become more diffused, but the system itself remains linked to a permanent presence of ancestral forces, a system in which there are no clocks that set limits on the duration of protection.[22] This conception of time and knowledge is very different to a chronological approach to protection in which the system shifts dramatically from strong monopolistic protection to no protection of knowledge.

The liberties that structure the public domains of intellectual property systems can bring about the non-consensual asset transfers of indigenous people's knowledge and material assets. The effects of intellectual property are part of the cumulative effects of the state's property order on indigenous people. The poor developmental position of indigenous groups described in the previous section is hardly puzzling when the extractive effects of state property orders on the tangible and intangible assets of indigenous people is summed. Plants that were important assets in their pre-colonial economies slip away from their control because indigenous people lose their land and their plants enter the public domains of intellectual property. There is also something that a summing of economic losses does not capture, and that is the effects of these extractive property orders upon the authority of indigenous people's ancestral systems. Their fight for the return of their assets is not just a fight for economic independence, although this is vitally important. It is also a fight to preserve or rebuild ancestral systems of decision making. In

---

[22] H. Morphy, *Ancestral Connections: Art and an Aboriginal System of Knowledge* (Chicago and London: University of Chicago Press, 1991), 89.

the case of Australia, these systems have helped them to adapt to changes over thousands of years of continuous occupation of the land.

There is the making of a deep dilemma here because as Maskus and Reichman have written, the relentless rise and spread of intellectual property standards 'requires a collective response aimed at preserving the roles of both knowledge and competition as international public goods'.[23] Should we create special intellectual property systems for indigenous people? My answer to this comes in two parts. If states do nothing to address the problem created by extractive property rights for indigenous people the state will remain non-developmental for indigenous people with all the familiar problems of poverty and inequality that this entails. At the same time, as chapter 5 argues, it should be possible to improve the asset position of indigenous people through a combination of simple rules, especially veto rules that will improve their bargaining power over their assets. For reasons that will become clear there are too many dangers associated with the creation of entire new systems of intellectual property protection for indigenous people. They already have ancestral systems that have served them well for tens of thousands of years.

1.3.   Extractive property and autonomous law

The opening section pointed out that autonomous law is important to the productive effects of property. Does the emergence of autonomous law offer prospects for reducing extractive behaviour by states when it comes to regulating indigenous peoples' assets? Autonomous law has clearly been important to progress on the protection and expansion of the rights of indigenous people in countries such as Canada, New Zealand and the United States, where treaties were negotiated with indigenous groups, albeit under conditions of unequal bargaining power. Perhaps autonomous law has been even more important in cases where treaties were not concluded, the Australian High Court's recognition of native title in the *Mabo* case being an example.[24]

But there is another way to view the role of autonomous law in settler states. Far from taming the exercise of power by the state over indigenous property rights, the autonomous legal order sets up the conditions under

---

[23] K. E. Maskus and J. H. Reichman, 'The Globalization of Private Knowledge Goods and the Privatization of Global Public Goods', in K. E. Maskus and J. H. Reichman (eds.), *International Public Goods and Transfer of Technology Under a Globalized Intellectual Property Regime* (Cambridge University Press, 2005), 3, 43.

[24] *Mabo v Queensland (No 2)* (1992) 175 CLR 1.

which indigenous peoples' property rights can be legitimately extinguished and circumscribed. Instead of remedying the extractive nature of the property rights system, the autonomous legal order legitimates its operation through subtle rule-based adjustments. New property rights emerge through bargaining contests amongst business elites and the capitalist state. Sometimes business elites move beyond simple bargaining and into sophisticated strategies of private governance, as in the case of the governance strategies that spawned the Agreement on the Trade-Related Aspects of Intellectual Property Rights, 1994 (TRIPS Agreement).[25] The extraordinary growth in intellectual property laws during the course of the twentieth century, which shows little sign of changing in the twenty-first, is an example of capitalism's perpetual motion of property rules. Reducing the extractive impact of property rights on indigenous people represents the greatest challenge for autonomous law because the extractive function of property is so important to the state and its partner elites. In the case of property rules, the separation of law and politics, which is one of autonomous law's chief features, is a thin separation, more like a curtain than a wall, offering courts the clearest glimpses of the needs of the political order in which they serve.[26]

As we will see from the case studies in this book, indigenous groups still face the risk of extractive behaviour. This risk, as my discussion in chapter 9 of India's traditional digital knowledge library suggests, is not confined to settler states. Autonomous law does two things. From time to time it recognizes, as the Australian High Court did in *Mabo*, an interest of justice capable of being protected by a right derived from the system of autonomous law. But for the most part autonomous law operates as a rule-adjustment system that serves the structural processes of capitalism. Propertization remains the most fundamental of these processes.[27]

So, while autonomous law is sufficiently open to bring moments of justice to indigenous groups, it does not produce a property order that is developmental for indigenous people. Instead there is a non-linear process of rule adjustment in which for moments of justice there are subsequent losses. The High Court moves away from the common law declaratory implications of discovering native title and into statute-led rule forensics that better serve the interests of the state.[28] The declaratory

---

[25] See P. Drahos with J. Braithwaite, *Information Feudalism: Who Owns the Knowledge Economy?* (London: Earthscan, 2002).

[26] On the importance of this separation, but also its limits see Nonet and Selznick, *Law and Society*, 59–60.

[27] J. Braithwaite and P. Drahos, *Global Business Regulation* (Cambridge University Press, 2000), 143.

[28] *Western Australia v Ward* (2002) 213 CLR 1.

discovery of native title in *Mabo* is the discovery of duty-based ancestral systems in which knowledge and land had become integrated to form a territorial cosmos. Duties towards it were the bedrock of the social systems that were developed for its study and understanding. Those who understood the laws of this cosmos the best, who became the most knowledgeable, became the law decision makers. It is hard for us to penetrate this cosmos with Hohfeldian inference rules about rights and duties or metaphors of property as a bundle of rights. Indigenous people were in some sense owned by the areas that their ancestors had created. Successive generations of duty bearers drawing on their knowledge devised complex systems of permissions to enable life and adaptation for the territorial cosmos for which they were responsible. What we would think of as customary rights over knowledge were indissolubly linked to what we think of as customary rights over land. Knowledge was at the very centre of what we call native title. To limit the recognition of native title to land is to only partially recognize it.

Perhaps the cycles of crisis and renewal, which Schumpeter suggested would completely transform the institutions of capitalism, will deliver a more equitable capitalist order for indigenous people. Perhaps not. As we will see, some indigenous groups are making more and more use of networks as part of their development plans. I term these 'indigenous developmental networks'. Faced by a state that is operating with a non-developmental property order, indigenous groups are compensating by organizing into developmental networks. Through colonization, states have enclosed the stateless societies of indigenous peoples along with their resources. Autonomous law cannot engineer the recognition of an independent sovereignty of these once stateless societies, especially one that threatens the property order of the state. But through developmental networks indigenous groups can increase their capacity to manage their knowledge assets under the property rules of the state.

Indigenous developmental networks face two key tasks when it comes to exploiting knowledge assets. The first is to develop a strategy of protection and the second is to enrol capacity into the network so that the full value of the asset can be understood for the purposes of exploiting it in non-indigenous systems of governance and regulation. We live, as a growing body of scholarship shows, in an era of regulatory capitalism where all the products that we buy, from food and medicines to the clothes that we wear, are the objects of multiple regulatory standards and systems.[29] This places huge capacity demands on those wishing to

---

[29] See D. Levi-Faur and J. Jordana (eds.), 'The Rise of Regulatory Capitalism: The Global Diffusion of a New Order', *The Annals* 598 (2005), 6–217; J. Braithwaite, *Regulatory*

enter markets with new products and services. In the case of indigenous people, meeting this capacity demand is contingent upon indigenous developmental networks forging close relations with science (see chapter 11). Indigenous people have to find ways to fit their knowledge assets into existing regulatory systems such as food and drug regulation or economic governance systems such as carbon markets or trade in eco-system services. This requires their assets to have a lot of what we might call epistemic mobility and can really only be achieved in cooperation with science.

There is another important reason why indigenous people see value in developmental networks. When one is confronted by small businesses a perfectly natural question from an economic growth perspective is to ask how one might scale up such businesses. Achieving economies of scale in order to lower costs of production is part of the natural growth logic of markets. The interviews I and Luigi Palombi conducted with indigenous groups (see next section) certainly confirmed that indigenous groups want economic independence from the state. Many are tired of or unhappy with receiving 'sit down money' (welfare payments) because they see its effects on their children. But there is for indigenous people an all-important issue of scale. They want a scale of business that preserves those things that they really care about – their 'Country' and their children. Controlling the scale of development is important to them. Indigenous developmental networks might be one way in which to manage scale.

1.4.   Data gathering

Jon Altman argues that the development problem facing Aboriginal people can better be understood through the use of an analytical frame-work that he calls the 'hybrid economy'.[30] In this framework the econ-omy consists of three sectors; the market, the state and the customary economy. Indigenous economic activity is best analysed in terms of the interactions and linkages amongst these three sectors. Activities within the customary economy such as hunting, gathering, fishing and trad-itional land management practices generate value, but quantifying this value in monetary terms may be difficult if the activity, as in the case of

Capitalism: How It Works, Ideas For Making It Work Better (Cheltenham: Edward Elgar, 2008).

[30] J. Altman, 'Development Options on Aboriginal Land: Sustainable Indigenous Hybrid Economies in the Twenty-First Century' in L. Taylor, G. K. Ward, G. Henderson, R. Davis and L. A. Wallis (eds.), *The Power of Knowledge, The Resonance of Tradition* (Canberra: Aboriginal Studies Press, 2005), 34.

traditional fire burning, generates benefits that cannot be captured through the market. One of Altman's key points is that growing the hybrid economy will require a focus on the linkages between the market and customary sectors.[31]

Between 2008 and 2010, along with Luigi Palombi, I conducted fieldwork in Australia, meeting with and interviewing indigenous and non-indigenous people. The fieldwork took place in the cities of Adelaide, Brisbane, Canberra, Darwin, Melbourne, Perth and Sydney, as well as central Australia (including Alice Springs), Queensland's Gulf Country (including Townsville), the Kimberley region in Western Australia (including Broome) and in South Australia in the Ceduna area. In 2011 I did some follow-up interviews. The number of informants interviewed for this project was 210.

The purpose of the interviews was to obtain data on the problems facing Aboriginal groups in cases where they wanted to use knowledge assets generated in the customary sector for the purposes of building an enterprise in the market sector. More specifically, we wanted to understand the effects of Australia's intellectual property regime on their capacity to exploit knowledge assets in the hybrid economy. To this end we spoke to indigenous entrepreneurs who were using plant knowledge to start or run a business, leaders in indigenous communities who were using the patent system as part of a business strategy, members of Aboriginal corporations[32] who had been or were involved in aspects of the bush food business, traditional land owners, and people working in land councils.[33] We gained insights into the regulatory effects of Australia's property systems on indigenous knowledge assets by interviewing individuals from state and federal government departments working on indigenous affairs, native title, biodiscovery, business development and the environment (this included departments with responsibility for water). We also followed the network connections of actors where our initial interviews suggested that these actors were part of a network that was important to understanding the use of indigenous knowledge assets. This led us, for example, to interview scientists researching fire or plant compounds, ethnobotanists, people working on biodiscovery in museums and herbaria and people in law firms involved in the

---

[31] *Ibid.*, 38–9.
[32] There are a range of incorporation options for indigenous people at both Federal and State level in Australia. See www.oric.gov.au/Content.aspx?content=CATSI-Act/default.htm&menu=catsi&class=catsi&selected=About%20the%20CATSI%20Act.
[33] Land councils are incorporated peak regional community organizations that provide an extensive range of services around the two basic goals of helping Aboriginal groups to regain land rights and then work with the land.

commercialization process. By following these network tracks we gained a fuller picture of the use that various networks in Australia make of indigenous knowledge assets.

Why did we focus on interviewing as many groups as we could in as many locations as we could? Our starting assumption was that we were confronted by a situation of diversity. We were assuming that the representativeness of a given indigenous group or individual for the broader indigenous population would be low. One can use the presence of different languages as a rough indicator of cultural diversity. Estimates of the number of languages spoken prior to colonization are in the order of 200–300, and 500–600 if dialects are included.[34] The number of languages surviving today appears to be under one hundred.[35] Under the assumption of diversity it followed that it was better to increase the number of groups and individuals for interview. The scale of diversity of Aboriginal group identity and social organization is something that is easily missed because our labels for indigenous groups lull us into assumptions of homogeneity. So, for example, Yolngu is generally used to refer to the Aboriginal population of North-East Arnhem Land, but the Yolgnu themselves, Howard Morphy has pointed out, use the names of smaller groups such as the clan or dialect group when speaking about groups to which they belong.[36] These clans have their own 'Countries' (areas of land or estates) to which they are specially linked.

Our interviews with indigenous people ended up covering far more than just intellectual property. Stories of the colonization process would often be related. The experience of colonization as an inter-generational memory appears to be strong. The problems of Australia's native title system, not surprisingly, were often mentioned. Gaining access to credit in order to start a small business was another issue that emerged. It was most often mentioned by indigenous women.[37] Our impression was that it is easier for indigenous men to borrow hundreds of thousands of dollars to invest in cattle stations than it is for an indigenous woman to borrow $5,000 to buy equipment so that she can extract oils from plants. Many of the problems we heard about are typical ones faced by any

---

[34] P. McConvell and N. Thieberger, *State of Indigenous Languages in Australia – 2001* (Australia, Canberra, State of the Environment Second Technical Paper Series (Natural and Cultural Heritage), Department of the Environment and Heritage, 2001), 16 available at www.environment.gov.au/node/21437.

[35] *Ibid.*   [36] Morphy, *Ancestral Connections*, 40.

[37] For a discussion of this issue see S. McDonnell, *Indigenous Women Entrepreneurs Within Torres Strait* (Discussion Paper No. 188, Centre for Aboriginal Economic Policy Research, ANU, 1999) available at http://caepr.anu.edu.au/sites/default/files/Publications/DP/1999_DP188.pdf.

small-business entrepreneur. They are harder for indigenous people living in remote locations to overcome because services such as financial services are hardly present, and it is difficult to access needed training in the skills to start and run a business (for example, how to write a business plan). This is also a small-business world complicated by kinship relations. We were told that traditional land owners can and do extract payments from indigenous business owners, something that causes resentment: 'If they [traditional owners] don't get off their arses they don't get a cut'; 'I'm not a bloody bank' (indigenous interviewees).

Business success brings another set of complications: 'you're acting white; you wanna be white' (indigenous interviewee). Economic success for an indigenous community appears to depend heavily on whether there is a leadership group planning for the future that is prepared to use company structures so that money can be reinvested for the community rather than redistributed within a community. It is critical that there be a leadership group. The price for one person trying to do all the work is exhaustion, burn-out and illness.

In 2006, of the 6 per cent of indigenous people who were self-employed in Australia, almost 90 per cent were located in urban and semi-urban areas.[38] The support services and networks for indigenous people wishing to start a business will probably improve as large businesses such as banks and mining companies develop programmes to assist indigenous individuals to pursue a business idea. For some time, state governments in Australia have had indigenous business advisory units, but more crucial to the long-term success of indigenous business entrepreneurship will be the creation of personal networks between experienced people from the Australian business community as genuine mentors and indigenous people wanting to take on the risks of running their own enterprise.

When we did get on to the topic of intellectual property and indigenous knowledge with our indigenous interviewees, three things became clear. The first is that many, if not all, indigenous people believe that the colonizers began a process of systematic misappropriation and misuse of indigenous knowledge assets. One interviewee put it this way: 'Our knowledge was exploited the minute white people set foot on Australia. It allowed white settlers to survive.'

The second is that indigenous people have a clear view that these knowledge assets are their intellectual property. At first, and somewhat

---

[38] *Indigenous Small Business Owners in Australia* (Canberra: Australian Taxation Office, 2009), 5, available at www.ato.gov.au/Business/Starting-and-running-your-small-business/In-detail/Industry-specific/Indigenous-small-business-owners-in-Australia/.

dimly on our part, we did not understand what indigenous people meant by their references to 'our intellectual property' or statements such as 'Intellectual property is everything we do'. But it became clear that for them their intellectual property does not depend on the intellectual property statutes that the colonizers transplanted from the UK, but rather on their systems of knowledge governance. The norms that guide the use and exploitation of indigenous people's knowledge are not the state's intellectual property laws, or even Ehrlich's 'living law' since this would implicate state law as a potential source of social analogues of law.[39] Instead, their intellectual property is constituted by ancestral law. For indigenous people achieving full recognition for 'their intellectual property' is not simply a matter of recognizing an economic claim. It is about recognizing an ancestral decision-making system that in various forms has been with them for a long time. It is about making sure that the Australian state treats their knowledge in the correct way. Many older indigenous people see the recognition of indigenous knowledge as vital to gaining the respect and interest of their children in a system of knowledge that seems to many of the younger generation to hold no economic promise, to hold no status for them in the modern world. Obtaining this recognition is part of a long-term agenda that will not disappear any time soon. One can expect patient persistence from them on this issue. Ancestral law should not be subsumed under the category of customary law for the reasons I explain in the next section.

The third thing to emerge clearly from the interviews was how little trust indigenous people have in Australia's intellectual property systems. Our interviews suggest that they are resorting to secrecy when it comes to protecting their knowledge assets. Does this matter? Is it a good strategy? Chapter 11 suggests some answers.

1.5.   Ancestral systems and customary law

Ancestral law should be separated from customary law, at least for present purposes. British common law is an example of a customary law system, but as we will see in chapter 2 the ancestral law of Aboriginal people has radically different cosmologies.[40] These cosmologies refer to a set of doctrines, precepts or directions left by ancestors for finding the

---

[39] Ehrlich used the concept of living law to refer to the normative analogues of state law constructed by people in their daily life. E. Ehrlich, *Fundamental Principles of the Sociology of Law* (1936), W. L. Moll, trans. (New Brunswick: Transaction, 2002).

[40] For a discussion of common law as customary law see R. Cotterrell, *The Politics of Jurisprudence: A Critical Introduction to Legal Philosophy* (London and Edinburgh: Butterworths, 1989), 27–30.

correct way or path in the world.[41] To add a further level of complexity, the evidence shows that Aboriginal languages did not contain simple equivalents to law.[42] Ancestral law does not fit particularly well into a Western jurisprudential typology of law. This is in part because this law appears to describe forces that can be harnessed by individuals to help bring about physical consequences in the world. Ancestral power can be drawn on by various means such as the singing of a song or the performance of a dance to help cure illness, to protect oneself or to attack one's enemy.[43] Ancestors remain in some form active agents in the world. It may be that it is better to speak of ancestral systems of which law in a variety of senses is a part. Ancestral law is more akin to a causal system of connections and consequences that individuals must understand if they are to survive and prosper. It is a system of binding guidance bequeathed to people by ancestors to help them make correct selections when confronted by problems and troubles. Once cut off from this ancestral system one loses one's way in life. It is this ancestral system that remains a source of authority for many Aboriginal people. The connection to this ancestral system remains strong because the connection with ancestors remains strong.

One implication of this distinction between customary law and ancestral systems of decision making is that it becomes more important to find indigenous people who know this system and less important to be engaged in the positivistic enterprise of codifying knowledge about customary practice. Court-based searches for customary solutions to conflicts will rely heavily on deductive or inferential processes involving rules as inputs. In an ancestral system, kinship relations link individuals to particular ancestors who reside in places and objects. When conflict about the use of a specific place or object occurs, it is those with the knowledge of the ancestral purposes for that place or object who are authorized to arrive at a solution. The use of resources by indigenous people is, where an ancestral system still operates, closely linked to ancestral purposes. In the hands of a state's law agencies the search for customary law is full of danger for indigenous people.[44] Those who find and declare the customary law risk turning it into static rules whether

---

[41] I. Keen, *Aboriginal Economy and Society: Australia at the Threshold of Colonisation* (South Melbourne, Vic: Oxford University Press, 2004), 211–12.

[42] Sutton, 'The Robustness of Aboriginal Land Tenure Systems, 7, 8–9; Keen, *Aboriginal Economy*, 212.

[43] Keen, 'Ancestors, Magic and Exchange', 515, 518–19.

[44] For discussion of courts and proof of customary law, see L. Sheleff, *The Future of Tradition: Customary Law, Common Law and Legal Pluralism* (London, Portland, OR: Frank Cass, 1999), ch. 19.

they intend to or not. Moreover, there is no guarantee that a court using rules of legal inference applied to whatever customary law propositions have made it into the courtroom will arrive at the same solution as a group of knowledgeable indigenous people reasoning about the application of ancestral purpose to the same problem.

At a practical level this does mean the agencies of the state keeping things out of the courts and working with those indigenous people who know the ancestral system and can use it to help indigenous groups adapt to the future. For state agencies, finding those with this knowledge is far from easy. In the words of one departmental official from South Australia describing the search process,

'Most of it's through the school of hard knocks. It took months of consultation to get a name and it turned out to be the wrong person.'

The same official then went on to describe the anger and criticism they would receive from indigenous groups for dealing with the wrong people. But, I would argue, it is still better to go through this 'school of hard knocks' to find those who know ancestral systems of decision making. The evidence from Australia's pre-history suggests a story of constant change and adaptation by indigenous groups.[45] Ancestral decision-making systems were an integral part of how indigenous groups reorganized to meet change over the 50,000 years or so of their occupation of Australia. This suggests that the most important feature of these systems is not their capacity to generate custom, but rather to generate adaptive behaviour and new conventions to deal with change.

Perhaps the most important reason for focusing on ancestral systems is that it helps us to understand that the Westphalian state, in the eyes of those indigenous groups in which the ancestral system remains strong, simply lacks the authority to make laws over the resources it is enclosing. When a plant has ancestral status for an indigenous group, that group will, if the system of ancestral law is still strong in that group, simply not recognize the authority of state law over that plant. Ancestral systems allow for changes in the customary uses of ancestral plants, but those changes have to be the outcome of negotiations by those who carry consensual authority within the system. State laws that permit, for example, the patent ownership of ancestral plants represent an illegitimate interference in a cosmological system in which indigenous people owe duties of care to their ancestors and to the living when making decisions about future plant uses. Decisions about these future uses have

---

[45] The evidence is brought together in P. Hiscock, *Archaeology of Ancient Australia* (London and New York: Routledge, 2008).

to emerge out of a kinship network in which those charged with the exercise of authority on behalf of the network fulfil their duties to the network and to ancestors. When, for example, the University of Hawaii took out patents over genetically modified varieties of taro there were protests from many groups in Hawaii because the first taro plant (kalo) was an ancestor by the name of Haloa.[46] The university found itself in the middle of public controversy, the researchers defending themselves on the basis that they were simply modifying kalo, as had Hawaiians through many centuries of cross-breeding. But this was not an answer in the eyes of the Hawaiian protest groups. For them, the university was making decisions about ownership of kalo for which it lacked authority.

One effect of an ancestral system is that future uses of resources that are likely to have widespread effects on groups have to be properly discussed. As we will see in chapter 2, ancestral systems spread duties of care over living organisms amongst many indigenous individuals through the use of totemic systems. Within this network of decentred responsibility, those who are charged with the care of a plant have special responsibilities to ensure the use of the plant stays true to ancestral purposes. It is important to repeat that an ancestral system does not prevent adaptive uses of plants and other resources, but it does require deliberation within indigenous groups. When patent systems allow for the unilateral acquisition of rights over ancestral plants they directly challenge the authority of ancestral systems. In chapter 5 I argue for a system of regulatory convening that draws more on the authority of ancestral systems.

The existence of ancestral systems within a state's borders does pose a greater challenge for a state than the existence of customary law. Much of the writing on indigenous knowledge and intellectual property looks to the recognition of customary law as part of the solution to problems of ownership and allowable uses of knowledge. Miranda Forsyth, drawing on a distinction between shallow and deep legal pluralism, has pointed out that this literature tends not to go beyond shallow legal pluralism in its analysis.[47] That is to say, it assumes the continuing authority of the state over property rules and construes the problem as one of integrating

---

[46] For an account see W. Ritte, Jr., and L. Malia Kanehe, 'Kuleana No Haloa (Responsibility for Taro): Protecting the Sacred Ancestor From Ownership and Genetic Modification' in A. Te Pareake Mead and S. Ratuva (eds.), *Pacific Genes & Life Patents: Pacific Indigenous Experiences & Analysis of the Commodification & Ownership of Life* (Wellington: Call of the Earth Llamado de la Tierra and the United Nations University Institute of Advanced Studies, 2007), 130.

[47] M. Forsyth, 'Do You Want it Gift Wrapped?: Protecting Traditional Knowledge in the Pacific Island Countries' in P. Drahos and S. Frankel (eds.), *Indigenous Peoples' Innovation: Intellectual Property Pathways to Development* (Canberra: ANU E Press, 2012) 189, 197–8.

customary laws into state-based intellectual property systems to help resolve disputes over the use of indigenous knowledge. When a state practises shallow legal pluralism it does not recognize the authority of an ancestral system, but rather it creates a customary analogue of the system and uses it as an input into its own legal system to arrive at a solution. If a state were to practise deep legal pluralism for an ancestral system, it would have to defer to the authority of decision makers within that system. The authority of decisions about the permissible uses of indigenous knowledge would no longer trace back to the foundational elements of a state's positive legal order but to an ancestral system of a once stateless society. One might try and accommodate the radical implications of deep legal pluralism with some theory of shared sovereignty, but this in the end would not change what is at stake here for the state – the displacement of its authority over indigenous people's systems of knowledge and a limitation on its own juridical capacity to command the enclosure of resources. This represents no small shift or adjustment in the concept of sovereignty over a state's property order. Sovereignty, property and territory are analytically inter-linked concepts that justify the legal order of the Westphalian state. As we will see in chapter 4, the juridical trend is towards a greater recognition of the sovereignty of enclosure practices, not less.

The United States has probably gone further than any other settler state in recognizing inherent powers of self-government of indigenous groups within its borders. Those powers are at their strongest when indigenous groups regulate affairs amongst themselves on land they have recovered from the US government and at their weakest when they attempt to deal with actions by non-indigenous people carried out away from their territory that affect their interests.[48] Deep legal pluralism for the indigenous knowledge systems of Native Americans is a long way off, as it is for indigenous groups everywhere, because states constitute themselves through processes of enclosure and extraction.

At a more philosophical level, one has to ask whether state-based legal pluralism can ever fully accommodate the combination of autonomy and obligations towards Country that stateless indigenous societies using ancestral systems forged so long ago. Much of what follows in the rest of this book assumes that indigenous people will face a world in which states will use weak legal pluralism when it comes to recognizing

---

[48] See C. E. Goldberg, 'A United States Perspective on the Protection of Indigenous Cultural Heritage' in C. B. Graber, K. Kuprecht and J. C. Lai (eds.), *International Trade in Indigenous Cultural Heritage: Legal and Policy Issues* (Cheltenham: Edward Elgar, 2012), 331.

indigenous peoples' control over their knowledge. Indigenous developmental networks are a pragmatic response by indigenous people to a world in which states will hold fast to their power of command over their property order.

1.6.   The quicksands of definition

Discussions of intellectual property and indigenous knowledge tend to end up in the quicksands of lawyerly definition. A good example is the work of WIPO. It established in 2000 an Intergovernmental Committee on Intellectual Property and Genetic Resources, Traditional Knowledge and Folklore with the aim of producing a draft legal instrument or instruments to protect traditional knowledge, traditional cultural expressions/folklore and genetic resources. At the time of writing there were three consolidated texts each containing definitions of traditional knowledge. These definitions contained bracketed options and alternative elements meaning that the set of possible definitions contains many thousands of members.

Traditional knowledge is perhaps the most open-ended concept that one might choose in this field. Some knowledge cannot be specified by means of rules and can only be passed on through relationships of close learning such as master and apprentice.[49] This form of personal knowledge depends on tradition. All societies, including capitalist societies, have traditional knowledge.

Not surprisingly, a range of definitions of traditional knowledge have emerged from the literature.[50] Traditional knowledge is sometimes linked to environmental or ecological knowledge or to local knowledge held by groups such as farmers and fishermen (who may or may not be indigenous). Other definitional strategies include contrasting traditional knowledge with scientific knowledge or specifying key properties for it such as oral transmission and its embeddedness in a non-materialist cosmology. All definitional strategies run into problems of one kind or another. For example, the contrast with science can be overplayed as both traditional knowledge systems and science depend on the making of observation statements and testing. In the end there is an irreducibly stipulative component in all these definitional strategies.

---

[49] M. Polanyi, *Personal Knowledge: Towards a Post-Critical Philosophy* (London: Routledge & Kegan Paul, 1958), 53.

[50] For a survey see G. Dutfield, 'Legal and Economic Aspects of Traditional Knowledge' in K. E. Maskus and J. H. Reichman (eds.), *International Public Goods and Transfer of Technology Under a Globalized Intellectual Property Regime* (Cambridge University Press, 2005), 495–520.

Indigenous knowledge is a much older phenomenon than intellectual property, but as a concept within Western scholarship it has had a short career, being most closely linked to anthropology and emerging as a distinct concept in the 1980s.[51] Its evolution as an international legal concept has been characterized by controversy over its definition.[52] Within anthropology the term 'indigenous' comes to be linked to cases of distinct tribal groups involved in a rights struggle with a state not founded by those groups.[53] The meaning of the term is thereby narrowed. Within international law the term 'indigenous' is open ended. The United Nations Declaration on the Rights of Indigenous Peoples avoids proposing a definition, stating that indigenous peoples 'have the right to determine their own identity or membership'. If being X depends upon a right of self-identification as X and this right is open to all then it follows that anyone may make use of the right to become X. A potential political problem arises for states as being indigenous gives access to a rights-based discourse in which the principle of self-determination features prominently. Within South East Asia and South Asia, some states such as India, Indonesia and Malaysia have attempted to characterize their respective populations at large as indigenous and to avoid the use of the term as a descriptor for minority groups such as hill tribes.[54] Some Asian states have argued that the concept of indigenous peoples should be confined to those groups living in the settler states born of the processes of European colonization.[55]

States that want to exclude the possibility of the term 'indigenous peoples' being applied as a legal descriptor to particular groups within their borders are seeking to maximize their sovereign authority over those groups. Their definitional manoeuvring, however, does not make the psychology of group identity go away and nor does it necessarily prevent a politics of resistance. Other practical consequences also flow from the wordplay by states around the meaning of 'indigenous'. Copyright law in Indonesia, for example, puts the Indonesian state in the position of the

---

[51] S. B. Brush, 'Indigenous Knowledge of Biological Resources and Intellectual Property Rights: The Role of Anthropology', *American Anthropologist* 95 (1993), 653, 659.

[52] For a detailed discussion see B. Kingsbury, '"Indigenous Peoples" in International Law: A Constructivist Approach to the Asian Controversy', *American Journal of International Law* 92 (1998), 414.

[53] S. B. Brush, 'Indigenous Knowledge of Biological Resources and Intellectual Property Rights: The Role of Anthropology', *American Anthropologist* 95 (1993), 653, 658.

[54] G. A. Persoon, '"Being Indigenous" in Indonesia and the Philippines' in C. Antons (ed.), *Traditional Knowledge, Traditional Cultural Expressions and Intellectual Property Law in the Asia-Pacific Region* (Alphen aan den Rijn: Kluwer Law International, 2009), 195, 196.

[55] Kingsbury, '"Indigenous Peoples"', 418.

holder of copyright in subject matters that make up Indonesian culture and folklore.[56] Moreover, in these regions, migration patterns, intermarriage and cultural cross-pollination make the ascription of indigeneity to particular groups a matter of debate and complexity. Chidi Oguamanam in a discussion of various meanings of 'indigenous' identifies problematic aspects for all of them.[57]

The United Nations Development Group in its guidelines suggests 'no formal universal definition [of indigenous] is necessary'.[58] In the absence of a definition that selects attributes of indigeneity, self-identification has become accepted by the United Nations as the principal mechanism for distinguishing indigenous groups from other groups. This approach has psychological realism. The consistent self-expression of an identity over time is evidence of a powerful group identity mechanism at work. Reliance on self-identification does not mean that one cannot look to corroborating factors such as cultural distinctiveness and historical links to territory for the purposes of developing a workable definition of indigeneity. Peru's approach to the meaning of indigenous peoples, for instance, has the element of cultural self-recognition, but it also links back to people who held rights and were occupying a particular area before the formation of the Peruvian state.[59] In Australia, the general legal approach to defining a person as Aboriginal or Torres Strait Islander is based on a combination of three elements: descent, self-identification and community acceptance.[60] A great strength of adopting self-identification as one core element in the definition of 'indigenous' is that it gives members of indigenous groups some definitional power over status. It enables a right of self-legislation, as it were, where previously colonial authorities simply legislatively imposed definitions upon indigenous peoples. That said there may be a case, as some have argued, for adding other characteristics to the principle of self-identification in order

[56] C. Antons, 'The International Debate about Traditional Knowledge, Traditional Cultural Expressions and Intellectual Property' in Antons (ed.), *Traditional Knowledge*, 39, 53.

[57] See C. Oguamanam, *International Law And Indigenous Knowledge: Intellectual Property, Plant Biodiversity, and Traditional Medicine* (Toronto, Buffalo, London: University of Toronto Press, 2006), 20–26.

[58] United Nations Development Group, *Guidelines On Indigenous Peoples' Issues* (New York and Geneva: United Nations, 2009), 8.

[59] See Article 2(a) of Peru's Law No. 27811, published 10 August 2002, entitled Law Introducing A Protection Regime For The Collective Knowledge Of Indigenous Peoples Derived From Biological Resources, available at www.wipo.int/wipolex/en/details.jsp?id=3420.

[60] For a discussion of this approach in Australian law see Australian Law Reform Commission, *Essentially Yours: The Protection of Human Genetic Information in Australia* (ALRC 96, volume 2, Commonwealth of Australia, 2003), ch. 36.

to obtain an understanding of indigenous that better identifies beneficiaries of indigenous peoples' rights and sets some limits on evasive
strategizing by states when it comes to delivering those rights.[61]

For my purposes 'indigenous knowledge' is a better term than
'traditional knowledge', even if traditional knowledge (or TK) is the term
with the greater currency. As I have indicated, all societies have traditional knowledge, including post-industrial capitalist societies, but not
all societies can be described as indigenous. More importantly, in the
chapters that follow I will refer to 'indigenous innovation systems' and
here the term 'traditional' performs a disservice because it implies a
knowledge system not open to innovation. There is recognition that
indigenous people have been and are innovative.[62] For example,
included in the draft text emerging out of the WIPO process is an
acknowledgement that 'traditional knowledge systems are frameworks
of ongoing innovation'.[63] My focus in this book is not so much on the
protection of existing traditional knowledge, but rather on the question
of what is needed to support systems of indigenous peoples' innovation.
I do not mean to imply that the former issue is unimportant, but it has
received considerable attention, as the WIPO process itself demon-
strates. Little attention has been paid to the latter question. As we will
see, indigenous people in Australia are regaining some control over their
land, but at a time when the climate and ecological systems around land
are shifting to as yet unknown new patterns. Indigenous people face an
innovation and adaptation challenge, much as they did when they first
arrived some 50,000 years ago.[64]

A focus on systems of innovation leads into a broader analysis of the
institutions that contribute to innovative performance.[65] A systems
approach to innovation requires one to identify the set of institutions
that matter to innovation as well as the distinctive linkages and interactions amongst institutional actors that characterize an innovation
system. In the context of modern economies, this usually involves an
examination of the linkages amongst firms and their industrial research

---

[61] See J. Scott and F. Lenzerini, 'International Indigenous and Human Rights Law in the
       Context of Trade in Indigenous Cultural Heritage' in Graber, Kuprecht and Lai (eds.),
       International Trade, 61, 65.
[62] The Convention on Biological Diversity (1992) in Article 8(j) requires its members to
       'respect, preserve and maintain knowledge, *innovations* and practices of indigenous and
       local communities' (emphasis added).
[63] See the draft 'The protection of traditional knowledge' available at www.wipo.int/edocs/
       mdocs/tk/en/wipo_grtkf_ic_21/wipo_grtkf_ic_21_ref_facilitators_text.pdf.
[64] On estimates of arrival see Hiscock, *Archaeology of Ancient Australia*, 44.
[65] See R. R. Nelson, 'National Innovation Systems: A Retrospective on a Study', *Industrial
       and Corporate Change* 1 (1992), 347.

laboratories, universities and government laboratories, as well as looking at the role of institutions such as tax and venture capital markets.[66] In chapter 2, I will set out what I take to be some of the distinctive institutional characteristics of Aboriginal people's innovation. As we will see in chapter 3, nineteenth-century capitalism was highly destructive of Aboriginal people's innovation. Rebuilding institutions of innovation is an ongoing process for Aboriginal people, but this rebuilding also coincides with the arrival of a knowledge economy that places more value on indigenous knowledge and innovation. The potential for cooperative approaches between the state and indigenous groups to common problems such as adaptation to climate change is high.

In the next section, I want to show how Aboriginal innovation systems relate to a conventional economic understanding of innovation. The first step to encouraging states to work in a non-extractive way with 'traditional knowledge' is to help them see that they are dealing not with systems of past achievement but with innovation systems that can contribute to the growth of new knowledge. From a policy point of view this means thinking about how to support indigenous peoples' innovation in much the same way that states internally debate how to support their national systems of innovation. Although it is clear from our fieldwork that Aboriginal groups want to use their knowledge assets to achieve a measure of economic autonomy, it does not follow that they support a conventional economic growth model. As we will see in the last two chapters of the book, their views of economic growth seem to be much closer to those of people like Schumacher, who emphasized a sustainable scale of growth, than to views that economies of scale would fuel growth without limits. Their property rights systems, which as we saw earlier were based on a combination of duties and use-permissions, did not leave what we would think of as environmental resources unallocated. Resources were allocated, but in ways that meant that knowledgeable people had primary responsibility for ensuring that the network of duties and use-permissions would produce healthy Countries.

Before moving to the next section I want to make some final terminological stipulations. I will refer to Aboriginal people or groups, or indigenous people or groups, these terms including the indigenous people of the Torres Strait Islands. Sometimes indigenous will either include or mean indigenous peoples outside of Australia. This should be clear from the context.

---

[66] For a discussion see *ibid.*, 347; P. A. Hall and D. Soskice (eds.), *Varieties of Capitalism: The Institutional Foundations of Comparative Advantage* (Oxford University Press, 2001).

1.7.   Innovation and useful knowledge

Innovation has come to be seen as made up of many different kinds of activities (for example, innovation in products, services, processes, marketing, organization and governance) carried out at different levels such as the individual, the group, the organization, an industry and a geographic region.[67] This multidimensional conceptualization of innovation allows one to research and test the different ways in which societies have been innovative. Sometimes the emphasis is placed on firms developing new products and processes. Greenhalgh and Rogers, for example, define product innovation as 'the introduction of a new product, or a significant qualitative change in an existing product' and process innovation as 'the introduction of a new process for making or delivering goods and services'.[68] On this definitional approach it is clear that Aboriginal people have been innovative. For example, the recorded knowledge of some Wagiman elders shows an extensive knowledge of the nutrional, therapeutic and technological uses of plants. For instance, the ironwood tree has featured in product and process innovation.[69] Its leaves can be used as a fish poison, as well as in the treatment of pain and its roots contain a wax that can be turned into a glue. Other examples of innovation include the knowledge that the tips of spinifex leaves can be used to treat warts and to increase the production of breast milk and that the seeds of *cycas canalis* (bush palm) can be turned into a damper that has the qualities of long-term storage and high food energy.[70]

We can deepen our analysis of Aboriginal people's innovation by drawing on Joel Mokyr's theory of useful knowledge.[71] His theory divides useful knowledge into propositional and prescriptive knowledge. Propositional knowledge consists of beliefs about the natural world and is generated primarily through observation. It includes 'practical informal knowledge about nature such as the properties of materials, heat, motion, plants and animals', along with many other kinds of practical

---

[67] For a full discussion of this approach see A. K. Gupta, P. E. Tesluk and M. S. Taylor, 'Innovation At and Across Multiple Levels of Analysis', *Organization Science*, 18 (2007), 885.

[68] C. Greenhalgh and M. Rogers, *Innovation, Intellectual Property, and Economic Growth* (Princeton and Oxford: Princeton University Press, 2010), 4.

[69] L. G. Liddy *et al.*, *Wagiman Plants and Animals: Aboriginal Knowledge of Flora and Fauna From the Mid Daly River Area, Northern Australia* (Darwin: Department of Natural Resources, Environment and the Arts, NT Government and the Diwurruwurru-jaru Aboriginal Corporation, 2006), 39.

[70] *Ibid.*, 34, 71.

[71] J. Mokyr, *The Gifts of Athena: Historical Origins of the Knowledge Economy* (Princeton and Oxford: Princeton University Press, 2002).

knowledge.[72] Prescriptive knowledge is knowledge of techniques. The techniques potentially available to a society at any given time depend on its stock of propositional knowledge. There is no neat one-to-one correspondence between propositional and prescriptive knowledge. Processes of selection determine which techniques are actually realized. Economic production involves agents using techniques that have been derived in some way from propositional knowledge. Techniques might be stumbled upon, but unless they generate a body of propositional knowledge their use and development is not likely to continue. The causal sequence that matters most to economic production is the one that travels from knowledge to technique. What is derived from propositional knowledge depends not just on the content of that knowledge but on institutional and cultural factors that affect who is allowed to contribute to the processes of derivation (for example, do the institutional arrangements allow for the full participation of women?) and the incentive settings of those who might potentially adopt or invent new techniques (so, for example, what are the rewards and punishments for innovation?).

Mokyr's theory of useful knowledge helps us to see that Aboriginal people were generating both prescriptive and propositional knowledge using their innovation system. Going back to the examples of Wagiman knowledge, the knowledge that the leaves of the ironwood tree can be used as a fish poison is an example of propositional knowledge. Prescriptive knowledge (technique) is needed to turn seeds into damper that can be stored. In the chapter that follows, we will see that the great strength of Aboriginal innovation lies in the generation of prescriptive knowledge about ecosystems and land. Aboriginal people invested a great deal in the production of useful knowledge around the techniques needed to maintain healthy 'Country'. Building up knowledge of their respective Countries and keeping them in a proper state were overriding obligations for indigenous people. In terms of the multidimensional conceptualization of innovation, the dimensions that characterize Aboriginal innovation are the group level of innovation and a concentration on methods, processes and systems aimed at intervening in the performance of ecological systems. The most obvious example of an innovative technique to manage systems was the use of fire, something I discuss in detail in the next chapter.

When it comes to assessing the character of Aboriginal people's innovation, there is something of a parallel with classical antiquity. Mokyr points out that the technological achievements of classical civilizations

---

[72] *Ibid.*, 5.

lay more in the realm of information processing than the mechanical – geometry, alphabetization and coinage being some examples.[73] In the case of Aboriginal people, the outcomes of information processing were for the most part mentally recorded and replayed in dance, ritual, singing and story. Much of this information processing was made concrete through maintaining and fulfilling obligations towards Country. The Aboriginal economy, as we will see in chapters 2 and 3, focused on accumulating human capital in order to develop services to Country. Their services to Country produced what we now term ecosystems services, which in turn helped indigenous groups to survive and prosper. The distinctive innovative achievement of Aboriginal peoples was not something that was understood by the arriving colonists of 1788 who were coming from an innovation culture that was all about harnessing the raw materials of nature such as coal, water and wool for the purposes of mechanization and the production of goods.

Today, there is a much greater recognition of the achievements of indigenous peoples everywhere. The problem of climate change has triggered a remarkable synthesis amongst the scientific disciplines, including the recognition of the Earth system. It is a time of big ideas for planetary health with some scientists, for example, proposing the idea of planetary boundaries.[74] The argument is that in certain key areas such as climate change, biodiversity loss and land use changes, we should, based on the best evidence, set limits beyond which we would not go in order to minimize the risks of damaging our natural life support systems. There are huge implications for multilevel governance from these ideas, implications that in the coming decades will animate policy networks as it becomes clearer and clearer that we need boundaries to manage the risks of crossing thresholds into dangers such as ocean acidification and water shortages. It seems reasonably clear that the property rights schemes of the Anthropocene, the period from the Industrial Revolution onwards, will have to be rethought in significant ways if we are to save ecosystems in decline. Understanding the duty-based institutional arrangements of Aboriginal societies for healthy Country is one important sources of ideas for rethinking our own property schemes.

[73] *Ibid.*, 19.
[74] See W. Steffen, J. Rockstrom and R. Costanza, 'How defining planetary boundaries can transform our approach to growth' available at www.energybulletin.net/stories/2011-05-25/how-defining-planetary-boundaries-can-transform-our-approach-growth.

2   Cosmology's country

2.1.   Cosmology and Plato's Dreaming

Aboriginal people have systematized beliefs about the origin of their worlds, their structures and nature, and the things that exist in them. More formally, they have cosmogonies, cosmologies and ontologies.[1] At first glance these may seem a long way removed from an inquiry into the economic use of knowledge assets by indigenous people deploying intellectual property rights systems. But as we will see in this chapter Aboriginal cosmologies (this single term will be used for convenience) give indigenous knowledge assets certain characteristics that set limits on what may or may not be done with knowledge. An indigenous person wishing to put a knowledge asset to business use cannot ignore these characteristics. We will also see that Aboriginal cosmologies help to explain the specific strengths of Aboriginal innovation. The importance of linking cosmology to economic institutions is not without precedent. Weber's sociology of capitalism links the rise of its economic institutions to ethical values derived ultimately from the nature of the supernatural realm.[2] Ian Keen points out that Aboriginal cosmologies are relevant to understanding how Aboriginal institutions were organized, including ancestral law and ownership and control of access to land.[3]

The term cosmology does a better job than the English words 'Dreamtime' or the 'Dreaming' of communicating the idea that we are dealing with beliefs about the nature of the world that are thought to be true. The use of Dreamtime to refer to Aboriginal cosmological beliefs goes back to a mistranslation of a word from the Aranda language that is better

---

[1] Metaphysics is generally divided into ontology and cosmology in which the former is an inquiry into the categories and concepts of existence and the latter is a more generalized account of the nature of the universe. See K. Campbell, *Metaphysics: An Introduction* (Encino, CA: Dickenson Publishing Company, 1976), 21–2.

[2] S. Kalberg, *Max Weber's Comparative-Historical Sociology Today* (Aldershot: Ashgate, 2012), 63.

[3] Keen, *Aboriginal Economy*, 210.

translated as 'eternal, uncreated, springing out of itself'.[4] Aranda was one of more than 200 languages that were being spoken in Australia prior to colonization by Europeans, along with many dialects. The term Dreamtime spread into popular usage, but its connotations of impermanence and imagination do not sit well with the fact that we are dealing with a metaphysical scheme.

Over time those who have closely studied Aboriginal languages and societies have developed conceptualizations of the Dreamtime that better convey its cosmological nature. Strehlow, basing himself on the original Aranda word, suggested 'having originated out of its own eternity' as the best approximation. Swain, using this as a springboard, has suggested that we are dealing with a class of eternal events that he labels 'Abiding Events' in order to link the events to place as well as time.[5] Dussart in her study of the Warlpiri people identifies five related meanings of the Dreamtime, the most common of which she labels the 'Ancestral Present'.[6] The Ancestral Present is that part of the space–time continuum shaped by Ancestral Beings and occupied by the Warlpiri. Dussart's use of the term Ancestral Present is designed to convey the idea that this space–time continuum is simultaneously past and present.

Aboriginal cosmologies represent a form of philosophical realism in which a set of entities and objects are claimed to have an independent and knowable existence, an obvious example of these entities being ancestors. On one view forms of Aboriginal institutional organization represent an integrated response to these realist cosmologies. Stanner, for example, argued against the Durkheimian view of Aboriginal cosmology as a derivative of Aboriginal social organization that serves some useful purpose such as social cohesion.[7]

The idea that social structure should form an integrated response to the cosmological nature of knowledge is to be found in the Western philosophical tradition. Plato's *Republic* is the most famous example of where a social and political system is designed in response to the objective nature of knowledge. In the *Republic* it is those philosophers who attain the highest level of knowledge who become philosopher rulers, the highest level of Plato's class of Guardians. Philosopher rulers are fit to

---

[4] T. Swain, *A Place For Strangers: Towards A History of Australian Aboriginal Being* (Cambridge University Press, 1993), 21.

[5] *Ibid.*, 22.

[6] F. Dussart, *The Politics Of Ritual In An Aboriginal Settlement* (Washington and London: Smithsonian Institution Press, 2000), 17–18.

[7] M. Charlesworth, 'Introduction' in M. Charlesworth, F. Dussart and H. Morphy (eds.), *Aboriginal Religions in Australia: An Anthology of Recent Writings* (Aldershot: Ashgate, 2005), 1, 8.

rule because they have a pure knowledge of the good. Such knowledge is possible because of the nature of knowledge itself. Knowledge and truth are based on a knower being able to apprehend the form of an object where form refers not to shape but rather the property or quality of being good that allows the knower of the form to see that different actions all share the property of being good. Forms for Plato have an existence that is independent of the physical world.

My point here is not that Aboriginal cosmologies can be likened to Plato's realist metaphysic. I suspect that apart from being in the general realist camp they have nothing much else in common. Rather Plato's *Republic* shows the importance of striving to understand the causal role that cosmology plays in political institutions. If we ignored Plato's theory of forms in the *Republic* we would miss what is of central importance to the way in which political and social life is therein organized. And, of course, no one does ignore the theory of forms. It is, as it were, Plato's Dreaming.

2.2.   Cosmologies and Countries

Western metaphysics is about space and time, but it is not about place. Abstract theories of space and time do not, for example, concentrate on the nature of the space–time continuum at Broken Hill in New South Wales. One of the things that strikes an outsider about Aboriginal cosmologies is their focus on explaining the origins of the physical features of particular areas of land. In Dreamtime stories ancestral beings in either animal or human form will often begin a journey in a specific place and end it in another known place. Along the way they will, through the exercise of their great powers, transform the landscape to give it the physical features by which it is known today. So, for example, in one Yolngu story pairs of guwaks, emus and possums leave from Burrwanydji near Donydji station and end up in Djarrakpi a brackish lake on the coast of the Gulf of Carpentaria, near Blue Mud Bay.[8] During the journey the emus form waterholes using their feet for drills. At Djarrakpi these beings engineer more topographical transformations. Lengths of string spun by the possums using their fur become gullies, sandbanks and coastal dunes and these become linked to specific clans. The emus, unable to find freshwater in the lake, throw their spears into the sea to form low-tide fresh water springs. Through their geo-magical powers the ancestors create the topography of an area that clan members come to know as

---

[8] The story is to be found in Morphy, *Ancestral Connections*, 220–2.

their 'Country'. Country is an emotional centre of being because it is a place that one knows intimately at many levels, where one has Country-men and rights along with the safety and security that these things bring. It is a place of belonging where one can truly 'sit down'.[9]

Aboriginal cosmologies are not just about the origins of Country. They also explain how people came to know about particular technologies such as fish traps, how animals and plants gained their names and why they have certain characteristics. The Lardil People on Mornington Island in the Gulf of Carpentaria have an important story in which three ancestors journey from the mainland to Mornington Island and other neighbouring islands. During their travels they build fishtraps, dugon traps and freshwater wells, as well as naming all the animal, plant and fish life.[10]

Some ancestral beings perform colossal acts of transformation, forming, sometimes in their death throes, mountains and rivers. Different tribes may have different versions of the same life events of these abnormally powerful ancestral beings. Probably the most well-known example of this is the myths around the Rainbow Serpent. Stanner, for example, recorded four versions of a Rainbow Serpent myth widely known amongst tribes on the north-west coast of the Northern Territory.[11] In the longest and most detailed version that Stanner obtained from some old people belonging to the Murinbata tribe the ancestral being Kunmanggur has two daughters and a son. The son is filled with lust for his sisters and eventually forces himself upon them. He then arranges a large dance and while Kunmanggur is distracted he spears him. Kunmanggur is badly wounded and in an effort to heal himself he begins to travel looking for treatment. He performs wonderous feats at various places, but eventually realizing that death is drawing near he turns to the sea, gathering up all the fire intending to deprive others of its use. At the last moment before Kunmanggur is completely submerged another ancestor manages to snatch an ember that he uses to give fire back to the people. Through his final thrashing movements in the sea Kunmanggur causes various creeks to form.

The Lardil also have an important Rainbow Serpent story in which Thuwathu (the Rainbow Serpent) builds a shelter from the heavy wet

---

[9] D. McKnight, *People, Countries, and the Rainbow Serpent: Systems of Classification Among the Lardil of Mornington Island* (New York: Oxford University Press, 1999), 81.

[10] Details of this story are to be found in McKnight, *People, Countries, and the Rainbow Serpent*, 78–9.

[11] W. E. H. Stanner, 'On Aboriginal Religion', *Oceania Monograph*, XXXI (1961), 81, 88–94.

season rains.[12] During a torrential rainstorm his sister Bulthuku asks him to make space for her baby daughter. Thuwathu refuses, saying there is not enough room. Bulthuku's baby dies and in her rage she sets fire to the shelter. Suffering mortal burns Thuwathu bursts from the shelter and begins a journey that forms the Dugong River. He attempts to return to his sister, but dies at a water hole before he can do so. His death leaves behind useful things such as red ochre (his blood) and boomerangs (his ribs).

The ancestors also leave behind an ancestral system, sometimes referred to as ancestral law (discussed in chapter 1). During our field-work many indigenous people referred to their law, sometimes contrast-ing its unchanging nature with the changing nature of Australian law. In the words of one indigenous woman: 'Your law changes all the time, ours doesn't'. It may be that there are two types of law embodied in the concept of an ancestral system. One may refer to the physical forces that govern an area in which ancestors have been active and the other to lessons of guidance of ancestral origin for people to use in social life.

Ancestors also leave behind a landscape that is more propitious for the survival of its inhabitants. There are waterholes and freshwater springs, names to help classify animal and plant life, as well as useful tools such as fish traps and many other things. The features of the landscape are evidence of ancestral travels, with ancestors sometimes leaving behind personal signs such as footprints or bodyprints on cave walls. These are not cosmologies made up of an abstract set of truths in the canonical form of a text or a set of equations. They are cosmologies that speak of great events, events that are made concrete because they are embodied in Country. Countries through their topography serve as partial physical records of these events. The details of the stories are transmitted through dance, singing, ritual and storytelling. Variations of the same story may occur amongst individuals who are members of the same group, or amongst different groups. Stanner, basing himself on his work with northern groups, concluded that there was no authoritative version of a story, but rather stories had a common core, this common core being adapted by individuals for creative and contextual purposes.[13]

Country and Countrymen do not correspond in any simple way to ownership and use rights. It is not a case of one tribe, one Country. As noted in chapter 1, terms such as 'the Yolngu people' mask a complex social organization built around clans or dialect groups. These clans have their own Countries to which they are specially linked. McKnight's

[12] McKnight, *People, Countries, and the Rainbow Serpent*, 195–6.
[13] Stanner, 'On Aboriginal Religion', 84–5.

detailed work on Mornington Island also shows that it is not a matter of one tribe, one Country. By 1914 the island had been divided into thirty-one Countries by the Lardil people. Access and use rights over a given Country depended on the kinship relationship one had to members of the Country. The Country of one's father or father's sister would give individuals specific rights in the division of game whereas the Country of one's sister-in-law would allow for general hunting rights but with an obligation to give big game to the senior member of the Country.[14]

Kinship structures matter greatly to indigenous business entrepreneurs. Our fieldwork in Broome showed that when indigenous entrepreneurs wanted to collect plants for their businesses they utilized their kinship web of relations in order to gain access to the best physical specimens that they could. The ability of an entrepreneur to run a successful wild harvest operation, for example, depends in part on gaining access to Countries where the best picking is to be found and which Countries an entrepreneur can access depends on her or his kinship connections.

One of the interesting features of the Lardil system of land tenure was the way it was adapted by the Lardil to help individuals from other Aboriginal groups deal with the consequences of colonization. A Presbyterian mission was established on Mornington Island in 1914 and this became a place where colonial authorities would sometimes send Aboriginal people from the mainland because they were seen as troublemakers or they were children who, it was thought, should be separated from their parents. The Lardil responded by finding places within their Countries for these strangers from the mainland so that they would over time be able to say that they had a place to 'sit down'. This particular example suggests that while Dreamtime cosmologies are key to understanding the forces that shape and govern an area, the division of an area into Countries and the creation of use rights over the resources of Countries has a pragmatic and negotiable component. Dreamtime cosmology does not pre-ordain a system of land tenure. The evidence suggests that Aboriginal systems of land tenure are flexible, allowing for changes in ownership groups.[15] Colonization was the greatest test of this flexibility because groups driven from their land sought refuge in the lands of others. As one of our indigenous interviewees remarked: 'desert people had to learn to live with saltwater people'.

---

[14] McKnight, *People, Countries, and the Rainbow Serpent*, 84.
[15] On the formation of new clans see H. Morphy, 'Myth, Totemism and the Creation of Clans', *Oceania*, 60 (1990), 312.

Different groups of ancestors shaped different areas of land in Australia. Exceptionally powerful totemic beings such as the Rainbow Serpent feature in more than one cosmology. However, ancestral beings have to be understood as local forces within a territorial cosmos. A Lardil person going to central Australia where the Warlpiri live is not equipped by virtue of Lardil cosmology to understand the forces that shaped Warlpiri Countries. One of the purposes of Welcome to Country ceremonies is to introduce visitors to the ancestral forces of an area in order to help those visitors to achieve safe passage while travelling in that Country. So, while cosmologies may have some similarities they are location specific, functioning as a key to understanding a particular area.

2.3.   Communicating with ancestors

At one level Dreamtime cosmologies appear to be stories of the past. Long ago, Dreamtime ancestors created present day topographies. But these Dreamtime ancestors did not in death leave the land they transformed, but rather they became part of it in some way and, crucially, they remain a part of it. Their topographical signatures are not simply the physical tracings of the departed, but rather places where they remain active. Ancestors can manifest themselves physically in the landscape in various ways such as an unusual weather phenomenon or the appearance of very large snake, leaving observers the task of finding the correct message being sent. Communication with Dreamtime ancestors is two way. Individuals travelling to particular Countries let an ancestor know of their journey: 'We sang songs to let the guwak and possum know that we were coming'.[16]

Dreamtime cosmology does not follow a simple model of time implied by the words yesterday, today and tomorrow. But this can probably be said of all theories of time. Indigenous cosmologies do seem committed to the claim that ancestors are simultaneously part of a distant past and the present – the Ancestral Present as Dussart puts it.[17] Linear models of the Dreamtime seem not to work as an explanation of it, but what does work is much less clear.[18] Perhaps, as Swain suggests, the Dreamtime does not have the dimension of time. Another complicating factor is that these cosmologies seem to suggest that ancestors have some degree of

---

[16] The artist Narritjin Maymuru describing a journey in Morphy, *Ancestral Connections*, 222.

[17] Dussart, *The Politics Of Ritual*, 18.

[18] For a summary of definitional approaches to the Dreamtime see Swain, *A Place For Strangers*, 14–22.

materiality.[19] They remain a watchful presence in the Countries they
have shaped. Aboriginal cosmologies are perhaps closer to some version
of physicalism than we realize. The word spiritual, frequently used to
describe the relationship that indigenous people have with their land,
probably misses in significant ways what indigenous people believe about
ancestors and land.

Each new generation of individuals can connect to the ancestral knowledge and forces that are a permanent part of their Country's cosmology.
Not all individuals have equal capabilities and competencies when it
comes to understanding and working with Dreamtime cosmological
knowledge. Some of this knowledge is believed to be powerful and
possibly dangerous.[20] Therefore one has to be properly trained in its
use. Secrecy and initiation are important mechanisms in the protection of
this kind of knowledge. Elkin's work on men of higher degree points out
that those chosen for this role were chosen because they had demonstrated skills of observation and memory that suggested they would be
able to meet the requirements of training and achieve the necessary
competency.[21]

If there is one thing that unites indigenous systems of knowledge it is
the principle that most or all knowledge that is part of an Aboriginal
group's system can be traced back to the acts of powerful ancestors in the
Dreamtime. Dreamtime stories are the threads that connect different
parts of an indigenous knowledge system. One can give independent
descriptions of a group's botanical taxonomies, for example, but the
ultimate origins of these taxonomies lie in the names and classifications
that ancestors created along with the landscape and the animals and
plants in it. The Dreamtime helps individuals make connections between
different parts or objects of a knowledge system, so that a place, a
painting, an object, a word and a ceremony can all be connected to the
Dreamtime and relations amongst these things established by virtue of
this connection.

In the next section I will argue that Dreamtime cosmology inclined
indigenous people towards a connectionist way of working with the land.
Cosmological connectionism saw indigenous people investing in
innovation that served to maintain the health of the land and its
ecosystems. The most obvious example of this service innovation was

---

[19] Keen, *Aboriginal Economy*, 211.
[20] I. Keen, *Knowledge and Secrecy in an Aboriginal Religion* (Oxford: Clarendon Press,
     1994), 106.
[21] A. P. Elkin, *Aboriginal Men of Higher Degree*, 2nd edn. (Queensland: University of
     Queensland Press, 1977), 10–15.

the use of fire to manage the landscape, an example I discuss in a later section of this chapter.

2.4. Cosmological connectionism

The empirical value of indigenous knowledge has come to be widely recognized (discussed in chapter 4), including in the scientific study of environmental and ecological problems. In this section I want to advance an explanation for the generative empirical power of Aboriginal knowledge systems by linking Aboriginal cosmologies to a connectionist way of working with the world. The model of cosmological connectionism matters to my overall argument in the following way. One can think of indigenous knowledge as useful knowledge in propositional form that can be extracted and used in other contexts (for example, indigenous knowledge about a plant's properties can be used by pharmaceutical companies in their R&D systems) or one can think about indigenous knowledge as part of a distinctive system of innovation that is capable of generating new knowledge. If one's purpose is primarily extractive then the cosmological context of indigenous knowledge propositions will not be of central interest. If, on the other hand, one is interested in supporting indigenous systems as innovation systems then understanding cosmological connectionism and its role in indigenous innovation is crucial. Without that understanding it will, amongst other things, not be possible to help indigenous people rebuild their institutions so that they can participate more fully as autonomous economic agents in the broader economy. As I pointed out in my introduction, Aboriginal people want more economic autonomy. They want to find ways to break their dependence on 'sit down money' (welfare payments).

Aboriginal systems of indigenous knowledge are better thought of as connectionist than holistic. Connectionism is an approach within the cognitive sciences that draws on the interactions of units in a network to create models that explain functions of the mind such as memory, learning and calculation.[22] Individual units are linked to form a discrete network. These units have varying degrees of activation and the interaction amongst units is weighted so that some connections become strongly active while others are suppressed or diminished. Learning is based on the different weights being adopted over time for connections. Influential in the development of connectionism has been the model of

---

[22] For a detailed discussion of the evolution of connectionism see W. Bechtel and A. Abrahamsen, *Connectionism and the Mind: Parallel Processing, Dynamics and Evolution in Networks*, 2nd edn. (Oxford: Blackwell, 2002), ch. 1.

the brain as a dense network of neurons. My use of connectionism does not follow the sense in which it is used to model processes of cognition. Rather I use connectionism to refer to the social networks that underpin the performance of indigenous knowledge systems. Indigenous social networks are distinctively different in terms of the units that they include compared to non-indigenous networks. Individuals are immersed in a social network that stretches well beyond the conventional understanding of a social network because the units of the network include plants and animals and the Country itself. Connectionism is a way of describing the fact that indigenous knowledge systems are the product of social networks that are characterized by variety in the types of units in the network, as well as density of connections amongst those units. The density of connection comes about because, as we saw in the previous section, communication with the non-human members of the network is seen as possible. Indigenous cosmology, kinship systems and totems operate together to create an intricate web of relations that for the most part remains opaque to outsiders.

An example of the way in which indigenous social networks are enlarged through links with animals comes from Deborah Rose's work with a community of Ngaringman and Nagaliwurru-speaking people in the Northern Territory.[23] The social identity of members of the community is in part constructed by reference to connections to other species such as flying foxes. Some individuals are Countrymen of flying foxes, meaning that they are close kin. When a flying fox person dies, flying foxes become a food taboo until other flying fox people lift the taboo.

There are aspects of Aboriginal kinship systems that are highly familiar to Westerners such as the use of mother for one's actual birth mother. The extension of mother to the sisters of one's mother is understandable. But as genealogical distance begins to wane the use of mother in Aboriginal societies becomes harder for outsiders to grasp, as it is in the case when it is applied to 'one's actual mother's mother's sisters' daughters'.[24] Aboriginal societies are sometimes described as kinship societies because no individual of a given tribe is left out of a kinship calculation.[25] In practical terms it may mean that an individual using this classification system can work out a kin relationship to a language group

---

[23] D. B. Rose, 'Consciousness and Responsibility in an Australian Aboriginal Religion' in W. H. Edwards (ed.), *Traditional Aboriginal Society: A Reader* (Melbourne: Macmillan, 1987), 257.

[24] P. Sutton, *Native Title in Australia in Ethnographic Perspective* (Cambridge University Press, 2003), 175.

[25] McKnight, *People, Countries, and the Rainbow Serpent*, 33.

of hundreds of people.[26] These kinship systems are open systems in the sense that they can be used to integrate strangers who through being addressed by a kinship term find themselves knowingly or unknowingly beginning a journey of integration into a kinship and marriage system.[27]

The kinship patterns of Aboriginal groups are affected by social categories according to which all individuals are classified. The most basic category is that of moiety. All individuals have, based on some social rule, a particular moiety and may also have a further section identity and perhaps a subsection identity. A crucial purpose of these classification systems is to deal with the problem of genealogical proximity in tribal groups and to ensure that people marry correctly. For example, the Yolgnu are divided into the Dhuwa and Yirritja moieties, with children following the moiety of their father and marrying into their mother's moiety.[28] Under the Yolgnu system everything – land, plants, animals, fish – fall into one or other moiety. The Lardil have an eight-class subsection system in which animals, plants, and natural objects function as totems. McKnight's tabulation of the Dreaming totems shows that Semi-moiety P includes in its totems the sea, saltwater, sparrow hawk, black duck, mangrove rat, hammernose shark, and the wild cucumber, while Semi-moiety S includes the death adder, rain, barracuda, the moon and the west wind.[29]

The kinship systems, classification schemes and totemic aspects of Aboriginal societies have been much studied and debated in the anthropological literature. It could be, to take one example of a debate, that the categories of moiety, sections and subsection are kinship categories or it may be that the classification scheme has a broader underlying logic that connects sets of natural objects, some of which are not obvious members of the set, to a cosmological structure.[30] My purpose in drawing attention to kinship systems and their totemic dimensions is simply to further illustrate how indigenous knowledge systems are part of social networks that are dense with human and non-human members. The connectionism that characterizes Aboriginal societies is hard for outsiders to comprehend because of the number and diversity of

---

[26] W. H. Edwards, *An Introduction to Aboriginal Societies*, 2nd edn. (Victoria: Thomson Social Science Press, 2008), 58.

[27] D. McKnight, *People, Countries, and the Rainbow Serpent: Systems of Classification Among the Lardil of Mornington Island* (New York: Oxford University Press, 1999), 33.

[28] Morphy, *Ancestral Connections*, 44.

[29] For the complete list see Table 9-1 in McKnight, *People, Countries, and the Rainbow Serpent*, 187–92.

[30] For a discussion of this debate see D. McKnight, *Going the Whiteman's Way: Kinship and Marriage Among Australian Aborigines* (Aldershot: Ashgate, 2004), ch. 5.

connections that link and bind human and non-human members in these societies. Even for insiders, understanding the connections takes time and involves a life-long process of initiation.

2.5.   'Elders with big brains'

Indigenous cosmologies saturate the indigenous socio-neural net, a term that I use to describe a social network the members of which think about the world in a distinctive way from other networks. In this section and the next I want to explore why the socio-neural nets of indigenous communities are likely to generate important empirical knowledge.

My explanation begins with some observations made to us during the course of our fieldwork by an ethnobotanist who for several decades has worked with Aboriginal groups in Australia's tropical north, recording the language and botanical knowledge of groups in which usually there remain only a handful of fluent speakers. In some cases he has had to work with the last remaining speaker. During the course of the interview he remarked that he worked with 'elders with big brains'. He went on to point out that 'the Aboriginal habitat is brain-filling'. This habitat lacks the kinds of information flows generated by smart information technologies to be found in cities. Instead indigenous individuals grow up in an environment in which they are linked to various plants and animals as 'Countrymen'. Living in this habitat, individuals have a constant daily interaction with plants and animals and are always acquiring new knowledge about them through use, observation, initiation and ceremony. An elder might know 600 or 700 plants and have a history of constant personal interaction with those plants and their associated Dreaming (interview, 2008). Remembering this much knowledge about plants is aided by 'memory enhancing scenarios' (interview, 2008) – ritual and ceremonies that help individuals to remember the knowledge they have acquired. The integration of indigenous individuals who have gone through these customary processes into their Country is deep: 'The elders are literally part of the habitat' (interview, 2008).

The hypothesis that the bush is a brain-rich environment is worth considering further. Indigenous people are born into social systems that from the very beginning multiply the number of connections with the environment that they have to understand and deal with. Their kinship systems link them to not just their own Country, but to the Countries of other groups, their ancestors and the events associated with those ancestors. In this connectionist world plants, animals, rocks, rivers and other things have multidimensional natures. A tree may have utilitarian functions such as providing shelter and being a source of medicine, but it may also be linked to a person by virtue of a kinship relation because it features in an ancestral story on that person's mother's side leading that person to say that 'this tree is my mother'.[31] From this kinship connection there may flow a set of rights and obligations with respect to a tree species.

Socio-neural nets that build dense multilevel connections in this way are potentially very rich sources of experience for the individuals that are born into them. One very important feature of these nets is that they dispose individuals to observe natural phenomena and events very closely. In a world full of multilevel connections, the sighting of, say, a snake is not necessarily a random event. It may be, but the snake may also be judged on the basis of its physical features to be a manifestation of the Rainbow Serpent. The judgement about whether or not it was may ultimately be made based on a discussion in the larger group and by an elder, but much depends on the report of those who made the sighting.

The connections that make up indigenous socio-neural nets mean that the indigenous habitat is a place rich in layers of experience. The Country is alive with the possibilities of different kinds of experiences, experiences to be shared and analysed around the campfire and perhaps to be further entrenched in memory through dance. Accessing these layers of experience depends on careful observation and then participation in broader interpretive circles of analysis.

Our interviewee's suggestion that 'the Aboriginal habitat is brain-filling' is a plausible hypothesis once we see that the connectionism of an indigenous socio-neural net creates the conditions for enriching the experiences of individuals. There is increasing evidence from neuroscience that experience, especially early experience, has a profound effect on the development of neural circuits.[32] The laboratory work shows that the young brain exhibits a great deal of plasticity with the formation of neural circuits that underpin capabilities such as vision and language being highly responsive to outside experience. The effects of early experience travel deep within brain chemistry, with, for example, the presence or absence of early mothering in young rats throwing genetic switches that cause life-long hormonal and therefore temperamental differences. This neuroscientific evidence points to a possibility that a prolonged experience of Country will have distinctive activation effects. Young indigenous children will be being introduced to a multilayered world of

---

[31] Keen, *Knowledge and Secrecy*, 107.
[32] See E. I. Knudsen, J. J. Heckman, J. L. Cameron and Jack P. Shonkoff, 'Economic, Neurobiological, and Behavioral Perspectives on Building America's Future Workforce', *Proceedings of the National Academy of Sciences*, 103 (2006), 10155.

experiences and those experiences will have profound neuronal impacts. Even without the aid of internet connections and reality TV shows, the Country will be switching on young indigenous minds. Or rather it might once have done so in a pre-colonial world where indigenous children automatically acquired the language of their parents.

One recurring theme in our interviews was the loss of indigenous knowledge. Rarely was it not mentioned by our indigenous and non-indigenous interviewees. One obvious factor in this loss is the way in which colonization broke the process of knowledge transmission between adults and children by interfering in the language development of indigenous children. McKnight's description of what happened on Mornington Island after a Presbyterian mission was established there provides us with an example of the neural dimensions of colonization. A mission school was built and attendance was made compulsory. English was taught and had to be spoken by indigenous children in the dormitories. The system became self-policing – the children 'themselves would make fun of homesick newcomers when these attempted to talk to one another in their own language. Before long, the newcomers forgot their mother tongue'.[33] By 1966 'the Lardil were rapidly losing their traditional culture' even though the old people were anxious to pass it on because those young people 'were not interested in the old ways'.[34]

2.6.   Observing and burning Country

Careful observation is important for the scientific method. It is also crucial to the operation of indigenous knowledge systems. To some extent the role of observation in indigenous knowledge systems is underplayed because we are more drawn to stories of the spectacular and the marvellous – the heroic acts and fights of ancestral beings or the powers of medicine men to fly, disappear into a tree or kill at a distance. The idea that indigenous knowledge is built up through the hard work of constant and detailed observation, committed to memory and passed on to the next generation makes for a less engrossing story. The mystical overshadows the mundane. Elkin's work on Aboriginal medicine men contains many descriptions of their spectacular origins and feats, as in the case of the Wardaman medicine man, who after having fought Wolgara, the spirit of the dead and being killed by him is cured of his wounds by a black hawk, has life breathed into him by a white hawk and so returns to his people with healing powers.[35]

[33] McKnight, *People, Countries, and the Rainbow Serpent*, 5.   [34] *Ibid.*, 6.
[35] Elkin, *Aboriginal Men*, 123.

Elkin's analysis also shows the importance of observation and training in explaining the powers of the medicine men; they learn from teachers and observation which illnesses are likely to be cured and which are not; they are careful observers of others and in this way gain crucial insights into their thinking; they 'possess a fund of knowledge concerning the signs which mark changes in the weather such as the sweating ground'.[36] One can also be sure that they understand the power of the placebo effect.

My claim is not that observation is the only source of knowledge in indigenous knowledge systems, but it is central to the way in which Aboriginal people work with their environment. This observational knowledge becomes part of indigenous knowledge systems where it grounds practices that help indigenous groups to manage and adapt to the changing conditions of the Countries in which they live. There is obvious utility in the art of careful observation in hunter-gatherer societies. The connectionist architecture that underpins these knowledge systems also helps to encourage careful observation. A large range of things can function as a totem in Aboriginal societies, including plants, animals, wind, rain, thunder, fire, mist, tools, food, as well as parts of the human body.[37] Totemic relationships are another way in which indigenous people collectively are likely to gather more observational data about the Countries on which they live because totemic relationships create more personalized and humanized relations with the non-human and are, therefore, more likely to make individuals pay attention to the behaviour of totemic entities and objects when they are sighted. Totemic relationships integrate individuals into the territorial cosmos and alert them to the possibility of signalling from the non-human in this cosmos. Indigenous people know that their Country is a place of fluctuating moods and forces, one where physical phenomena are veiled communications of changes or dangers and that the first step in understanding these is careful watchfulness.

Cycles of observation and experimentation by indigenous people lead eventually to institutional practices. Institutionalizing practices is important to managing food sources, health and the environment over the long run. Going back to the discussion of useful knowledge in chapter 1, once, for example, a technique for storing food is discovered it makes sense to entrench its use through custom. An example of an innovation that became an institutional practice is the customary use of fire by indigenous people. The success of this innovation (methods of burning) would

---

[36] *Ibid.*, 10–11.
[37] W. E. H. Stanner, 'Religion, Totemism and Symbolism' in W. E. H. Stanner (ed.), *White Man Got No Dreaming* (Canberra: Australian National University Press, 1979), 106, 127–9.

have been based on careful observation. Exactly when these methods were employed on a large scale to intervene in natural systems is not clear.[38] Even if fire technology was not systematically used from the first arrival of indigenous people, some 50,000 years ago, it is clear that by the time the colonizers arrived in 1788 indigenous people had been managing the land and its ecosystems through the use of fire for thousands of years. The early colonizers reported on the seemingly endless burning of the country. Few seemed to see any good in it. Arthur Phillip (first Governor of New South Wales) complained that his desire to turn 'swine into the woods to breed have been prevented by the natives so frequently setting fire to the country'.[39] But there were some who paid more attention to the effects of fire. Thomas Mitchell an early Australian explorer describes in one of his journals the type of landscape that indigenous methods of burning had produced and how the importance of burning Country was not really understood by colonists:[40]

Fire is necessary to burn the grass, and form those open forests, in which we find the large forest-kangaroo; the native applies that fire to the grass at certain seasons, in order that a young green crop may subsequently spring up, and so attract and enable him to kill or take the kangaroo with nets. In summer, the burning of long grass also discloses vermin, birds' nests, etc., on which the females and children, who chiefly burn the grass, feed. But for this simple process, the Australian woods had probably contained as thick a jungle as those of New Zealand or America, instead of the open forests in which the white men now find grass for their cattle, to the exclusion of the kangaroo ...

The squatters, it is true, have also been obliged to burn the old grass occasionally on their runs; but so little has this been understood by the Imperial Government that an order against the burning of the grass was once sent out, on the representations of a traveller in the south. The omission of the annual periodical burning by natives, of the grass and young saplings, has already produced in the open forest lands nearest to Sydney, thick forests of young trees, where, formerly, a man might gallop without impediment, and see whole miles before him. Kangaroos are no longer to be seen there; the grass is choked by underwood; neither are there natives to burn the grass, nor is fire longer desirable there amongst the fences of the settler.

---

[38] Peter Hiscock suggests that indigenous people may have started using fire well after their first arrival. See P. Hiscock, *Archaeology of Ancient Australia* (London: Routledge, 2008), 27. Burning may have started at different times in different regions. See T. Denham, R. Fullagar and L. Head, 'Plant Exploitation on Sahul: From Colonisation to the Emergence of Regional Specialisation During the Holocene', *Quaternary International*, 202 (2009), 29–40.

[39] Arthur Phillip quoted in S. J. Pyne, 'Firestick History', *Journal of American History*, 76 (1990), 1132, 1134.

[40] T. Mitchell, *Journal of an Expedition into the Interior of Tropical Australia* (1848), ch. X, available as an e-book http://gutenberg.net.au/pages/mitchell.html.

Not many of the colonists had Mitchell's powers of observation. Indigenous people kept on using fire technology in a bid to keep their Country
healthy. But they risked violence from the colonists if they were caught in
the act of setting fire to country.[41] Indigenous fire regimes stopped being
implemented as indigenous people were driven off Country or became
too scared to keep up the practice. Today many indigenous people would
see 'unhealthy' Country in many parts of Australia, Country that has not
been managed properly. The open forests with their carpets of native
grasses that Mitchell saw have in many cases descended into a dangerous
wild capable of releasing fires that travel at the speed of hurricanes
leaving behind ashes and the charred remains of what once lived there.

Scientific interest in the value of indigenous burning methods in
Australia has been slow to develop. Burning practices were seen as
dangerous by most of those working in the cattle industry. Forestry
managers in the Northern Territory would call in fire-fighting teams
when they spotted fires started by Aboriginal people:[42]

'Whitefella science came into Darwin in the 1960s led by the foresters. They
decided that all blackfella burning had to be suppressed' (interview, 2008).

The work of a senior forester, Chris Haynes appears to have been something of a turning point in developing a genuinely scientific approach to
the study of indigenous burning practices (interview, 2008). He began
to the study Aboriginal fire technology closely, developing hypotheses
about its importance.[43] In 1969 Rhys Jones proposed the 'fire-stick
farming' hypothesis, the idea that indigenous people had farmed the land
using fire as their technology of choice.[44] It was a radical hypothesis that
spurred further work. Some 200 years after colonization, scientists began
to consider the possibility that the Australian wild was more akin to a
managed park that had been built through firestick technology.

Today much more scientific attention is given to indigenous fire
burning methods. The knowledge of these fire practices appears to be

---

[41] D. Ritchie, 'Things Fall Apart: The End of an Era of Systematic Indigenous Fire
Management' in J. Russell-Smith, P. Whitehead and P. Cooke (eds.), *Culture, Ecology
and Economy of Fire Management in North Australian Savannas: Rekindling The Wurrk
Tradition* (Victoria: CSIRO Publishing, 2009), 23, 33.

[42] P. M. Cooke, 'Buffalo and Tin, Baki and Jesus' in J. Russell-Smith, P. Whitehead and
P. Cooke (eds.), *Culture, Ecology and Economy of Fire Management in North Australian
Savannas: Rekindling The Wurrk Tradition* (Victoria, Australia: CSIRO Publishing,
2009), 69, 79.

[43] On the importance of Chris Haynes' work see P. M. Cooke, 'Buffalo and Tin, Baki and
Jesus' in Russell-Smith, Whitehead and Cooke (eds.), *Culture, Ecology and Economy of
Fire Management*, 80.

[44] R. Jones, 'Fire-Stick Farming', *Australian Natural History*, 16 (1969), 224.

the greatest for the Arnhem Land region. There is a practical motivation for this greater interest. As Jeremy Russell-Smith and others have pointed out there is in fire-prone Australia a need to support the use of fire as a tool for managing the landscape to meet a range of goals.[45] Based on satellite and other evidence the northern part of Australia experiences massive and highly destructive wildfires, especially in the late dry season. By way of example for the period 1997–2001 an annual mean of 373,000 square kilometres of tropical savannas were burnt or fire affected, this representing almost 20 per cent of the tropical savannas region.[46] Late season fires, in particular, may burn for months, only being extinguished by the arrival of wet season rains. Fires on this scale cause many environmental 'bads' including greenhouse gas emissions, the degradation of ecosystems and the loss of biodiversity. In the words of one scientist we interviewed, these late season fires 'open the bush to a lot of nasty predation'.

How did indigenous people respond to the threat of these wildfires? In Arnhem Land there are areas that have been in the hands of traditional custodians for many decades, allowing those custodians to use a traditional system of fire management.[47] Burning begins in the early dry season and is first targeted upon the higher parts of Country where the moisture content of the grass has fallen. This moisture content acts as a natural control upon the extent of the burn. Burning, because of its potential dangers, is done under the guidance of knowledgeable elders. It continues throughout the dry season, moving into lower areas and reaching a peak in the coolest months of the dry season. As groups move about on their Countries, carrying out burning, a mosaic pattern of blackened and green patches develops. The goal of the method is to produce a large number of smaller cooler fires that pose less risk for people and Country.

2.7.   Cosmological connectionism and innovation

I suggested in my introduction that Aboriginal people invested resources in maintaining healthy 'Country'. The use of fire was clearly the single most important technique because of its pervasive effects on ecological

---

[45] J. Russell-Smith, P. J. Whitehead, P. M. Cooke and C. P. Yates, 'Challenges and Opportunities for Fire Management in Fire-prone Northern Australia' in Russell-Smith, Whitehead and Cooke (eds.), *Culture, Ecology and Economy of Fire Management*, 2.

[46] J. Russell-Smith *et al.*, 'Contemporary Fire Regimes of Northern Australia, 1997–2001: Change Since Aboriginal Occupancy, Challenges for Sustainable Management', *International Journal of Wildland Fire*, 12 (2003), 283, 287.

[47] D. Yibarbuk *et al.*, 'Fire Ecology and Aboriginal Land Management in Central Arnhem Land, Northern Australia: a Tradition of Ecosystem Management', *Journal of Biogeography*, 28 (2001), 325.

systems.[48] In this section I want to show how the use of fire can be seen as the outcome of their innovation system and what it reveals about the characteristics of this innovation system.

The first thing to note is that we are dealing with innovation in the form of a method (process innovation) and not a simple act of starting a fire. Achieving a 'cool burn' that causes minimal damage to trees and insect life, but at the same time stimulates grasses into growth, requires an intimate knowledge of how to manage the fire as well as a judgement about exactly the right time and conditions under which to burn so as to produce the right level of regrowth. During the course of the fieldwork, we participated in an indigenous fire workshop in which the method was explained and demonstrated by indigenous experts.[49] It soon became clear that a great deal of experience is required to use the method safely and to produce the right results. Even an expert may on occasion make a mistake, choosing the wrong time to burn. Wrong burning produces thick scrub, a tangled wild. Correct burning produces an open park-like landscape in which native grasses and insects thrive.

Standing in the bush, surrounded by grass ready to burn, the wind drifting about, watching an indigenous man calmly twisting together some paper bark, light it and then start a series of fires that come together into one wall of flame makes one realize how much depends on accurate judgement about exactly when and where to start the fire. The flames must not reach too high because it is a basic law that the canopy must not burn. The fire has to move and stop in a predictable way. Lives depend on this. After one demonstration I walked over the ground that ten minutes before had been burned. The ground felt warm on the palm of my hand, but not hot. Ants were moving about. The first metre or so of the trunks of the trees had been blackened but the canopy had not been touched. In the distance the wall of flame had been reduced to a trickle, heading towards the lagoon that would bring it extinguishment.

The mosaic method of burning requires supervision by 'masters of the method', as one of our interviewees put it. It is not a matter of just strolling into the bush and randomly setting bits of it alight. During our work in the Gulf Country we were told of incidents in which Aboriginal youths would without supervision set fire to Country. Not surprisingly, these incidents caused great concern amongst senior people because the

---

[48] For the effects of fire on the ecology of the savanna see J. Russell-Smith, T. Start and J. Woinarski, *Effects of Fire in the Landscape* available at www.savanna.org.au/land_manager/downloads/sav-burning-fire-plants.pdf.

[49] The Indigenous Fire Workshop Program, 12 July 2010 to Friday 16 July 2010. The workshop was hosted by the Chuulangun community which is based at Chuulangun on the upper Wenlock River, Northern Queensland.

youths were doing something that was dangerous to themselves and others.

The use and development of the method is intimately linked to cosmologies:

The secret of fire in our traditional knowledge is that it is a thing that brings the land alive again. When we do burning the whole land comes alive again – it is reborn. But it is not a thing for people to play with unless they understand the nature of fire … the fire-drive is itself regarded as a sacred and very serious act, often first enacted by the major creative beings for that area.[50]

From the place-time cosmologies of indigenous people it follows that indigenous innovation is place-based innovation. It takes place on 'Country', where indigenous people observe and interact with the plants and animals to which they are cosmologically linked in some way. Their Country is their laboratory. Individuals can, of course, leave the place of their cosmological affiliation, but remain part of a network, communicating with its other members and contributing to its production of knowledge. Place anchors indigenous networks of innovation, but these networks can extend beyond place.

The mosaic method of burning is an example of how indigenous innovation depends on careful observation. Devising this method of burning and finding out its practical benefits could only have been done through cycles of observation and experimentation. For example, on the Arnhem Land Plateau indigenous people employed burning techniques for a variety of purposes, including to stimulate the growth of fruit trees and the shooting of new grass so that kangaroos would grow fat.[51] Discovering the linkages between fire, the seasons (Aboriginal calendars contain more seasons than just dry and wet) and species of flora and fauna requires observation and experimentation over a long period of time. Indigenous people using the method were engaged in a process of incremental innovation.

It was also a process of innovation featuring the presence of uncodified knowledge. The information theoretic perspective on innovation draws a distinction between codified and uncodifed information, with the latter

[50] D. Yibarbuk cited in M. Langton, '"The Fire at the Centre of Each Family": Aboriginal Traditional Fire Regimes and the Challenges for Reproducing Ancient Fire Management in the Protected Areas of Northern Australia' in *Fire, The Australian Experience, Proceedings of the 1999 Seminar* (National Academies Forum, 2000), 3, 7–8.
[51] For these and examples of other purposes see M. Garde in collaboration with B. Lofty Nadjamerrek, M. Kolkkiwarra, J. Kalarriya, J. Djandjomer, B. Birriyabirriya, R. Bilindja, M. Kubarkku and P. Bliss, 'The Language of Fire: Seasonality, Resources and Landscape Burning on the Arnhem Land Plateau' in Russell-Smith, Whitehead and Cooke (eds.), *Culture, Ecology and Economy of Fire Management*, 85.

being best transferred by means of personal communication.[52] A subset of uncodified information may also be uncodifiable and therefore only capable of being transmitted through personal teaching. This, as we saw in chapter 1, is Polanyi's argument. As I have already indicated, burning was done under the supervision of a knowledgeable elder and could only have been passed on through personal training.

Aboriginal people's systems of innovation were less oriented towards direct product innovation and more oriented towards the use of methods to improve the ecological systems they observed on their Countries. If we look at the technological products of Aboriginal people prior to colonization they largely consist of the wooden and stone tools and hunting implements that one might expect of hunter-gatherer societies.[53] But different theories of innovation illuminate different dimensions of a society's achievements in innovation. The information theoretic perspective locates innovation in collective processes of generating information to reduce uncertainty.[54] By experimenting with fire techniques Aboriginal people were able to implement a system of management to regulate or enhance the performance of ecological systems. Bowman suggests that the 'great triumph of the Pleistocene Australians was the taming of wildfires through the development of "igniculture"'.[55] A system for the regulation of wildfires produced other desirable effects in other systems. One study of an area in north-central Arnhem Land on which this traditional method of burning had been more or less continuously used to present time showed that the method promoted ecological integrity as measured by a number of indicators such as biodiversity, the presence of rare native fauna and threatened fire-sensitive vegetation types.[56] Through fire regimes, indigenous groups shaped ecosystems to produce a diversity of flora and fauna that helped foraging indigenous groups to survive.[57] Services by indigenous groups to Country were rewarded by improved ecosystems services.

Summing up, we can see that indigenous innovation has at least the following features. It is a place-based form of innovation that is deeply integrated into a cosmological connectionist scheme in which all

---

[52] T. Mandeville, *Understanding Novelty: Information, Technological Change, and the Patent System* (Norwood, NJ: Ablex Publishing Corporation, 1996), 50.
[53] Keen, *Aboriginal Economy*, ch. 3.   [54] Mandeville, *Understanding Novelty*, 49.
[55] D. Bowman, 'Bushfires: a Darwinian Perspective' in G. Cary, D. Lindenmayer and S. Dovers (eds.), *Australia Burning: Fire Ecology, Policy and Management Issues* (Victoria: CSIRO Publishing, 2003), 3, 10.
[56] Yibarbuk *et al.*, 'Fire Ecology', 325.
[57] R. B. Bird, *et al.*, 'The "Fire Stick" Hypothesis: Australian Aboriginal Foraging Strategies, Biodiversity, and Anthropogenic Fire Mosaics', *Proceedings of the National Academy of Sciences*, 105 (2008), 14796.

innovation has threads leading back to ancestors. The cosmological scheme disposes those in the system to careful observation. The innovation system depends on the transmission of knowledge that has to be learnt through personal training. The goals and expression of innovation have less to do with products and everything to do with services to Country. It is a system of innovation that specializes in the maintenance or enhancement of ecological systems.

2.8.   Humiliation and pride in innovation

Under the leadership of scientists such as Jeremy Russell-Smith, the links amongst indigenous fire technology, land management practices, wildfires and biodiversity have come to be much better understood. Using remote sensing technologies, methods have been developed to assess the impact of wildfires and fire regimes in Australia.

As states have lurched towards reducing their carbon emissions, new and unexpected opportunities have arisen for indigenous people to make some economic gains from their innovation systems. The mosaic method of burning is important to controlling the danger of late season uncontrolled wildfires in Australia's savanna country. Reducing the incidence of these fires reduces the overall carbon emissions from savanna burning. When the mining company ConocoPhillips gained permission to build a Liquid Natural Gas plant in Darwin in the late 1990s, a condition imposed by the Northern Territory government was that it offset the emissions from the plant by 100,000 tonnes. Conoco went looking for a greenhouse gas offset strategy, investigating 'various schemes and scams to get offsets' (interview). Ultimately it settled on a carbon abatement scheme that relies on the knowledge and skills of indigenous groups to carry out the managed burning of the savanna landscape. The work and methodologies developed by Jeremy Russell-Smith's group became the basis for a seventeen-year contract in which Conoco agreed to pay $10 a tonne for a minimum of 100,000 tonnes.[58] Known as the West Arnhem Land Fire Management Agreement it involved agreements and partnerships between Conoco, the Northern Territory government, Aboriginal traditional owners and groups, the Northern Land Council, Northern Territory Bushfires Council and the Tropical Savannas CRC.

At the time of our interviews in 2008 we were told that almost all the money went into paying indigenous groups to carry out the fire

---

[58] A brief description of the West Arnhem Land Fire Management Agreement is to be found at http://www.conocophillips.com.au/EN/responsibilities/health/environment/wafma/Pages/WAFMA.aspx.

management. A helicopter has to sweep into remote places to drop incendiaries where thousands of years ago indigenous people would have carried out the burning on foot. Now an indigenous expert sits in a helicopter advising on exactly where those incendiaries have to be dropped (interview, 2008). How much is left over for indigenous groups involved in the burning once all the costs of burning are met was not something for which we were given figures, but according to some of our interviewees it was not a lot. The Conoco deal has been important in helping one indigenous elder to get his group back onto Country (interview, 2008).

There will be different views about whether the price that Conoco is paying for the offset is too expensive or too cheap. But this arrangement has set the stage for bigger thinking and projects involving the use of indigenous people's skills of land management. Four new carbon abatement projects have been proposed for different areas of northern Australia, capable of generating a large volume of carbon credits and at the time of our interviews the proposal was to aggregate these credits under one trading desk.[59] Where this will go in the medium term will obviously be affected by the price of carbon and whether there are investors that will be prepared to take the risk in backing these kinds of projects. But these projects are examples of how indigenous people using their specialized skills of fire technology and knowledge of Country might be able to generate revenue streams in emerging carbon markets.[60] There is a cautionary note that should be sounded here. When investment banks such as Goldman Sachs enter markets in conservation, biodiversity and carbon trading they can structure products in these markets in ways that very few other players understand. Generally the real beneficiaries from these kinds of opaque deals turn out to be insiders. The Conoco deal, which is a simple carbon credit offset arrangement, has not benefited all traditional owners (TOs) in the area: 'Most of the TOs still get CDEP [welfare payments] and most do not know about the scheme' (indigenous interviewee, 2008).

This particular case study illustrates a theme taken up in detail in chapters 10 and 11 – the utilization of indigenous knowledge assets by indigenous people in today's economic context depends heavily upon the

---

[59] For the details see www.edgefunders.org/wp-content/uploads/2012/01/Savannahburning. pdf.

[60] For a model of the effect of this carbon revenue on land management see L. L. Douglass, H. P. Possingham, J. Carwardine, C. J. Klein, S. H. Roxburgh, J. Russell-Smith and K. A. Wilson, 'The Effect of Carbon Credits on Savanna Land Management and Priorities for Biodiversity Conservation', *PLoS ONE* 6(9) (2011): e23843. doi:10.1371/journal. pone.0023843.

creation of trusted networks in which scientists become key partners. It is these trusted networks that will provide safe ground for exchanges of knowledge and where mutual respect between scientists and indigenous people can grow. For most of the period of colonization the worth of fire knowledge and techniques of indigenous people were not recognized. Aboriginal people who attempted to manage their Country through fire technology risked the humiliation of a beating by those pastoralists who saw no good in the method.

As I have explained, systematic scientific investigation of indigenous people's fire technology took a long time to develop. Hugely important steps were taken when the scientists in the savanna project realized they were dealing with Aboriginal 'masters of the method' from whom they could genuinely learn (interview, 2008). The danger for indigenous groups is that once their fire knowledge is recorded and analysed it will be utilized by commercial networks in which the state, scientists and the Conocos of this world become the dominant players and indigenous groups the public sideshow. Chris Haynes, for example, argues that the planned burning of Kakadu National Park using helicopters does not match the tradition of burning known by indigenous people in the region as *anwurrk*.[61] One indigenous interviewee from the Kimberley made a similar point suggesting that fire bombing by helicopter was not a substitute for the more controlled on-the-ground burning that indigenous people had practised.

The takeover of indigenous knowledge of high conservation value by networks of commercial partners made up of private investment partners, investment banks and others to the exclusion of knowledgeable indigenous people from decision making about their revealed knowledge is a constant danger. In the final two chapters I argue that indigenous people are trying to meet this danger through indigenous developmental networks that lead the decision making about the use of their knowledge assets. But I also argue that the formation of these networks is a slow process that has to overcome a trust trap.

The Chuulangun fire workshop I mentioned in the previous section was attended by non-indigenous people, but it was probably more important for the indigenous people who had also come. Lots of indigenous communities have lost fire knowledge. The workshop was following a 'bridging principle' of putting this knowledge back into communities. Indigenous fire management is a service that requires intense

---

[61] C. Haynes, 'Realities, Simulacra and the Appropriation of Aboriginality in Kakadu's Tourism' in I. Keen (ed.), *Indigenous Participation in Australian Economies: Historical and Anthropological Perspectives* (Canberra: ANU E Press, 2010), 165, 176.

coordination. For example, in the Chuulangun area there are twenty-two clan estates that have to be 'kept in the loop when it comes to burning country'. Further afield is the 'mob on the coast' and if they burn at the wrong time when the fuel load is too high and there are winds from the Antarctic, destructive walls of flame over twenty metres high can race inland. The case for building and spreading expertise in fire technology is strong. If indigenous fire management is to work it has to be coordinated by experts, not amateurs. In the words of one indigenous man 'building the confidence to put the first match to the ground is critical'.

Over the five days of the Chuulangun fire workshop I heard indigenous people speak with pride about the importance of their fire knowledge. It was not a hubristic pride, but a quiet pride in the collective achievement of previous generations that was at last being seen by others. Creating a pride that reinforces a sense of worth in one's culture is fundamental to creating confidence, both personal and collective, in younger indigenous people. Colonization created many lasting legacies, one of them being a loss of confidence by many young indigenous people in their ancestral culture. As one senior indigenous man explained to me, when indigenous elders are trying to persuade young indigenous people to embrace cultural practices such as dance, indigenous elders have to find ways to get these young people to 'drop shame'.

During the workshop I sat down next to an old indigenous man who had not spoken at the workshop. We talked a bit about Country. Later I found out it was Tommy George, a Senior Elder of the Kuku-Thaypan clan. He had escaped being caught by the police during the period when Aboriginal children were being forcibly separated from their families. He went on to become one of the great experts in indigenous knowledge systems, recognized by indigenous and non-indigenous people alike. Tommy George would have over the decades seen the gradual deterioration of much Country as it stopped being managed by indigenous people. But at the workshop he sat quietly listening to a younger generation of indigenous leaders trained in English, speaking to attentive groups in which stood uniformed members of rural fire services from around Australia. Some progress has been made since Governor Phillip saw indigenous burning practices as an obstacle to releasing his swine into native forests.

3   Loss

3.1.   The first pistol

In January of 1788 the ships of the first fleet, which Great Britain had sent to establish the colony of New South Wales, sailed into Botany Bay. An empire in the grip of an industrial revolution was about to confront stateless indigenous societies that had lived in a vast continent for an estimated 50,000 years.

By 1788 the musket and pistol were well developed pieces of military technology in Europe. Soon after the arrival of the fleet in Botany Bay, an officer demonstrated the power of the pistol to a group of Aboriginal people by firing at a bark target. Watkin Tench, an officer on one of the ships who wrote an account of the fleet's arrival, described the incident in the following way:[1]

> Our first object was to win their affections, and our next to convince them of the superiority we possessed: for without the latter, the former we knew would be of little importance ... The Indians, though terrified at the report, did not run away, but their astonishment exceeded their alarm, on looking at the shield which the ball had perforated.

News of the musket travelled fast through indigenous communities and while it was feared, the Aboriginal guerilla fighters who resisted the white invaders progressively worked out its limitation in terms of distance and accuracy. Standing at a safe distance they would sometimes attempt to provoke the musket holder to fire his hard-to-reload musket through gestures such as slapping their buttocks, a somewhat derisory assessment of this European technology.[2] In the widespread conflicts that followed two things helped to crush the resistance of Aboriginal fighters. The musket and the pistol were replaced by the rifle and the revolver. Rapidity

---

[1] Watkin Tench, *A Narrative of the Expedition to Botany Bay* (1789) available as an E-text at http://setis.library.usyd.edu.au/ozlit/pdf/p00039.pdf, chapter VIII.
[2] For an account of Aboriginal resistance see H. Reynolds, *The Other Side of the Frontier* (North Queensland: James Cook University, 1981).

of fire was no longer constrained by the slowness of reloading. The other major factor was the creation of the native mounted police. Colonizing empires rarely succeed in their conquests without the assistance of some local people who are persuaded in one way or another to join the colonizer's forces. The creation of the native mounted police in New South Wales, Queensland and Victoria countered, at least to some extent, the tactical advantages that Aboriginal fighters had based on their knowledge and skills in the bush.[3] In Queensland, the Native Police operating on horseback and armed with rifles had considerable success in finding Aboriginal camps and killing the inhabitants. Killing old people was a priority because they were seen as having special knowledge and powers.[4] In central Australia, the Native Police, which had been established in 1884 under the command of William Willshire to deal with problems of cattle killing, captured many indigenous people. According to the official reports indigenous suspects were generally killed while trying to escape.[5]

The guerilla resistance by many Aboriginal groups in the face of the colonial invasion led, according to Reynolds, to some 20,000 Aboriginal people being killed by the colonists, with Aboriginal people killing between 2,000 and 2,500 Europeans.[6] Massacres of indigenous people continued into the twentieth century, the killings at Coniston in central Australia in 1928 being an example. A recent analysis of these killings points to a number of deaths that is at least more than twice the official figure of thirty-one deaths and may well be five or six times higher.[7]

After 1788 the Aboriginal population declined, but the extent and causes of that decline are uncertain. Smith, in a very detailed analysis of the Aboriginal population changes published in 1980, observed that there had been no real attempt to understand the relative contributions of massacres, diseases, land loss and other factors to the depopulation that followed the arrival of the colonists.[8] Work since 1980 suggests that by far the single biggest killer of indigenous Australians was smallpox.[9] In the case of Australia, the evidence points to smallpox preceding the

---

[3] *Ibid.*, 85.
[4] J. Richards, 'The Native Police of Queensland', *History Compass*, 6 (2008), 1024, 1026.
[5] A. Nettlebeck and R. Foster, *In The Name Of The Law: William Willshire and the Policing of the Australian Frontier* (South Australia: Wakefield Press, 2007), 31–5.
[6] Reynolds, 99.
[7] B. Wilson and J. O'Brien, '"To Infuse an Universal Terror": a Reappraisal of the Coniston Killings', *Aboriginal History*, 27 (2003), 59.
[8] L. R. Smith, *The Aboriginal Population of Australia* (Canberra: Australian National University Press, 1980).
[9] See J. Campbell, *Invisible Invaders: Smallpox and Other Diseases in Aboriginal Australia 1780–1880* (Victoria: Melbourne University Press, 2002).

arrival of the colonists. The most likely source appears to be fishermen from Sulawesi (an island in Indonesia) searching for trepang for the Chinese market. Commonly referred to as the Macassans, somewhere between two and three thousand made the trip to northern Australia each year during the wet season, living on the beaches, intermingling with Aboriginal people and collecting trepang.[10] The illegal collecting of trepang by Indonesian fishermen remains a problem today. Of the diseases brought by the Europeans, tuberculosis accounted for the most indigenous lives.

Reviewing the literature and data, Smith put the Aboriginal population in 1788 at approximately 314,000, a figure not much different from the 300,000 estimated by Radcliffe-Brown in 1930.[11] Smith points out the highly conservative nature of Radcliffe-Brown's estimate and the weakness of his own assessment and concludes that the best we can say is that the pre-contact population was several hundred thousand without being able to say how many hundred thousand.[12] Butlin argues that the estimate of 300,000 completely ignores the effects of smallpox and that the figures for the indigenous population of south-eastern Australia were at least five times higher than assumed in that estimate.[13] Butlin does not argue that population estimates for northern Australia have to be increased by a similar factor, but based on his analysis one could easily double or even triple the size of the pre-contact population. There are other estimates for the 1788 population, including 750,000 or 1.25 million.[14] The numbers given for the Aboriginal population towards the end of the nineteenth century and into the first part of the twentieth are probably better estimates because colonial administrators began to record more and more information about Aboriginal populations in their districts and states. The Australian Bureau of Statistics, relying on individual state censuses, places the indigenous population at approximately 93,000 in 1901.[15]

Even if one begins with a conservative estimate of the indigenous population in 1788, it is clear that there was a massive decline in the population in the 100 or so years that followed the first steps of white

---

[10] *Ibid.*, 72–3.   [11] Smith, *The Aboriginal Population of Australia*, 69.   [12] *Ibid.*, 77.
[13] See N. Butlin, *Our Original Aggression: Aboriginal Populations of Southeastern Australia 1788–1850* (Sydney: George Allen & Unwin, 1983).
[14] For a discussion see J. Mulvaney, "'Difficult to Found an Opinion': 1788 Aboriginal Population Estimates' in G. Briscoe and L. Smith (eds.), *The Aboriginal Population Revisited: 70,000 years to the Present*, Aboriginal History Monograph 10 (Canberra: Aboriginal History Inc., 2002), 1.
[15] See www.abs.gov.au/ausstats/abs@.nsf/94713ad45ff1425ca25682000192af2/bfc28642d31 c215cca256b350010b3f4!OpenDocument.

colonists along Botany Bay and Port Jackson. By the end of the nine-teenth century the indigenous population was probably in the range of 10 to 30 per cent of what it had been in 1788. Population density was a key factor in explaining the varying impact of disease in different parts of Australia. In areas of arid Australia where population density was low, perhaps 25 per cent of the population died of smallpox whereas in the Murray-Darling Basin, where tribes and clans lived much more closely to each other, the percentage is likely to be closer to 50 per cent.[16] The non-indigenous population grew from less than 1,000 at settlement to over 400,000 in 1850 to about 3.8 million in 1901.[17] In Southern Australian cities like Adelaide, Aboriginal people become a rarity.[18] The indigenous population kept on falling till the 1930s when it seems to have stabilized at around 75,000.[19]

3.2.   The loss of knowledge

The decline in the indigenous population throughout the nineteenth century also represented a loss of knowledge. All societies have in their people a stock of knowledge, experience and skills. Economists describe this as human capital. When societies are confronted by great crises and threats such as epidemics and invasions they draw upon the skills, knowledge and experience of their members in formulating responses to the immediate crisis as well as longer-term plans for recovery. Human capital is a foundational resource for all societies whether they are capit-alist societies or hunter-gatherer societies. After 1788 the indigenous societies of Australia found themselves entering a century in which they experienced a rapid decline in the stocks of human capital that they had built up through their knowledge and innovation systems.

Human capital has become an increasingly important concept in explaining sources of economic growth in market economies.[20] The concept of human capital includes experience and skills because these things in addition to formal training often enable an individual to gain greater economic returns. Prior to colonization, indigenous people would have built up human capital through processes such as the education and training of their young (initiation and ritual), learning to use technologies such as fire to manage the land for a variety of purposes,

---

[16] Campbell, *Invisible Invaders*, 223.
[17] Historical population statistics are available from the website of the Australian Bureau of Statistics.
[18] Nettlebeck and Foster, *In The Name Of The Law*, 52.
[19] Smith, *The Aboriginal Population of Australia*, 210.
[20] See Greenhalgh and Rogers, *Innovation*, 229–31.

investigating the medicinal properties of plants, exchanging knowledge about those plants, studying weather patterns and so on. The investment by indigenous societies in training, education and the therapeutic investigation of plants to treat illnesses, would all have helped to improve their productive capacity to manage the land and their food supply. One can see indigenous societies as being involved in a process of human capital accumulation, although obviously this process of accumulation did not take place in the context of a capitalist market aimed at producing more and more goods. As chapter 2 argued, cosmological connectionism provided indigenous societies with strong incentives to invest in human capital accumulation in order to learn more about Country and to better provide services to Country. Services to Country helped ecosystems to produce a biological diversity that was important to the foraging strategies of indigenous groups. This was very much a services economy.

An explanation for the low level of goods production in hunter-gatherer economies is advanced by Sahlins: wants were scarce in relation to means and so a low level of goods production satisfied wants.[21] Institutions to support the generation of wants were simply not created in these societies. Sahlins also argues that there is evidence to support the conclusion that at least some hunter-gatherer societies (he draws on data from Arnhem Land) had become efficient in the production of subsistence goods and had made leisure abundant.[22]

Although human capital and services were at the centre of indigenous peoples' economies, this capital does not appear to have been managed for the purposes of economic growth. Cosmological connectionism set up a cycle of services in which the overriding duties of the participants were services to Country. Clearly, human capital accumulation in Aboriginal societies was highly specialized. This was both a strength and a weakness. Increasing specialist skills in managing Country was a strength when it came to living on Country, because those skills enabled people to better manage Country. But it became a weakness once the connection with Country was broken. The place-time cosmology of one Country could not be mapped on to that of another. Those indigenous groups that were forced off their traditional Countries became, in a way, strangers in strange lands.

All the survival strategies available to indigenous groups under colonization were high risk. Where the colonists saw obviously fertile land they would often resort to extreme violence in order to take it from the indigenous owners. The fighting around the Hawkesbury riverbank land,

---

[21] M. Sahlins, *Stone Age Economics* (New York: Aldine de Gruyter, 1972), 13.
[22] *Ibid.*, 14.

near what was to become Sydney, was intense for this reason, with the bodies of Aboriginal people at one campsite 'left hanging on gibbets, to terrorise their kinsfolk'.[23] If Aboriginal groups shifted to more remote locations they risked their known food supplies. The malnutrition that followed when indigenous groups lost access to the places where they had usually hunted and gathered food was recorded by a few nineteenth-century observers.[24] Some indigenous groups chose a survival strategy based on becoming fringe dwellers around white settlements, but being in such close proximity carried risks, even in cases of a small white settlement in a remote part of Australia. McKnight, for example, describes how the establishment of Burketown in 1865 in the Gulf country with a small non-Aboriginal population of less than a hundred brought with it, amongst other things, opium, alcohol, venereal diseases, and whooping cough. Disease, along with the fact that the police and pastoralists shot the local Aboriginal inhabitants, 'had a catastrophic effect on the neighbouring tribes'.[25]

By focusing on the human capital dimensions of Aboriginal societies we get a better understanding of why colonization had such devastating effects on them. The explanation lies in the attack on indigenous institutions of human capital accumulation. The institutions that indigenous people had created for the purpose of increasing knowledge and services to Country came under extreme pressure. As we saw in the previous section, the smallpox epidemics of the nineteenth century were responsible for the greatest number of deaths in Aboriginal societies, but it was colonization that was responsible for the attack on Aboriginal institutions of property and knowledge through the imposition of legal systems and policies such as assimilation. The policies of colonization concerning land rights and the education of indigenous children made the process of inter-generational transfer of human capital amongst indigenous groups extraordinarily difficult. As Aboriginal groups were dispossessed of land they not only lost the land as an asset, but they also began to experience the break-up of the institutions that had grown around the land and that had carried an understanding of the land across generations. The distinctive economy that Aboriginal people had built up through an accumulation of specialist human capital around services to Country was swept away in many parts of Australia.

[23] H. Goodall, *Invasion to Embassy: Land in Aboriginal Politics in New South Wales, 1770–1972* (New South Wales: Allen & Unwin, 1996), 28.
[24] See, for example, the extract by the nineteenth-century historian Samuel Bennett in H. Reynolds (ed.), *Aborigines and Settlers: the Australian Experience 1788–1939* (New South Wales and Victoria: Cassell Australia, 1972), 77–8.
[25] McKnight, *People, Countries, and the Rainbow Serpent,* 4.

3.3.   Loss of Country

The taking of Aboriginal land by the colonists can be divided into a formal process of rule imposition and a practical process of dispossession. As we saw in the first section of this chapter, the practical process of dispossession consisted of fighting a war of invasion and then occupying the territory that had been taken. The occupation and use of conquered Aboriginal territory was stimulated by structural changes in the nature of British capitalism. In particular, the London wool market in the early nineteenth century shifted to a dependence on imported wool.[26] Responding to this change in demand, Australian colonial authorities in the 1820s began to grant larger tracts of land, much of which was turned to sheep grazing. The official release of land did not keep pace with demand and so squatting on a large scale became common. Many made the journey from England, eager to build a fortune on the sheep's back. By 1850 colonial Australia was supplying almost 50 per cent of Britain's wool needs, much of this expansion in wool production being financed by London commercial credit.[27] Changes in British industrial and financial capitalism created an aggressive hunger for pastoral property in Australia. Squatters supported by London financiers became a powerful interest group and were in 1847 able to secure changes to the law granting them long-term leases at comparatively little cost. As is often the case, secure property was the outcome of merchant investment and not its cause. Wealth buys the laws needed for secure property. In the words of a critic at the time: 'The price he [the squatter] has to pay for these privileges, counting three sheep to an acre, is a fifth of a penny per acre.'[28] To purchase the land as freehold would have cost at least one pound per acre. Millions of acres that had for tens of thousands of years been the subject of indigenous systems of ownership, fell into the hands of 'shepherd-kings'.[29] The resulting changes to land use patterns must have seemed utterly astonishing to indigenous people. Where there had been indigenous tribes and native forests and animals there were now white people and white sheep in ever growing numbers.

The formal process of imposition involved the application of the common law system to the territory of what became Australia. Under

---

[26] P. McMichael, *Settlers And The Agrarian Question: Foundations Of Capitalism In Colonial Australia* (Cambridge University Press, 1984), 55.

[27] *Ibid.*, 101–3.

[28] Robert Lowe, a barrister and member of the Legislative Council cited in S. H. Roberts, *The Squatting Age In Australia 1835–1847* (Carlton, Victoria: Melbourne University Press, 1975), 271.

[29] Robert Lowe's phrase cited in *ibid.*, 270.

the system Aboriginal people became subjects of the Queen. The system did not formally recognize the ancestral systems of Aboriginal people, even though many officials and commentators of the time likened various indigenous groups' control of land to British categories of property ownership, including exclusive rights.[30] At the time colonial authorities took the view that any customary rights, if they existed, were extinguished by the manner of the Crown's occupation of Australian territory. More than 200 years later this was found to be the wrong view of the law. The Australian High Court in its *Mabo* decision found that the reception of British law into Australian colonies did not produce the chain of extinguishment supposed by colonial legal authorities.[31] Legal truth depends on factual truths. The application of the English common law relating to property ownership in Australia rested on two linked falsehoods identified by the court. Essentially these were that indigenous people were barbarous and that they had no system of laws. Assuming these two claims to be true allowed the common law of England to fill a legal vacuum, namely the territory of New South Wales over which the British Crown claimed sovereignty. The common law operated on the principle that the Crown was the root of all individual title held by the subjects of the Crown. It followed that once the common law applied to a territory the Crown became the owner of the territory. The common law enabled the Crown's ownership of the land, but what was it that enabled the application of the common law? The answer lies in the operation of the extended doctrine of *terra nullius*. Originally the doctrine allowed a state to acquire sovereignty over an uninhabited territory through an act of occupation. In its extended version a state could through an act of occupation claim sovereignty over a territory that was already inhabited but where the inhabitants had very low levels of social and political organization and so could be considered primitive. The High Court reconsidered the operation of Australian common law based on the evidence of highly organized indigenous systems, including systems of property ownership. It declared the existence of a native title that could and did survive settlement. Settlement established sovereignty, but the sovereignty of the Crown of itself did not lead to an extinguishment at common law of native title. Whether or not the Crown had extinguished native title depended on the manner in which it had exercised its sovereignty over a given area of land.

---

[30] See I. Keen, 'The Interpretation of Aboriginal "Property" on the Australian Colonial Frontier' in Keen (ed.), *Indigenous Participation*, 41.

[31] *Mabo v Queensland (No. 2)* 175 CLR 1.

The *Mabo* judgment arrived some 204 years after colonization. During this period the various Australian colonies introduced private property institutions into their jurisdictions, those institutions providing various classes of owners such as pastoralists, farmers and miners with incentives to make investments. At the same time indigenous people had under the rules of the colonial economy close to no land assets. Faced by pressure from indigenous people for the return of some of their land, as well as from politically influential anti-slavery interests in England, the colonial authorities settled on the creation of reserves. These were small areas of Crown land set aside for use by Aboriginal people. As Heather Goodall has shown for New South Wales, the creation of these reserves was the product of complex politics in which different interest groups such as the squatters and miners took different views of the nature of the rights that came with reserves.[32] Thirty-five reserves were created in 1850 in New South Wales. They were approximately one square mile each in area. Prior to colonization indigenous groups had control of Countries that were hundreds or thousands of square miles in size. One can only speculate what they thought of the grant of thirty-five 1-square-mile reserves.

However, at least in NSW, the squatters' desperate need for labour resulted in, at least for a little while, a measure of coexistence between them and many Aboriginal groups, thereby allowing those groups to gain access to some of their traditional lands. Indigenous groups found ways to integrate their ceremonies into the cycle of pastoral management. Even if indigenous groups were from time to time able to reach access arrangements to their lands, the overarching reality of the nineteenth and twentieth centuries became insecurity of access. Land use in the colonies became the subject of political contests amongst squatters, miners, farmers and the urban classes, contests that Aboriginal people had little chance of influencing. So, for example, as the squatters lost influence and their runs were broken up into smaller holdings for other uses such as wheat farming, indigenous groups found themselves having to fight for access.[33]

Faced by this politics of land use and the ever-increasing use of their land, Aboriginal groups kept pressing for a return of a portion of their traditional lands. In NSW, the government responded by creating thirty-two reserves (the reserves of 1850 appear to have simply faded away). By 1911, 115 reserves had been created in NSW.[34]

The reserve system that was put in place in NSW and in the other colonies did not provide Aboriginal groups with security of property

---

[32] Goodall, *Invasion to Embassy*, 54–6.   [33] *Ibid.*, 70–1.   [34] *Ibid.*, 96.

rights in either the economic sense or the moral sense in which philosophers sometimes use the property concept. The full moral sense of property is used by John Locke when he refers to 'lives, liberties and estates' as property.[35] Property for Locke in this sense included rights of personal security, as well as the security of one's things and land. The reserve system did not deliver either security of estates or personal security for indigenous people. By way of example, the Weipa reserve in far north Queensland was cut by the government in 1959 from 354,828 hectares to 124 hectares in order to accommodate the bauxite leases of the mining company Comalco.[36] In NSW reserve lands in 1938 amounted to about 15,000 acres. By 1964 this had been cut to about 1,500 acres, the rest being revoked or leased to white people.[37]

The reserves also became places of great personal insecurity. The welfare of indigenous people living on reserves was placed in the hands of regulatory authorities in the form of protection boards or chief protectors.[38] These regulatory authorities were given formal powers of control over indigenous adults and their children. The power to declare indigenous children to be wards of the state was often threatened by white authorities when indigenous activists were fighting for their rights, with examples of these threats to be found in the 1970s when indigenous activism over land rights reached very high levels.[39] The practical exercise of these powers was driven by the goal of assimilation. The NSW Board, faced by funding problems, also seized the farm blocks of some Aboriginal farmers in order to lease them out. The return of soldiers from the First World War brought more demand for land. In NSW this contributed to a 'relentless second dispossession' in which many of the reserves for indigenous people were reduced in size through official revocation.[40] The failure to protect the property rights of Aboriginal people in the full Lockean sense continued. In 1936 the Board gained the power to move Aboriginal people to specific locations in order to manage them more efficiently according to Board policy. This power to concentrate Aboriginal people in a few locations, often away from Countries, led them to refer to the 1936 amendments as the 'Dog Act'.[41]

---

[35] J. Locke, *The Second Treatise Of Government (1690)* (Indianapolis: Bobbs-Merrill Educational Publishing, 1952), para. 123.

[36] F. Brennan, *Land Rights Queensland Style: the Struggle for Aboriginal Self-management* (University of Queensland Press, 1992), 8.

[37] Goodall, *Invasion to Embassy*, 321–2.

[38] For the history of these boards and protectors see *Bringing Them Home: Report of the National Inquiry into the Separation of Aboriginal and Torres Strait Islander Children From Their Families* (Commonwealth of Australia, 1997), ch. 2.

[39] Goodall, *Invasion to Embassy*, 341.   [40] *Ibid.*, 125.   [41] *Ibid.*, 193.

Obviously in those areas where the 'Dog Act' was used to its fullest extent, Aboriginal people would have had to struggle to maintain their indigenous knowledge systems because, amongst other things, they were not on the lands and sites to which they needed access in order to carry out ceremonial activities and teach their children.

In the nineteenth century and for much of the twentieth century indigenous people were deprived of the economic rights and personal security that liberal philosophers such as John Locke identified as being necessary to the expression of a full and free life. This failure to extend the protection of liberal conceptions of property to indigenous people was made easier by the fact that liberal philosophers like Locke peddled arguments deliberately aimed at excluding indigenous people from those protections.[42]

The last three decades or so of the twentieth century in Australia saw indigenous people begin to make significant gains in terms of land rights. The collective struggles of indigenous people opened up three basic pathways to acquiring land with varying degrees of control over that land. Land rights legislation enacted by the states forms one such pathway. The details of this legislation vary with some states creating one central land-owning body and other states working with a more decentralized model of a number of land-owning bodies.[43] The election of the Whitlam Labour government in 1972 eventually brought land rights legislation to the Northern Territory, legislation that created strong freehold rights over indigenous land.[44]

A second pathway is through the processes that operate under the Commonwealth's Native Title Act of 1993, a law that was passed by the then Labour government in response to the *Mabo* decision. The Liberal government in 1998 made some long amendments in response to the High Court decision in the *Wik* case, a case in which a majority of the court found that the grant of a pastoral lease did not necessarily extinguish native title. Indigenous people had to contend with politicians who wanted to deliver 'bucket loads of extinguishment' to white constituencies worried about the security of what their colonial predecessors

---

[42] See J. Tully, 'Consent, Hegemony and Dissent in Treaty Negotiations' in J. Webber and C. M. Macleod (eds.), *Between Consenting Peoples: Political Community and the Meaning of Consent* (Vancouver: UBC Press, 2010), 233.

[43] The centralized model is to be found in South Australia (Aboriginal Lands Trust Act 1966) and Tasmania (Aboriginal Lands Act 1995). In other states ownership is divided amongst land trust bodies. See, for example, Aboriginal Lands Act 1970 (Victoria) and Aboriginal Lands Act 1991 (Victoria) and Aboriginal Land Act 1991 (Queensland).

[44] Aboriginal Land Rights (Northern Territory) Act 1976 (Commonwealth).

had taken from Aboriginal people.[45] This pathway is well trodden with the National Native Title Tribunal, which registers applications for native title, reporting that as of June 2012 it had 471 applications in its system.[46] Negotiating rather than litigating native title issues has seen the registration of some 646 Indigenous Land Use Agreements that together cover 18 per cent of the land mass of Australia.[47]

A third pathway to land for indigenous people has been through land acquisition programmes. Placing much more emphasis on the goal of indigenous self-determination, the Whitlam government in the early 1970s started funding the purchase of pastoral leases for indigenous communities. Through the 1980s and 1990s various government agencies spent millions of dollars on the acquisition of some seventy leases.[48] In 1995 the Indigenous Land Corporation (ILC) was formed as a statutory authority under Commonwealth legislation. It has acquired some 231 properties totalling some 5.7 million hectares.[49]

How much land has been recovered by indigenous people through these pathways? Estimates of the amount of land under indigenous ownership have to contend with definitional and rule complexity brought about by state and Commonwealth legislative systems that regulate this ownership. In 2000 Pollack estimated that indigenous people owned, controlled or had some management capacity over 16 to 18 per cent of land in Australia.[50] He also identified a huge diversity when it came to ownership and governance arrangements for this land.

One can be critical of the statutory complexity that surrounds this ownership, but it is clear that indigenous people have some degree of ownership over a significant percentage of land in Australia, a monumental achievement when one keeps in mind that the baseline of ownership is the trivially small reserves of the nineteenth century. As indigenous groups regain land and/or increase their degree of control over land they also increase their opportunities to strengthen and rebuild their indigenous systems of knowledge. As we saw in chapter 2 under

---

[45] The phrase was uttered by Deputy Prime Minister Tim Fischer in 1998 in an ABC interview.

[46] See National Native Title Tribunal, *Annual Report, 2011–2012*, 37 available at www.nntt.gov.au/.

[47] See *ibid*.

[48] See E. Young, 'Rhetoric to Reality in Sustainability: Meeting the Challenges in Indigenous Cattle Station Communities' in Taylor *et al.* (eds.), *The Power of Knowledge*, 116, 119.

[49] Figure obtained from the website of the Indigenous Land Corporation. See www.ilc.gov.au.

[50] D. P. Pollack, 'A Quantitative Assessment of Indigenous Landholdings in 2000', Discussion Paper 221/2001, Centre for Aboriginal Economic Policy Research, available at http://caepr.anu.edu.au/sites/default/files/Publications/DP/2001_DP221.pdf.

conditions of cosmological connectionism indigenous people were able to create knowledge assets that allowed them to manage ecosystems, the knowledge assets around the use of fire being a prominent example. These knowledge assets have income-generating potential for indigenous groups. The use of customary fire knowledge to generate income by providing a carbon offset service is one example of this. The combination of land ownership and cosmological connectionism opens a door to creation and use of distinctive knowledge assets in a range of environmental services, especially in northern Australia where indigenous ownership of land amounts to some 30 per cent.[51] Basically indigenous people can make economic gains from their knowledge assets if governments are willing to pay for the utilization of those knowledge assets as a public good or if they can find ways to privately capture some of the social benefits of those knowledge assets. As we will see in the next chapter there has been a widespread recognition in various international treaties that indigenous knowledge has important social benefits. But we will also see that this recognition has taken the form of 'soft' principle. This has left states with lots of discretion as to how to regulate indigenous knowledge assets. As we will see in the following chapters, Australia has done comparatively little to address the extractive effects of its intellectual property rights systems.

---

[51] For a discussion of the possibilities for indigenous people in northern Australia see J. Altman, K. Jordan, S. Kerins, G. Buchanan, N. Biddle, E. J. Ens and K. May, 'Indigenous Interests in Land & Water' in *Northern Australia Land and Water Science Review*, 2009, ch. 7.

4   Symbolic recognition

4.1.   'Savages'

In his short essay, 'The Noble Savage', Charles Dickens concludes that 'if we have anything to learn from the Noble Savage, it is what to avoid. His virtues are a fable; his happiness is a delusion; his nobility, nonsense.'[1] Dickens' venomous characterization of tribal cultures was not the only view of them. Other European writers presented a more romantic conception of the virtues of 'savages', although almost none used the term 'noble savage'.[2] European intellectual traditions invested the category of 'savage' with qualities ranging from inherent moral goodness to murderousness. These categorical versions of the 'savage' did not remain confined to European parlours, but travelled with colonists, serving to filter their perceptions of indigenous people.

Governor Macquarie in a letter written in 1814 describes indigenous Australians as 'Savages' prone to 'great Indolence', but 'honestly Inclined' and having qualities that 'if properly Cultivated' might make them 'progressively Useful to the Country'.[3] The explorer Thomas Mitchell provided a very different image of indigenous people in his journals describing them as the 'children of nature'.[4] The dominant category of thought that European intellectuals had bequeathed to their colonizing settlers about indigenous people was the 'savage', a category usually counter-poised to that of civilization.[5]

---

[1] The essay was first published by Dickens in 1853. For a discussion of it and Dickens' other writing on indigenous peoples see F. Orestano, 'Dickens on the Indians' in C. F. Feest (ed.), *Indians and Europe: An Interdisciplinary Collection of Essays* (Aachen: Edition Herodot and Rader Verlag, 1987), 277.

[2] See T. Ellingson, *The Myth of the Noble Savage* (Berkley and Los Angeles: University of California Press, 2001).

[3] Macquarie's letter is extracted in Reynolds (ed.), *Aborigines and Settlers*, 109–11.

[4] See the entry dated 11 May, Mitchell, *Journal of an Expedition*, ch. IV.

[5] For examples of these images see the documents assembled in Reynolds (ed.), *Aborigines and Settlers*, ch. 7.

These categories and the lines of reasoning they underpinned did little to stimulate settler society into taking an interest in the knowledge systems of Aboriginal groups. The states of Europe measured their superiority and progress in terms of technological achievements, with the great trade fairs of the nineteenth century being places where this technological prowess was exhibited. The Industrial Revolution had created great demand for raw materials of all kinds, from the food needed by growing cities to the coal and ore essential for iron and steel production. Primitive industrial capitalism set in train processes of resource extraction from the earth's natural systems that continue today, albeit on a much larger scale than anything in the nineteenth century. Australia's colonial economies were built on natural resource extraction in the agricultural, maritime, mining, and pastoral sectors to service the needs of a resource-hungry mother country. Whale oil, wool and gold were amongst the first important exports.

This extractive approach to the land led to an extractive attitude towards indigenous knowledge. Generally speaking, the colonists were interested in indigenous knowledge that helped them to explore the country and exploit its resources. As the journals of explorers like Mitchell and Sturt make clear indigenous guides helped expeditions by leading them to waterholes and showing them food sources. Indigenous knowledge and labour in collecting and then diving for pearl shell along the coastlines of Western Australia provided the start for an industry in which Broome was to become the world centre.[6] The pastoralists who occupied vast tracts of indigenous land came to realize the practical value of indigenous people's knowledge about the land's food and water resources. For example, before the use of artesian bores the early cattle industry in central Australia was dependent on the local knowledge of Aboriginal people about rainfall patterns and water sources.[7]

There are examples of individuals taking a more systematic interest in indigenous knowledge institutions, an obvious example being the anthropological work of the explorer and administrator Alfred Howitt in the second half of the nineteenth century.[8] A wider interest in fact gathering and reporting on the indigenous way of life did occur towards the end of the nineteenth century in Australia, mainly as a result of the publication of Darwin's *Origin of the Species* (1859), which had stimulated an interest

---

[6] See J. Bailey, *The White Divers of Broome* (Sydney: Pan Macmillan, 2001), ch. 2.
[7] See A. Paterson 'Early Pastoral Landscapes and Cultural Contact in Central Australia', *Historical Archaeology*, 39 (2005), 28.
[8] A. W. Howitt, *The Native Tribes of South East Australia* (London: Macmillan and Co., 1904).

in aboriginal societies everywhere.[9] But for the most part attitudes towards indigenous culture were based on a general curiosity or where individuals were engaged in an agricultural, mining or pastoral enterprise, a utilitarian approach. Official government policies towards indigenous people at the beginning of the nineteenth century were based, as Reynolds has pointed out, on a principle of benevolence.[10] According to a House of Commons Select Committee of 1837, the British Empire had a duty in its dealings with 'the untutored and defenceless savage' to provide an opportunity to become a part of 'that civilization, that innocent commerce, that knowledge and that faith with which it has pleased a gracious Providence to bless our own country'.[11]

But behind this benevolence there lay the razor's edge. Britain in the nineteenth century became a leader in developing trusteeship arrangements, which, in the case of aboriginal people, cut them off from their land and in many cases their children.[12] The basic assumption was that the Empire had a great deal to teach, but not much to learn from indigenous people.

4.2. Recognition and ritualism

If now we jump to the end of the twentieth century we find evidence of a remarkable transformation in official Australian attitudes to the value of indigenous knowledge. For example, when in 1999 the Commonwealth enacted the centrepiece of its environmental protection strategy in the form of the Environment Protection and Biodiversity Conservation Act 1999, it included amongst its objects the recognition of 'the role of indigenous people in the conservation and ecologically sustainable use of Australia's biodiversity' and the promotion of 'the use of indigenous peoples' knowledge of biodiversity'.[13]

The point that I am making about recognition is a limited one. As generations of socio-legal scholars have shown, one cannot read off from the law on the books anything about the internalization of law, its administration and implementation or its effects on social attitudes and behaviour. Still, the existence of a statute listing the recognition and promotion of indigenous knowledge as part of its purpose is evidence of at least symbolic change, a change that stands in marked contrast to

---

[9] Nettlebeck and Foster, *In The Name Of The Law*, 51–2.
[10] Reynolds (ed.), *Aborigines and Settlers*, 151.
[11] For an extract of the Committee's report see *Ibid.*, 152–3.
[12] On Britain and the trusteeship principle see S. J. Anaya, *Indigenous Peoples in International Law*, 2nd edn. (Oxford University Press, 2004), 32.
[13] See section 3(1)(f) and (g).

the views of colonizing authorities that I described in the previous section. Beyond this symbolic change is the empirical question of the extent to which a change in the language of the law is part of some deeper attitudinal and behavioural change or whether this language simply represents a game of symbolic politics in which indigenous people and their supporters are given mythical assurances while being denied tangible benefits.[14] Statutes can also be vehicles for different kinds of ritualism such as rule ritualism (producing rules rather than solutions), legal ritualism (ignoring the spirit of the law) and participatory ritualism (setting up procedures of non-genuine inclusion).[15] As we will see in the coming sections of this chapter, symbolic recognition of indigenous knowledge systems in treaty law has become widely used. Whether or not indigenous groups make gains beyond symbolic recognition within the borders of the states that enclose them depends, as I argued in chapter 1, on whether property systems operate in an extractive or developmental way. This becomes a matter of empirical investigation. The chapters that follow present some fieldwork findings for how things are working out in Australia when it comes to indigenous knowledge. Rule ritualism, as we will see in chapters 7 and 8, is an ever-present danger when the state comes to addressing the protection of indigenous knowledge. Indigenous people have also made great strides in participation in multilateral fora dealing with indigenous knowledge, but at the same time much of standard setting in intellectual property has shifted to the bilateral or regional level where the problem is old-fashioned exclusion from deal making that affects their interests. In the remainder of this chapter I want to show how international treaties project symbolic assurance and reward when it comes to indigenous knowledge while at the same time setting very few standards that encroach on a state's sovereignty when it comes to devising systems of protection for indigenous knowledge.

4.3.   Journeys to treaties

The Environment Protection and Biodiversity Conservation Act 1999 was, in part, Australia's response to its obligations under the Convention on Biological Diversity (CBD) of 1992. The CBD, which was the result

---

[14] The classic work on this form of politics is M. Edelman, *The Symbolic Uses of Politics* (Urbana: University of Illinois, 1964).

[15] For a discussion of these different types of ritualism see J. Braithwaite, T. Makkai and V. Braithwaite, *Regulating Aged Care: Ritualism and the New Pyramid* (Cheltenham: Edward Elgar, 2007) ch. 7.

of a 1988 initiative of the United Nations Environment Programme, was opened for signature at one of the most important environmental summits of the 1990s, the United Nations Conference on Environment and Development. Held in 1992 and also referred to as the Rio Summit (or Conference) or the Earth Summit, this conference also saw the United Nations Framework Convention on Climate Change (UNFCCC) opened for signature and the adoption of three agreements:

> the Rio Declaration on Environment and Development;
> Agenda 21 (a very long blueprint for implementing principles of sustainable development); and
> the Forest Principles (short for 'Non-legally binding authoritative statement of principles for a global consensus on the management, conservation and sustainable development of all types of forests').

The text of these agreements all provide examples of recognition by states of the value of indigenous knowledge, including the following:

> CBD – Article 8j. It requires states to 'respect, preserve and maintain knowledge, innovations and practices of indigenous and local communities that is relevant to the sustainable use of biodiversity'.
> Rio Declaration – Principle 22. It states that '[i]ndigenous people and their communities and other local communities have a vital role in environmental management and development because of their knowledge and traditional practices'.
> Agenda 21. This contains a separate chapter on indigenous people. Amongst other things, this chapter suggests that states could 'adopt or strengthen appropriate policies and/or legal instruments that will protect indigenous intellectual and cultural property and the right to preserve customary and administrative systems and practices'.[16]
> Forest Principles. Article 5a states that '[n]ational forest policies should recognize and duly support the identity, culture and the rights of indigenous people, their communities and other communities and forest dwellers'.

The inclusion in the CBD and other treaties of language declaring the importance of indigenous knowledge is an example of how indigenous people have had success at the international level. This engagement by

---

[16] Chapter 26 is available at http://sustainabledevelopment.un.org/content/documents/ Agenda21.pdf.

indigenous people with the international level of decision making has a long history going back to the nineteenth century when some indigenous groups and individuals embarked on a strategy of appealing to imperial seats of power in an attempt to obtain the justice that was being denied to them by the colonial representatives of these imperial powers. For example, New Zealand Maori delegations travelled to Britain in 1882, 1884, 1914 and 1924 to meet with the reigning monarch of the time in attempts to gain justice.[17] In 1923 Deskaheh, a chief of the Cayuga, travelled to the League of Nations as a spokesman for the Six Nations of the Iroquois League.[18] He wanted the League of Nations to help the Iroquois gain the sovereign independence that had been agreed to by King George III through his Governor General of Canada, Frederick Haldimand, but was now opposed by the Canadian government. Working with various humanitarian organizations in Geneva such as the International Association for the Defence of Indigenous Peoples, Deskaheh attracted a good deal of sympathy and public support for his cause, but ultimately, because of the opposition of Canada and Great Britain, he failed to get the League of Nations' help. Both Canadian and Iroquois politics turned against him. Leaving Geneva in 1924 and weakened by illness, he died in New York in 1925.

Indigenous people in Australia also used the international level to try and obtain favourable interventions. In 1846 a group of Tasmanian Aborigines living on Flinders Island sent a petition to Queen Victoria in a bid to prevent the return of a superintendent who had terrorized them with pistols and jailings.[19] Amongst the petitions organized by the Aboriginal leader, William Cooper, was a petition of 1934, containing 1,814 signatures of Aboriginal people, to King George V asking for Aboriginal representation in the Australian Parliament.[20] It was never forwarded by Commonwealth authorities to London. Anthony Fernando, the son of an Aboriginal mother, left Australia for Europe in the early 1900s. Deported to Britain in 1923 for distributing pamphlets in Italy declaring the extermination of indigenous people by the British in Australia, he spent his days in lonely activism in England, at one stage regularly protesting outside Australia House in London in a coat covered

---

[17] Douglas Sanders, 'The Formation of the World Council of Indigenous Peoples', April 1980, available at www.nzdl.org.
[18] See J. Rostkowski, 'The Redman's Appeal For Justice: Deskaheh and the League of Nations' in Feest (ed.), 435.
[19] A copy of the petition is available at www.indigenousrights.net.au/files/f85.pdf.
[20] Cooper's story is told in B. Attwood and A. Markus, *Thinking Black: William Cooper and the Australian Aborigines' League* (Canberra: Aborigines Studies Press, 2004).

with toy white skeletons. The skeletons, he said, depicted the fate of his people. He died in a mental hospital in Essex in 1946.[21]

The United Nations Charter of 1945 and the evolution of the United Nations system that followed created in the second half of the twentieth century many more opportunities for indigenous political networks to press for just treatment. The Charter itself states that the purposes of the United Nations include cooperation in 'promoting and encouraging respect for human rights and for fundamental freedoms for all'.[22] Other major human rights instruments such as the Universal Declaration of Human Rights (1948), the International Covenant on Economic, Social and Cultural Rights (1966) and the International Covenant on Civil and Political Rights (1966) inscribed their rights and principles with a universal quality that was full of evocative promise for indigenous groups: 'All peoples have the right of self-determination'.[23]

Universality and independent existence were two general qualities predicated on human rights by major human rights conventions. These qualities opened the way to a re-engagement with an earlier European natural law tradition of the sixteenth and seventeenth centuries that had theorized rights and obligations in ways that were more sympathetic to the interests of indigenous people than the later legal positivist tradition that in international law made law the instrument and protector of state interests.[24] Conceptually, human rights bearing the qualities of universality and independence allow any action, whether by a state or non-state actor, to be judged under human rights standards. Seeing the possibilities, indigenous people became increasingly active participants in the international networks that were forming around human rights standard-setting initiatives.

The formal entry of indigenous peoples into the UN system owes much to the personal leadership of individuals such as George Manuel from the Shushwap Tribe in British Columbia.[25] In the early 1970s he forged links with indigenous groups around the world, including from New Zealand, Australia and the Sami from Sweden. A world conference of indigenous people in 1974 laid the path to the formation of the World Council of

---

[21] See F. Paisley, 'Australian Aboriginal Activism in Interwar Britain and Europe: Anthony Martin Fernando', *History Compass*, 7 (2009), 701.

[22] See Article 1.3.

[23] Article 1.1 of the International Covenant on Civil and Political Rights.

[24] Representatives of this tradition included Vitoria and Grotius. For a discussion see Anaya, *Indigenous Peoples*, 16–19. On the role of legal positivism see P. Keal, '"Just Backward Children": International Law and the Conquest of Non-European Peoples', *Australian Journal of International Affairs*, 49 (1995), 191.

[25] See P. McFarlane, *Brotherhood to Nationhood: George Manuel and the Making of the Modern Indian Movement* (Toronto: Between the Lines, 1993).

Indigenous Peoples in 1975. The National Indian Brotherhood of Canada had been granted non-governmental organization status in 1974 by the Economic and Social Council of the United Nations, a position that the World Council took over. The Declaration of Principles of the World Council provides an example of the way in which indigenous groups used the language of human rights to frame and communicate their interests. Article 2 of that Declaration, for example, uses the words of the International Covenant on Civil and Political Rights on self-determination: 'All indigenous peoples have the right to self-determination'.

Indigenous networks still had to confront the reality of state power in international human rights fora, but they did so collectively and under conditions of greater transparency than when they faced governments alone in the alleyways of domestic power. State representatives could no longer openly speak in the way that Thucydides famously describes the Athenians speaking to the Melians: 'the standard of justice depends on equality of power to compel and that in fact the strong do what they have the power to do and the weak accept what they have to accept'.[26] Human rights, as the opening words of the Declaration on Human Rights make clear, offer another foundation for justice.

4.4.   Treaties and indigenous knowledge

Steadily over the last half and especially in the last quarter of the twentieth century a body of treaty-based principles dealing directly with indigenous people and indigenous knowledge or capable of being applied to protect their interests in indigenous knowledge has developed and deepened. Symbolic recognition, at the treaty level, is widespread. An extensive literature analysing the treaty language on indigenous knowledge, its implications and effects has grown. There are many hundreds of technical working papers available from the websites of the World Intellectual Property Organization (WIPO), the Secretariat of the CBD, and other international organizations working on this topic. In the sections that follow I want to revisit briefly some of the major treaties and initiatives dealing with indigenous knowledge in order to show three things:

1. Much of the treaty language dealing with indigenous knowledge has a permissive form that more or less preserves state sovereignty over property standards and rules.

---

[26] Thucydides, *History of the Peloponnesian War*, Book 5, 89 extracted in C. Brown, T. Nardin and N. Rengger (eds.), *International Relations in Political Thought: Texts from the Ancient Greeks to the First World War* (Cambridge University Press, 2002), 54.

2. The global level of governance has delivered principles that are important to the design of property standards for indigenous knowledge, but it has not delivered property systems for the protection of indigenous knowledge.
3. The practical effect of all the treaty activity dealing with indigenous knowledge has been to partition in various ways indigenous knowledge systems, the most obvious example being that land issues (real property) have become separated from knowledge issues (personal property-intellectual property). These conceptual partitions have no place in the cosmological connectionist model of knowledge that I described in chapter 2.

4.5.   The International Labour Organization

An early organizational player on the rights of indigenous people was the International Labour Organization (ILO). One of the products of the Versailles peace accord, the ILO was born in 1919 with a tripartite structure that gave formal voices to business, states and the labour movement. It was the labour movement that took up the cudgel against discriminatory and exploitative practices and laws that imperial powers allowed to apply to indigenous workers in colonies. A treaty in 1936 dealing with the recruitment of indigenous workers was followed by others dealing with contracts of employment and the use of penal sanctions against indigenous workers.[27] These early ILO standards constitute a recognition that indigenous people were and usually still are amongst the most disadvantaged workers in an economy. From setting standards to protect indigenous workers, the ILO moved to setting standards for indigenous people around their cultural, spiritual, social and economic interests. These came in the form of the Convention on Indigenous and Tribal Populations (No. 107) 1957, which was in turn revised by the Convention Concerning Indigenous and Tribal Peoples in Independent Countries (No. 169) 1989 (Convention 169). Of the ILO conventions that were expressly aimed at indigenous workers or people Australia ratified only one, a 1947 convention dealing with contracts of employment.

Today it is the CBD that occupies centre stage when the focus is on the protection of indigenous knowledge, but I would argue that it is Convention No. 169 that comes closest, perhaps of any treaty in this area, to a

---

[27] See Recruiting of Indigenous Workers Convention 1936; Contracts of Employment (Indigenous Workers) Convention 1939; Penal Sanctions (Indigenous Workers) Convention 1939; Contract of Employment (Indigenous Workers) Convention 1947.

practical recognition of the cosmological connectionism described in chapter 2. We will see that the CBD in fact entrenches the Westphalian system of sovereignty over biological resources. States have clamoured to join the CBD (it has more than 190 members). Only twenty-two have joined Convention No. 169. Unlike the CBD, it has a part devoted to land rights.

Importantly, the ILO 'has the most sophisticated dialogic machinery for securing compliance of any international organization'.[28] Ministers from states do not always enjoy reporting processes at the ILO concerning their state's compliance with ILO treaty standards. An example of an ILO procedure in action is the complaint brought by the Ecuadorian Confederation of Free Trade Union Organizations against the Ecuadorian government in 1999 under Article 24 of the Constitution of the International Labour Organization. The basic claim was that the Ecuadorian government had struck an oil deal involving the territory of the Independent Federation of the Shuar People without consulting the Shuar people, thereby breaching a number of the provisions of Convention 169. A reading of the report of the ILO Committee set up to hear the complaint provides a sense of why the ratification of Convention 169 remains low.[29] Basically, the Committee found that the Ecuadorian government had not complied with its obligation of prior consultation and it asked for detailed reporting on how the government was going to bring its approach in line with Convention 169.

Part II of Convention 169 is devoted to land issues. It accomplishes what the CBD does not, a recognition of the special importance of land to the cosmology of indigenous peoples (See Article 13(1)). It requires rights of ownership to traditionally occupied land to be recognized (Article 14(1)). States have to specially safeguard the rights of indigenous people to the natural resources that are part of their land (Article 15(1)). Land includes the concept of territory, a concept that includes the 'total environment' used by indigenous people (Article 13(2)). Here we are getting close to the idea of the territorial cosmos described in chapter 2. This extended sense of land is important for many reasons. For example, in Australia the sea was for many indigenous groups part of their

---

[28] Braithwaite and Drahos, *Global Business Regulation* (Cambridge University Press, 2000), 239.

[29] Report of the Committee set up to examine the representation alleging non-observance by Ecuador of the Indigenous and Tribal Peoples Convention, 1989 (No. 169), made under article 24 of the ILO Constitution by the Confederación Ecuatoriana de Organizaciones Sindicales Libres (CEOSL) (2001) available at www.ilo.org/dyn/normlex/en/f?p=1000:50012:0::NO::P50012_COMPLAINT_PROCEDURE_ID, P50012_LANG_CODE:2507223,en.

cosmology. In interviews I carried out in Queensland some scientists took the view that one of the advantages of bioprospecting in the sea was that one would not have to deal with indigenous people.

If our fieldwork has one clear message it is that rebuilding indigenous institutions of human capital and innovation has little chance of success unless indigenous groups have been able to obtain some control over their land. Yet contemporary treaty processes dealing with indigenous knowledge have created a set of conceptual reserves in which land is separated from knowledge and knowledge itself is subdivided into knowledge of folklore, genetic resources, food and agriculture, desertification and so on. ILO Convention No. 169 with its integrated approach to land rights, natural resources, culture, customary law, consultation and participation, an approach that is tied to complaints procedures that can be started by non-state actors, is an approach that should have been built upon and strengthened. This has not happened. Instead, as the rest of this chapter shows, states have strengthened their regulatory power over indigenous knowledge assets.

4.6.   Folklore in Tunis

Another early standard-setting effort that is sometimes discussed in the context of indigenous knowledge (more usually traditional knowledge) is the Tunis Model Law on Copyright for Developing Countries 1976. An initiative supported by WIPO, the United Nations Educational, Scientific and Cultural Organization (UNESCO) and a committee of experts convened by the Tunisian government, the Model Law recognizes copyright in works of national folklore. I mention it here because it neatly reveals how the existing copyright regime and manoeuvring of states in that regime have helped to create classification boxes for indigenous knowledge.

The Tunis Model was part of a trade-off in which the interests of some developing states in the protection of cultural material of national importance would be recognized in exchange for these states adopting a copyright model that would allow them to join international copyright treaties, especially the Berne Convention for the Protection of Literary and Artistic Works (1886) (Berne Convention). The authority of the international copyright regime had been questioned as a result of a dispute between developed and developing countries over access to Western scientific and technical texts. In 1967 India had led an initiative that saw some protection for folklore in the Berne Convention in the shape of provisions for the rights of unknown authors in unpublished works. But these provisions had little practical impact.[30] The bigger game in 1967 for India and other developing countries was to push for a system of non-exclusive licensing in relation to uses of copyright works for educational purposes. This triggered a crisis that threatened to undermine the Berne-based regime on which so many Western publishing cartels depended.[31] The 1976 Tunis Model Law was part of a process of trying to encourage developing countries to join the Berne system, thereby turning it into a global and stable system. The Model Law created property rights of indefinite duration in 'national folklore' to be administered by a state 'competent authority', presumably thus labelled in order to distinguish it from other state authorities. One wonders whether indigenous groups in various developing countries saw any use to them in these rights of the nation state over national folklore. More generally, even though a number of developing states used copyright law to protect folklore this seems to have generated no practical results.[32] Today folklore continues to find mention in WIPO in the negotiations over traditional cultural expressions.

4.7.   The Convention on Biological Diversity

The copyright dramas of the late 1960s show the beginnings of a coalitional muscle, albeit a small one, being flexed by developing states. They also show states, developing and developed alike, behaving on the assumption that they are the ones to command through law property rights over knowledge. This Westphalian model of resource enclosure is to be seen in full flight in the CBD. The preamble to the CBD reaffirms that states have 'sovereign rights over their own biological resources', a principle repeated in Article 3 with respect to 'resources'. Article 15(1) recognizes sovereign rights over 'natural resources' and goes on to say that national governments have the authority to determine access to genetic resources. There is probably no real way to reconcile this state authority over biological resources with those indigenous groups who see authority as residing in ancestors, ancestors that may have a plant form.

Article 8(j) is the key provision on, amongst other things, the knowledge and innovation of indigenous communities. It creates open standards. States have to 'respect, preserve and maintain' such knowledge,

---

[30] On the fate of Article 15(4) of the Berne Convention see D. Zografos, *Intellectual Property And Traditional Cultural Expressions* (Cheltenham: Edward Elgar, 2010), 14.

[31] See Drahos with Braithwaite, *Information Feudalism*, 76–7.

[32] C. Antons, 'Intellectual Property Rights in Indigenous Cultural Heritage: Basic Concepts and Continuing Controversies' in Graber, Kuprecht and Lai (eds.), *International Trade*, 144, 148–9.

'promote' its wider use with the 'approval and involvement of the holders of such knowledge' and 'encourage the equitable sharing of benefits'. It heavily qualifies whatever imperative mood it creates: states 'shall, as far as possible and as applicable, [s]ubject to national legislation . . .'. Article 10(c) requires states to 'protect and encourage customary uses of biological resources'. There are no rules of property for indigenous people in the CBD.

The CBD has had a remarkable catalysing effect in terms of work programmes both within and outside of the CBD. Within the CBD, a Working Group on Article 8(j) was established in 1998. By the time of the sixth meeting of the Conference of the Parties to the CBD in 2002 it seemed as if every international body was busy with indigenous knowledge issues of one kind or another. This Conference of the Parties took note of the work on indigenous communities and knowledge by the following organizations:[33]

> Intergovernmental Committee on Intellectual Property, Genetic Resources, Traditional Knowledge and Folklore of WIPO;
> Permanent Forum on Indigenous Issues established by the Economic and Social Council;
> the Working Group on Indigenous Populations of the United Nations Commission on Human Rights;
> the United Nations Development Programme;
> the United Nations Environment Programme;
> the United Nations Educational, Scientific and Cultural Organization;
> the United Nations Conference on Trade and Development;
> the World Health Organization;
> the International Labour Organization;
> the Food and Agriculture Organization;
> the World Trade Organization;
> the Working Group on Indigenous Populations of the Commission on Human Rights.

The CBD is much like a glass that is at once half full and half empty. Its catalytic effect on indigenous knowledge has seen the emergence at the global level of a large dialogic web around indigenous knowledge.[34] Included in this web are the organizations mentioned above, their state members, indigenous groups and their representative organizations,

---

[33] See COP 6 Decision VI/10.
[34] On the role of dialogic webs in regime formation see Braithwaite and Drahos, *Global Business Regulation*, 553–7.

business organizations, companies, different kinds of NGOs (environmental, developmental, food etc.) all meeting formally and informally to develop agendas, policy proposals and draft text. This dialogic web offers a deliberative potential for indigenous people that would have seemed impossible through the worst times of colonization. At the global level of governance, dialogic webs have created a regime rich in principles, standards and guidelines that are relevant for state property orders, important examples being the CBD's principles of prior informed consent and fair and equitable benefit sharing, the Bonn Guidelines and the standards in the Nagoya Protocol on Access to Genetic Resources and the Fair and Equitable Sharing of Benefits Arising from their Utilization to the Convention on Biological Diversity (2010) (Nagoya Protocol). This regime for biological resources has hooks that link it interpretively to the human rights regime as well as to international law more generally.[35] But for all the interpretive richness of the interconnected principles to which one might point as supporting the interests of indigenous people these principles do not create a system of property rights that enable indigenous people to control the economic and other benefits of 'their intellectual property' (see chapter 1 on the meaning of this phrase).

As the opening chapter pointed out indigenous groups in settler states do badly on many socio-economic measures. Chapter 1 suggested that the explanation for this lies in non-developmental states imposing extractive property orders upon indigenous people. Over time the deliberative potential of the principles that have been recognized at the global level of governance for indigenous people may come to drive the design of property rights systems that are truly developmental for indigenous people. But there are plenty of opportunities for states to slow this process down if they so desire. Here the empty part of the glass comes into view. Structurally, the CBD has strengthened a state system of resource enclosure in which it is the state that commands through law who has and does not have property rights over resources. The stateless ancestral systems of indigenous people are now subject to the authority of state property systems. The fate of open-ended standards that recognize the interests of indigenous people, such as Article 8(j), depends heavily on state processes of interpretation and implementation.

The Nagoya Protocol is intended to give effect to one of the CBD's trinity of goals – the fair and equitable sharing of benefits flowing from the

---

[35] By way of example Article 3 of the CBD refers to 'the Charter of the United Nations and the principles of international law' and the preamble of the Nagoya Protocol refers to the UN Declaration on the Rights of Indigenous Peoples.

use of genetic resources.[36] There are a number of provisions and stand-ards in the Nagoya Protocol that affect the position of indigenous people in the international regime that states are developing for genetic resources.[37] Some of these standards circle back to a state's existing domestic property system. So, for example, a state has an obligation to ensure that the benefits relating to the use of genetic resources belonging to indigenous people are shared with them.[38] But what genetic resources are held or not held by an indigenous community is expressly recognized as being a matter of domestic legislation. Similarly, the obligation to obtain prior informed consent from an indigenous community for access to genetic resources depends on a domestic specification by a state as to whether a community in fact has the right to grant access.[39] For indigenous people the benefits of the Nagoya Protocol are contingent in various ways upon a state's property regime, as well as its choice of policy instrument (for example, a legislative measure as opposed to a policy measure).

The extent to which indigenous groups benefit from a combination of principles and open standards depends ultimately upon their interpret-ation and translation by a state into specific property rights that enable indigenous people to exercise *dominium* over their assets. *Dominium* within a state property order does two things. It creates for holders a degree of autonomy over resources and it also contributes to freedom from interference. Freedom from interference is a negative conception of freedom prized by the liberal tradition.[40] Negative liberty lines up neatly with a negative right of exclusion, a core right of property. Property rights allow individuals to create a zone of non-interference in the assets in which they have invested. What this classical view of property and freedom suggests is that the standards that matter crucially to economic autonomy of indigenous peoples, as well as their freedom within states, are property rights. It is property standard setting over which states retain, as the CBD makes clear for biological resources, a firm sovereign grip. States may, of course, harness the resources of the global regime to design property rights that will genuinely improve the development prospects of indigenous groups within their borders, but the point is that states have a choice. How well Australia has chosen is something we will see in the coming chapters.

---

[36] The other two goals are the conservation of biological diversity and the sustainable use of its components. See Article 1 of the CBD.

[37] See, for example, Article 5(2) and (5), Article 6(2) and (3)(f), Article 7, Article 12, Article 21 and Article 22 of the Nagoya Protocol.

[38] Article 5(2) of the Nagoya Protocol.   [39] Article 6(2) of the Nagoya Protocol.

[40] P. Pettit, *Republicanism: A Theory of Freedom and Government* (Oxford: Clarendon Press, 1997), 17–18.

4.8.   World Intellectual Property Organization

The General Assembly of WIPO in 2000 established the Intergovernmental Committee on Intellectual Property and Genetic Resources, Traditional Knowledge and Folklore (IGC). What has followed is in its own quiet way a tribute to the philosophy of doing things slowly, in this case negotiating an agreement that might benefit indigenous peoples. The broad aim of the IGC is to produce a legal instrument or instruments to protect genetic resources, Traditional Knowledge and Traditional Cultural Expressions/Expressions of Folklore. So far three separate draft texts have been assembled on the protection of traditional knowledge, traditional cultural expressions and genetic resources (along with the traditional knowledge associated with those genetic resources). Each of these assemblages is described by WIPO as 'work in progress'. It is also complex work. Each text is made up of alternatives, options and bracketed text, meaning that the number of possible combinations in each of the texts numbers in the hundreds of thousands. If, for example, we have to choose a combination of only five articles from twenty-five draft options there are 53,130 possible combinations. The WIPO Secretariat in one of its early reports did see virtue in a more integrated approach to traditional knowledge, but states have taken the negotiating process in the opposite direction.[41]

The WIPO drafts are a good example of how far states have moved away from recognizing the implications of cosmological connectionism for state lawmaking. Knowledge in an ancestral system takes on a flow characteristic. It may touch many different objects such as plants, paintings or ceremonial objects or be incorporated into rituals and activities, but the knowledge remains part of a unified system. Legal approaches that divide this system into different categories of protection based on a selection of objects and activities create more regulatory options for states. For example, if the unified system is divided into, amongst other things, traditional knowledge and traditional knowledge associated with genetic resources, this allows a state to develop different rules for regulating knowledge in these boxes. Whatever the intention of the WIPO negotiating process, one likely long-run effect of it will be to separate indigenous knowledge into fields of detailed statutory rule making. States in this WIPO process are drafting treaties that will open up the options of rule ritualism and legal ritualism when it comes to national

---

[41] See WIPO, *Intellectual Property Needs and Expectations of Traditional Knowledge Holders: WIPO Report on Fact-Finding Missions on Intellectual Property and Traditional Knowledge (1998–1999)* (Geneva: WIPO, 2001), 25–6.

implementation. They will have the option of writing lots of rules to preserve their interests (rather than solving the problems that indigenous people want solved) and they will through rules be able to manoeuvre past the spirit of the principles on intellectual property to be found in the UN Declaration on the Rights of Indigenous Peoples (UNDRIP).

4.9.   Farmers, food and agriculture

Human life depends on plant life. It follows that those who over the millennia have nurtured plant life have performed a special service that deserves recognition. In 2001 a treaty was concluded that contained this symbolic recognition. Article 9.1 of the International Treaty on Plant Genetic Resources for Food and Agriculture (2001) (PGR Treaty) recognizes 'the enormous contribution that the local and indigenous communities and farmers of all regions of the world, particularly those in the centres of origin and crop diversity, have made and will continue to make for the conservation and development of plant genetic resources'. But the same treaty, just like the CBD, goes on to reinforce the Westphalian system of resource enclosure. It recognizes the 'sovereign rights of States over their own plant genetic resources for food and agriculture' (see Article 10.1). The protection of traditional knowledge, which falls under the concept of Farmers' Rights in the treaty, is to be guided by the 'needs and priorities' of states and 'subject to its national legislation' (see Article 9.2).

The PGR Treaty in its preamble describes plant genetic resources as 'raw material indispensable for crop genetic improvement'. This characterization of plant genetic resources as raw material would not be accepted by indigenous groups in Australia, and, it is safe to assume, by many other indigenous peoples. The archaeological evidence for Australia shows that indigenous groups had a range of technologies at their disposal to modify their environment, including plant life.[42] The debates in Australian archaeology are not about whether indigenous people transformed the Australian environment, but when this transformation occurred and the extent of it.[43] By the time of the Holocene we have considerable evidence of plant exploitation along with evidence of regional specialization. When the colonists arrived in 1788, indigenous groups had been applying their technologies to plants for tens of thousands of years. Plants, land and technologies were all united by cosmologies, cosmologies that drove a service-based innovation and that

[42] See Denham, Fullagar, Head, 'Plant Exploitation', 29.
[43] See Hiscock, *Archaeology of Ancient Australia*, ch. 4.

assigned status, control and custody in relation to plants and other resources. There was no Grotian negative commons full of raw material waiting to be appropriated by the colonists and their sheep. This was a European philosophical fantasy, albeit a convenient one for those in the colonization business.

The PGR Treaty is a good example of how symbolic recognition of indigenous peoples' interests can be accomplished without disturbing the property rights systems that matter to those industries working with plant genetic resources. Intellectual property rights over biological materials in European countries and the United States have a history of evolution in the nineteenth and twentieth centuries in which the plant breeding industry, the pharmaceutical industry and the biotechnology industry have had an influential role. For example, for a long time in both the United States and European countries there were arguments against the patenting of plants. These included the view that plants were products of nature rather than inventions, they were living organisms, they could not be described properly for the purposes of patent law and that they were the product of well-known techniques that made them obvious.[44] Two things happened. The objections to patentability were eventually overcome, but they also stimulated the development of specially designed systems of plant protection. The US Plant Patent Act of 1930 is an early example of such a system. Demand for a treaty approach saw the adoption of the International Convention for the Protection of New Varieties of Plants 1961. Today the kinds of biological materials that are patentable in a given country depends ultimately on a complex mix of treaty membership, treaty implementation, national law and judicial interpretation, patent office interpretation and the claims-drafting ingenuity of patent attorneys. Basically, by the time the PGR Treaty was concluded in 2001 and came into operation in 2004 there were long-established systems of property rights protection for biological materials that have their origins in the developmental processes of nineteenth-century industrialized capitalist nation states.

Not surprisingly, the PGR Treaty is careful not to disturb either international treaties dealing with intellectual property or national intellectual property systems. It establishes a multilateral system to facilitate access to particular listed plant genetic resources.[45] Access to resources protected by property rights, including intellectual property, has to be

---

[44] G. Van Overwalle, 'Patent Protection For Plants: A Comparison of American and European Approaches', *Idea*, 39 (1999), 143, 148–59.
[45] Article 10.2.

consistent with relevant treaties and national laws.[46] Those receiving plant genetic resources from the multilateral system must not 'claim' intellectual property over those resources 'in the form' in which they were put into the system.[47] This raises the possibility of intellectual property claims (for example, patent claims) over re-engineered or extracted versions of this material. The only way to guard against this would be for a country to put plant genetic resources into the system in a way that claimed every conceivable form. Not easy to do. The other point is that there is not an outright prohibition on obtaining intellectual property on material from the system. Rather one cannot claim intellectual property rights that 'limit the facilitated access' that the PGR Treaty promises. One can then argue about what property claims do or do not limit access. In this particular playground of treaty words there is enough to keep lawyers happy.

That said treaty vagueness or ambiguity is not a good way to engender trust in a treaty system. The long-term use of the PGR Treaty, which is meant to prevent the erosion of resources on which all food security depends, will be interesting to see. Use of the multilateral system also relies on a standard material transfer agreement. Such an agreement has been adopted, but it simply uses the same wording and therefore reproduces the vagueness of the PGR Treaty when it comes to a recipient's right to claim intellectual property over material received from the system.[48]

The PGR Treaty also introduces a principle known as Farmers' Rights.[49] This was a principle that was formulated in 1985 by the Rural Advancement Foundation International, a highly influential and adept NGO working on rural issues. The aim behind introducing Farmers' Rights into the framework of the Food and Agriculture Organization was to counter Plant Breeders' Rights.[50] The preamble of the PGR Treaty makes clear that the basis of Farmers' Rights lies in the collective labours of countless generations of farmers to conserve and improve plant genetic resources. Under the PGR Treaty, Farmers' Rights do not generate property rights for individuals.[51] Rather the principle recognizes that a

---

[46] Article 12 (3)(f).   [47] Article 12(3)(d).

[48] See Article 6.2 of the Standard Material Transfer Agreement, available at ftp://ftp.fao.org/ag/agp/planttreaty/agreements/smta/SMTAe.pdf.

[49] Article 9.

[50] This is made clear by Pat Mooney, the founder of RAFI, in P. R. Mooney, 'The Parts of Life: Agricultural Biodiversity, Indigenous Knowledge, and the Role of the Third System', *Development Dialogue* (1–2) 1996, 7, 25.

[51] Made clear at the Twenty-Sixth Session of the FAO Conference, Rome, 9–27 November 1991. See www.fao.org/docrep/x0255e/x0255e03.htm.

collective debt is owed to farmers as a class, a debt that states should find ways to repay. The PGR Treaty includes local and indigenous communities in its recognition of contributors to plant genetic resources and expressly links the promotion of Farmers' Rights to the protection of traditional knowledge.[52]

The PGR Treaty, just as the CBD, is important at the level of symbolic principle for indigenous groups. But just like the CBD it strengthens a system of Westphalian resource enclosure. It does not set standards of protection for indigenous knowledge, but leaves this to states. Similarly, like the CBD, it establishes a principle of fair and equitable sharing of benefits, but the detail of how this is to work is left in the hands of states.[53] Going back to the argument of chapter 1, it is clear that when it comes to enacting developmental property rights for indigenous groups the PGR Treaty leaves the design discretion of states intact. Where states have less discretion is in the design of intellectual property rights. This is not an effect of the PGR Treaty, but rather the detailed standards to be found in the intellectual property regime. The PGR Treaty simply genuflects before this regime.

4.10.   Dialogue, dialogue everywhere, nor any property to be seen[54]

As the earlier section in this chapter on the CBD made clear, there are a large number of international organizations working on some aspect of indigenous knowledge, some of which we have already discussed. To date very little of this work has led to standards of protection that have the specificity associated with property rules and standards of protection.

Indigenous groups were not part of the inner circle of elites that in the 1980s shaped the text of the Agreement on Trade-Related Aspects of Intellectual Property Rights (1994) (TRIPS Agreement). But indigenous knowledge became the subject of discussion in the World Trade Organization as part of the built-in review processes of the TRIPS Agreement, in particular Article 27(3)(b), which allows WTO members to exclude from patentability plants, animals, biological processes for the production of plants or animals and plant varieties. Within the WTO developing country coalitions became progressively more and more active, including on intellectual property issues. Countries from Africa and South America created a broader critique of the TRIPS Agreement using the principles of the CBD, including the claim that the TRIPS

---

[52] Article 9(1) and (2)(a).   [53] Article 10(2) and Article 13.
[54] With deepest apologies to Coleridge.

Agreement undermined rather than fostered the sovereignty of states over their genetic resources.[55] These broader issues were given further life in the WTO's Doha Ministerial of 2001, which instructed the Council for TRIPS to examine the relationship between the TRIPS Agreement, the CBD and the protection of traditional knowledge and folklore.[56]

As the WTO's Doha Round has slowly drifted through years of negotiation and deadlines, searching for finality, there has been no shortage of ideas and proposals on the issue of indigenous knowledge. Perhaps the most significant development has been the introduction by a group of developing states, including India, China and Brazil, of draft text for a mandatory disclosure obligation to be imposed on patent applicants when they apply for a patent involving biological resources and/or associated traditional knowledge.[57] Were this to become part of the TRIPS Agreement it would represent an important linkage between the CBD's principles of prior informed consent and benefit sharing, the requirements of the Nagoya Protocol and the obligations of patentees in the world's major patenting jurisdictions. It would also represent a negotiating achievement by developing country coalitions in the heartland of international economic law, an area historically dominated by Western countries.

The work of UNESCO has generated a set of treaty standards on tangible and intangible heritage that are important for indigenous groups and their knowledge systems.[58] The principal point I wish to make here is that UNESCO's treaty work has not generated property standards in indigenous knowledge, but it has generated principles that are relevant to the safeguarding and protection of indigenous knowledge as part of cultural heritage. At a structural level the work of UNESCO contributes to the process of conceptual and legal fragmentation of the place-time cosmologies of indigenous groups. UNESCO and its treaties are part of a long list of fora and international norms that indigenous people have to manage. What UNESCO can and cannot do for indigenous people is set

---

[55] For a detailed summary of issues and points made by WTO members going back to 1999 see Note by Secretariat, 'The Relationship Between the TRIPS Agreement and the Convention On Biological Diversity', IP/C/W/368/Rev.1, 8 February 2006.

[56] See para. 19, WT/MIN(01).DEC/1.

[57] See Communication from Brazil, China, Colombia, Cuba, India, Pakistan, Peru, Thailand and Tanzania, WT/GC/W/564/Rev.2, TN/C/W/41/Rev.2, IP/C/W/474, 5 July 2006. A revised draft article was submitted in April of 2011. See TN/C/W/59.

[58] For an analysis of UNESCO's work on indigenous cultural heritage see R. J. Coombe with J. F. Turcotte, 'Indigenous Cultural Heritage in Development and Trade: Perspectives From the Dynamics of Cultural Heritage Law and Policy' in Graber, Kuprecht and Lai (eds.), *International Trade*, 272.

by the deep structure of the international norm-making system. UNESCO operates in an international legal system divided into international economic law and public international law.[59] As Fiona Macmillan has argued, while the latter system has found space for the interests of indigenous peoples the former has remained largely closed to them. Her argument is consistent with my argument in this chapter that treaties have generated very few property standards of protection for indigenous groups and their knowledge systems. Worth noting also is that economically powerful states police the systemic divide that Macmillan describes. The United States withdrew from UNESCO in 1984 as part of a forum-shifting strategy because it did not like the economic implications of the work that UNESCO was doing, including the implications for copyright protection.[60]

UNESCO's conventions are a part of public international law.[61] They draw support from human rights principles, something made clear by UNESCO's Universal Declaration of Cultural Diversity of 2001. This convention links an obligation to defend cultural diversity to a full implementation of cultural rights, these rights being part of the indivisible and interdependent family of human rights.[62] The defence of cultural diversity implies a particular commitment to the rights of those belonging to minorities and indigenous peoples. In an annex, the Declaration contains an action plan for its implementation, which expressly mentions the protection of indigenous peoples' traditional knowledge.[63] The Declaration is important because it signals UNESCO's recognition of indigenous peoples in its standard-setting work. It also contributes to a web of interlocking principles in international public law that support the rights, freedoms and position of indigenous peoples.

The World Heritage Convention (WHC) of 1972 represents the tangible end of the heritage spectrum, but what is noteworthy about its evolution is how its operational rules are slowly recognizing the unity of the tangible and intangible that indigenous groups have always seen. The creation in 1992 of a category of cultural landscapes for inclusion on the World Heritage List is a good example of this evolution, as is the recognition of the importance of communities in implementing the goals of the convention. This recognition of the role of communities in the

---

[59] See F. Macmillan, 'International Economic Law and Public International Law: Strangers in the Night', *International Trade Law and Regulation*, 10 (2004), 115.

[60] The US rejoined in 2003. Braithwaite and Drahos, *Global Business Regulation*, 568–9.

[61] F. Bandarin, 'International Trade in Indigenous Cultural Heritage: Comments From UNESCO in Light of its International Standard-Setting Instruments in the Field of Culture' in Graber, Kuprecht and Lai (eds.), *International Trade*, 306, 320.

[62] See Articles 4 and 5.   [63] See Annex II, paragraph 14.

world heritage system has helped to spread a philosophy of co-management in which indigenous groups and the state become partners in managing cultural landscapes.[64] The WHC does create an important global governance system for heritage of all kinds, but it is a system that does not disturb the property rights regimes of states. Systems of co-management in which indigenous groups are partners may help them to negotiate access issues to listed cultural landscapes, but it is the real property systems and intellectual property systems of states that will determine categories of ownership rights in these cultural landscapes.

The same deference to the property regimes of states can be seen in UNESCO's Convention for the Safeguarding of the Intangible Cultural Heritage (ICH) (2003). Article 3(b) makes it clear that the ICH does not affect the rights and obligations of states under international intellectual property rules. Like the Universal Declaration of Cultural Diversity of 2001, the ICH draws on existing human rights principles in framing its obligations.[65] The ICH creates mechanisms for the listing by states of intangible cultural heritage in need of safeguarding, building in requirements of participation by groups and communities in the general process of safeguarding. A state that wants to increase its bureaucratic management of indigenous cultural heritage would see no problems in the ICH. If one looks at, for example, China's long report to the Intergovernmental Committee for the Safeguarding of Intangible Cultural Heritage, one can see the strong beginnings of a bureaucratic administrative paradigm for the regulation of intangible cultural heritage.[66] There is no a priori path to knowing how such a paradigm will work out for indigenous groups within states. The point is that the ICH articulates principles relevant to a paradigm of state management and administration of indigenous peoples' intangible cultural heritage.

Debates concerning the links between trade and culture were at the heart of the negotiations that led to UNESCO's Convention on the Diversity of Cultural Expressions (DCE) 2005.[67] In its preamble the DCE recognizes the 'importance of traditional knowledge as a source of intangible and material wealth, and in particular the knowledge systems of indigenous people'. It has a long list of objectives such as fostering interculturality and encouraging dialogue among cultures.[68] Its overall objective is to strengthen the capacity of people to engage in

---

[64] See Bandarin, 'International Trade in Indigenous Cultural Heritage', 306, 314.
[65] See Article 2(1).
[66] See Periodic Report No. 06611/China, available at www.unesco.org/culture/ich/index. php?lg=en&pg=00460.
[67] Bandarin, 'International Trade in Indigenous Cultural Heritage', 306, 320.
[68] See Article 1.

processes of cultural production and reproduction ranging from creation to use and enjoyment. Like the ICH, the DCE is careful not to disturb other treaty obligations of states.[69] This is not a convention that contains or affects property standards in indigenous knowledge. Ultimately who gains and who loses economically from increasingly global value chains for the production of cultural services and goods depends on who holds what intellectual property rights in those chains of production.

4.11.   UN Declaration on the Rights of Indigenous Peoples

UNDRIP was adopted by the General Assembly in 2007. As a declaration it does not bind states. However, some of the obligations it declares may be legally binding on states by virtue of other parts of international law. Article 1 makes clear that UNDRIP has to be read against the background of international human rights law. The recognition in the seventh preambular paragraph of the 'inherent rights of indigenous peoples' opens the way to a recognition of ancestral systems of decision making (see chapter 1). The rights declared in UNDRIP serve and protect a connectionist view of land and knowledge, thereby forming an important bulwark against the process of fragmentation of indigenous knowledge that I described earlier.[70] These rights provide other state standard-setting exercises such as those that states will have to engage in under the Nagoya Protocol with guidance as to how those standards should be set to serve the interests of indigenous peoples. The final preambular paragraphs of the Nagoya Protocol refer to UNDRIP and make it clear that nothing in the Protocol reduces the existing rights of indigenous peoples.

Clearly UNDRIP is of potentially huge importance in helping states to create developmental property systems for indigenous people. As I explained in chapter 1 it is property systems that ultimately are responsible for the realization of economic autonomy. The next frontier for indigenous people is the design of developmental property systems, as well as the removal of extractive systems. By way of example, Article 31 of UNDRIP sets up a cluster of rights of maintenance, protection, control and development over cultural heritage, traditional knowledge, seeds and other things. It goes on to state that indigenous peoples have 'the right to maintain, control, protect and develop their intellectual property over such cultural heritage, traditional knowledge, and traditional cultural expressions'. These are, going back to the language of the

---

[69] Article 20.   [70] See Articles 25, 26, 27 and 31.

preamble, inherent rights, but they do not necessarily have developmental effects for indigenous people because they are not, as yet, underpinned by property systems of states or only weakly so. Article 31 represents a starting point. It says to states these are the broad property rights and subject matters that concern indigenous peoples and to which your property systems must give effect. How individual states respond at the national property systems level will determine whether UNDRIP's recognition of the inherent rights of indigenous peoples will see for them a new developmental dawn. Australia along with Canada, New Zealand and the United States voted against UNDRIP's adoption, although all four states have since endorsed it.[71] Whether these states reform their intellectual property systems in ways that are developmental for their indigenous peoples remains to be seen. Australia's representative, Robert Hill, expressing deep disappointment with the text of UNDRIP, stated the following:

With regard to intellectual property, Australia does not support the inclusion in the text of intellectual property rights for indigenous peoples. Australia extends protection to indigenous cultural heritage, traditional knowledge and traditional cultural expressions to the extent that it is consistent with Australian and international intellectual property law. However, Australia will not provide sui generis intellectual property rights for indigenous communities as envisaged in the declaration.[72]

---

[71] Draft resolution A/61/L.67 that contained the draft Declaration was adopted by 143 votes to 4, with 11 abstentions. See UN General Assembly, 61st Session, 13 September 2007, A/6/PV.107, 19. Australia endorsed the Declaration in April of 2009.

[72] For the text of Robert Hill's speech see UN General Assembly, 61st Session, 13 September 2007, A/6/PV.107, 11–12.

5   Rules and the recognition of ancestors

5.1.   Be careful what you wish for: when rules rule

Summing up the argument of the previous chapter we can say that the global level of governance is full of treaty language recognizing the importance of indigenous peoples' knowledge. Essentially states have adopted a symbolic mode of recognition when negotiating treaties dealing with issues of indigenous knowledge and intellectual property. Through this mode states have carefully preserved their sovereign powers of command over property systems as they relate to indigenous knowledge, while strengthening the principle of sovereignty over the control of biological resources. The one area where there has been a significant erosion of state property sovereignty has been over intellectual property standards and principles, but this erosion has not favoured indigenous peoples, but rather multinationals and their globalized systems of production.

In this chapter I want to outline the possible danger of the increased involvement by states in the regulation of indigenous knowledge systems. States may, of course, choose to maintain extractive systems for indigenous people while trotting out ritualistic solutions that do nothing to increase the developmental prospects of indigenous people within their borders. They may not even bother with the pretence of ritualism. Another kind of danger, which is at the opposite end of the spectrum to disguised inaction, is the danger of over-regulation by rules.

The rise in the use of statutory law by states to govern has been relentless. In the case of intellectual property, the second half of the twentieth century has seen a dramatic increase in the output of intellectual property statutes as states have sought to meet their international obligations or chased rents in high-technology markets through more intellectual property law. This rise in statutory intellectual property law has triggered a growth in administration (for example, a patent law requires a patent office to administer the law, trade mark law requires a trade mark office and so on). Administration means a bureaucracy with its own agendas and maximizing set of behaviours. One possible future for indigenous knowledge might be an escalation of rule-based governance encased in the positive law of states. One can see increasing use of rules by states at the regional and national levels of regulation when it comes to indigenous knowledge.[1]

At this point it is worth reminding ourselves of the discussion in the early part of chapter 4 of examples of indigenous people appealing to European power centres to stop the predatory activities of settler colonists. These appeals invoked the principle of non-interference in one's affairs. This principle lies at the very heart of the liberal conception of liberty. Indigenous people in the nineteenth and twentieth centuries were making journeys to the metropoles of Europe in the hope of finding ways to make settler colonists honour this principle in their conduct with indigenous people. Many of them realized that the prospects for indigenous sovereignty in the legal form of statehood were slim and so they were pushing for a form of sovereignty based on the principle of non-interference. Fernando was relying on this principle when he suggested in a letter to a Swiss newspaper that the control of Aboriginal reserve lands in Australia should be passed to independent countries such as Switzerland.[2] It was only through such independent international control that the liberty and rights of indigenous people could be secured. Those indigenous groups and individuals like Deskaheh and Fernando who left their homelands to travel to the power centres of Europe did so because they saw little prospect of changing their powerlessness with settler societies.

[1] There is considerable activity in the Pacific Island Region. At least seven Pacific Island countries are in the process of drafting national legislation dealing with traditional knowledge. See M. Forsyth, 'Lifting the Lid on "The Community": Who Has the Right to Control Access to Traditional Knowledge and Expressions of Culture', *International Journal of Cultural Property*, 19 (2012), 1, 6. For further discussion of national developments in the Pacific Islands see M. Blakeney, 'The Pacific Solution: The European Union's Intellectual Property Rights Activism in Australia's and New Zealand's Sphere of Influence' in Drahos and Frankel (eds.), *Indigenous Peoples' Innovation*, 165; Forsyth, 'Do You Want it Gift Wrapped?', 189. In Africa a Model Law on the Protection Of the Rights of Local Communities, Farmers and Breeders and for the Regulation of Access to Biological Resources was adopted by the Organization for African Unity in 1998. In August of 2010 the Diplomatic Conference of the African Regional Intellectual Property Organization adopted the Swakopmund Protocol on the Protection of Traditional Knowledge and Expressions of Folklore. There are also examples of national laws from South America such as Peru's Law No. 27811, published on 10 August 2002, entitled Law Introducing A Protection Regime For The Collective Knowledge Of Indigenous Peoples Derived From Biological Resources, available at www.wipo.int/tk/en/laws/tk.html. WIPO's website contains many examples of national laws on the protection of traditional knowledge.
[2] Paisley, 'Australian Aboriginal Activism', 701, 706.

The strategy by indigenous groups of seeking to enrol international networks in order to loosen the dominance of individual states over them has borne fruit. The widespread recognition of indigenous peoples' interests in various treaty regimes, including their interests in protecting their knowledge systems, is evidence of this. One danger they now face, however, is that states will regulate their knowledge systems through complex rules. This danger is, as I have argued, already evident in the way that the international regime is dividing and boxing up these know-ledge systems into categories such as farmers' rights over plant genetic resources (the PGR Treaty) or 'traditional knowledge associated with genetic resources within the scope of the [CBD] Convention' (Article 3 of the Nagoya Protocol) or the WIPO draft international instruments mentioned in chapter 4 that divide indigenous knowledge into traditional cultural expressions, traditional knowledge and genetic resources and associated traditional knowledge. The use of complex rules to regulate indigenous knowledge systems advances like a rapidly falling shadow.

Complex rules as a regulatory instrument have well-known problems. Rules that require a long list of factors to be taken into account by a decision maker increase rather than decrease certainty.[3] In areas such as tax and financial regulation the use of complex rules has opened up many more interpretive doors than it has shut.[4] Similarly, rules that require high levels of technical expertise to interpret can create incentives for the caste of interpreters to behave in self-serving ways. State regulation of indigenous knowledge through complex rules is likely to drive indigen-ous people into the arms of lawyers. Complex rules may also have a pervasive effect on the daily lives of people, circumscribing in various ways what they can and cannot do. This feature of complex rules leads Richard Epstein to argue that there may be no gains for people's welfare from complex rules – the rules may raise administrative costs while not improving people's welfare and perhaps diminishing it.[5] A society cannot do without administration, but it may be able to do with less of it. Epstein's starting point to achieving more with less is to look for simpler rule solutions in complex areas of law such as property, contract and torts. His list of simple rules for property includes self-ownership

---

[3] Uncertainty is one of the features distinguishing complex rules from simple ones. The other features are density, technicality and differentiation. For a discussion see P. Schuck, 'Legal Complexity: Some Causes, Consequences, and Cures', *Duke Law Journal*, 42 (1992), 1.

[4] J. Braithwaite, 'Rules and Principles: A Theory of Legal Certainty', *Australian Journal of Legal Philosophy*, 27 (2002), 47.

[5] R. A. Epstein, *Simple Rules for a Complex World* (Cambridge, MA: Harvard University Press, 1995).

(autonomy), first possession and voluntary exchange.[6] Simpler rules will often lead to lower administrative costs and improve people's incentive settings. One need not go along with all the details of Epstein's libertarian-style arguments to see the force of the argument that rule complexity and its attendant administrative costs may reduce people's welfare.

The use of complex rules and the regulatory power that accrues to the state as a result of the need to administer these rules can be seen in the model law that has been developed for Pacific Island countries.[7] The indicators of rule complexity identified by Schuck can be seen everywhere; a ten paragraph rule stipulating uses of traditional knowledge that require informed consent (uncertainty); its application to all traditional knowledge and expressions of culture (density of coverage); the fact that the model law has to fit with the existing international intellectual property regime (differentiation) and that specialist lawyers will be needed to advise on its operation (technicality). The rise in the regulatory power of the state comes in the form of the creation of a national cultural authority with a long list of regulatory functions that include keeping a record of traditional owners and developing standard contractual terms for the use of traditional knowledge. The cultural authority also has the power under certain conditions to make a determination that it is the traditional owner of the knowledge or cultural expression.[8]

The colonization of indigenous people was a process of brutal enclosure of *stateless societies* by states. The rise of statutory rule-based regulation of indigenous knowledge systems might represent the final act of enclosure in that long historical process. The ancestral systems of decision making described in chapter 1 were decentred and networked systems of decision making for the use of knowledge and resources. But what one can see evolving in many national statutory systems for indigenous knowledge are centralized forms of regulation in which state authorities are being given powers of intervention and determination over indigenous knowledge systems. State laws establishing cultural authorities with regulatory powers to determine ownership issues over indigenous people's knowledge would in Kafka's hands have made a chilling tale. Some of Max Weber's observations about bureaucracy also draw attention to its darker dimensions. Weber linked the rise of

---

[6] R. A. Epstein, *Simple Rules for a Complex World* (Cambridge, MA: Harvard University Press, 1995), 53.
[7] See Model Law for the Protection of Traditional Knowledge and Expressions of Culture (2002).
[8] See Section 19(1) of the model law.

bureaucracy to processes of industrialization. Bureaucracy is characterized by formal rationality, a type of rationality that deals with problems
through the creation and use of rules applied universally and dispassion-
ately. Weber believed that bureaucracy was an indispensable organizational form for both modern states and economic enterprises, but he also
saw in it the dangers of power: 'Therefore, as an instrument of rationally
organizing authority relations, bureaucracy was and is a power instrument of the first order for one who controls the bureaucratic process'.[9] It
is also clear that for Weber the economic effects of bureaucracy did not
necessarily travel in the direction of economic efficiency.[10] In the end
much of the effects of bureaucracy depend on those who are its true
controllers.

There is nothing surprising in Weber's observations for indigenous
people in Australia who have seen 'rational' state bureaucracy march
through their lives, separating them from their land and from their
children. The rise of a bureaucratic administrative paradigm for indigenous peoples' knowledge systems may disrupt and damage those systems
in all sorts of unforseen ways. There are foreseeable dangers of giving
bureaucracies in countries with corruption problems regulatory powers
over ownership and licensing of indigenous knowledge. New sui generis
systems for the protection of indigenous knowledge may well create new
licensing rents, but there is no guarantee that indigenous people would
be the beneficiaries or that these systems would be a path to the kind of
economic autonomy desired by indigenous groups.[11]

5.2.   Getting what you wish for: the recognition of ancestors

So far I have argued that complex rules and the bureaucratic administrative paradigm are governance forms that should be avoided when it
comes to indigenous peoples' knowledge. Does this mean that we should
follow Richard Epstein's prescription of simple rules when it comes to
thinking about the governance of indigenous knowledge? Certainly there
is virtue in thinking about the role of simple rules in helping to protect the

---

[9] M. Weber, *Economy and Society: An Outline of Interpretive Sociology*, vol. 3 (G. Roth and
C. Wittich eds., New York: Bedminster Press, 1968), 987.
[10] M. Weber, *Economy and Society: An Outline of Interpretive Sociology*, vol. 3 (G. Roth and
C. Wittich eds., New York: Bedminster Press, 1968), 989–90.
[11] On the problems of licensing rents, see R. Hilty, 'Rationales for the Legal Protection of
Intangible Goods and Cultural Heritage', Max Planck Institute for Intellectual Property,
Competition & Tax Law Research Paper No. 09–10 (2 August 2009), available at
SSRN: http://ssrn.com/abstract=1470602 or http://dx.doi.org/10.2139/ssrn.1470602.

intellectual property of indigenous people. His rules of self-ownership and first possession offer support for indigenous intellectual property rights. Although these rules are often linked to Locke's labour theory of property (I own my labour and I am entitled to the fruits of my labour) Epstein does not defend them on the basis of this theory, but rather in terms of the positive welfare consequences they generate. The autonomy that is protected by self-ownership and a property right linked to first acquisition generate much better consequences for humans than other rules concerning the self and the acquisition of property. If the colonists who arrived in 1788 in Australia were part of a society that took these two simple rules seriously, the history following their arrival would have taken a different path. Indigenous people would be less attracted by Epstein's suggestion for a simple prescriptive rule that after a time gives good title to an illegitimate dispossessor of property. The argument is again consequentialist – the future gains from the certainty that such a rule brings outweighs the costs of uncertainty and administrative complexity that follow an open-ended commitment to restitution of property illegitimately taken. One can debate the application of a prescriptive rule on consequential grounds. Such a rule might have stopped indigenous groups in Australia from obtaining recognition of native title.

The list of simple rules for indigenous property, including intellectual property would, if formulated by indigenous people sitting in peace and quiet, almost certainly have variations or be different to the ones listed by Epstein. For example, a simple rule that indigenous people might well choose in Australia is a veto rule when it comes to negotiations over projects that affect their property. A simple veto rule would, for example, allow them to say no to mining projects they really do not want to take place on their land.[12] Indigenous people having to deal with mining companies in Australia have to cope with procedural complexity and strategic decisions about whether to reach a negotiated settlement with a mining company or take their chances in arbitration.[13] Interestingly, Australian government inquiries have in the past been supportive of giving indigenous groups a veto right over mineral developments.[14]

---

[12] In Australia the general position is that the Crown owns mineral resources. See Industry Commission, *Minerals Processing In Australia*, vol. 1, Report No. 7 (Canberra: Australian Government Publishing Service, 1991), 9.

[13] For a discussion of indigenous people's negotiating leverage with mining companies see J. Altman, 'Benefit Sharing is No Solution to Development: Experiences from Mining on Aboriginal Land in Australia' in R. Wynberg, D. Schroeder, R. Chennells (eds.), *Indigenous Peoples, Consent and Benefit-Sharing: Lessons from the San-Hoodin Case* (Dordrecht: Springer, 2009), 285, 291–3.

[14] Industry Commission, *Minerals Processing In Australia*, vol. 1, Report No. 7 (Canberra: Australian Government Publishing Service, 1991), 18.

Epstein's first possession rule is linked to a concept of ownership that may not have much resonance for some indigenous groups. Indigenous groups may well want to exclude others from using ancestral plants, not because they are owners of the plant, but rather because they have custodial duties with respect to that plant and others do not. In other words, their version of the first possession rule might be a first duty rule that requires others to recognize those who have first duties over particular resources. Duty-based concepts such as stewardship, trusteeship, guardianship and custodianship play a much greater role in explanations by indigenous people of how they relate to their knowledge and environmental resources than do ownership rights (see chapter 2). One can also see the same duty-based concepts underpinning the claim started in 1991 by a group of Maori people before the Waitangi Tribunal in New Zealand concerning the protection of their knowledge.[15] Their description of their interests did not rely on first ownership rules so much as the obligations they had by virtue of ancestral and kinship systems to properly care for entities and processes designated under these systems to be treasures to be so cared for: 'Each taonga [treasures] work has kaitiaki [guardians with obligations] – those whose lineage or calling creates an obligation to safeguard the taonga itself and the mātauranga [knowledge] that underlies it'.[16]

The simple rules that Epstein formulates for a property order are unlikely to be the same ones as indigenous groups would choose, but the goal of formulating simple rules should be a part of a strategy for developing property rules for indigenous intellectual property. An analysis that sees problems in rule complexity but which travels in a slightly different direction to Epstein's for solutions is John Braithwaite's analysis of the role that principles can play in regulation of complex economic phenomena.[17] Drawing on comparative data from a study of rule-intensive regulation of nursing homes in the United States and the principle-oriented regulation of Australian nursing homes, Braithwaite hypothesizes that for complex changing phenomena in which there are

---

[15] For the history of the claim see Waitangi Tribunal, *Ko Aotearoa tēnei: A Report into Claims Concerning New Zealand Law and Policy Affecting Māori Culture and Identity*, vol. 1 (Wellington, New Zealand, Legislation Direct, 2011), 3–10. For a discussion of the Tribunal's report see S. Frankel, 'A New Zealand Perspective on the Protection of Mātauranga Māori (traditional knowledge)' in Graber, Kuprecht and Lai (eds.), *International Trade*, 439.

[16] Waitangi Tribunal, *Ko Aotearoa tēnei: A Report into Claims Concerning New Zealand Law and Policy Affecting Māori Culture and Identity*, vol. 1 (Wellington, New Zealand, Legislation Direct, 2011), 44.

[17] J. Braithwaite, 'Rules and Principles: A Theory of Legal Certainty', *Australian Journal of Legal Philosophy*, 27 (2002), 47.

high economic stakes, principles will deliver more legal certainty than rules. Complex rules with lots of elements allow for more interpretive options and therefore less certainty. This uncertainty is deliberately generated by well-resourced players in areas such as tax law when they want to avoid compliance with the rules.

Combining Epstein's and Braithwaite's analyses suggests that simple rules and principles offer the beginnings of a regulatory system that engages seriously with indigenous peoples' knowledge systems.[18] These simple rules and principles would form the legal framework of a regulatory system for indigenous intellectual property. The distinction between rules and principles has been drawn in different ways. For my purposes principles suggest a generalized orientation or direction in which a regulatory system should travel while the application of rules within that system settles specific issues or problems. Principles permeate and orient a system and are suggestive of solutions to specific problems. Simple rules help settle a solution. An example of a principle would be one that recognized an indigenous group's ancestral system of decision making and an example of a simple property rule would be a first duty rule in which the holders of duties under an ancestral system would be entitled to make decisions about a resource to which they were ancestrally related.

Another example of a regulatory principle that indigenous people might conceivably choose is a principle of disclosure for when their knowledge or materials are used by the state or third parties. As we saw in chapter 1, indigenous people see themselves as links in chains of custodianship of knowledge that go back thousands of years. They owe duties to their ancestors under these chains of custodianship. A principle of disclosure would help them to fulfil these duties. An example of a simple rule that flows from the application of the principle to the patent system is a rule that prohibits the grant of a patent or makes it a ground for the revocation of a patent if an applicant fails to disclose in the patent application that it has utilized the knowledge and/or materials of indigenous people. As I indicated in chapter 4, states have deliberately generated a vast menu of complex rule options around the disclosure obligation in the patent system so that they can play the games of rule and legal ritualism.

At this point a rule-minded lawyer might agree that while principles and simple rules represent a starting point there are many particular problems generated by the recognition of indigenous intellectual property for which more complex rules would be needed. The basic problem is that systems of ancestral decision making about treasured works

---

[18] See *ibid.*, 50–52.

(to borrow the taonga concept) would have to have rules of coexistence with existing intellectual property systems. The lawyer's point would be that even if one started with simple rules, complex rules would inevitably follow. For example, a simple first duty rule would raise questions relating to whether this rule would apply to treasured works that were for the purposes of copyright in the public domain and if so what the consequences of applying the first duty rule might be. By way of example, the Waitangi Tribunal heard evidence from a descendant of the Maori leader, Te Rauparaha, the composer of the famous haka dance *Ka Mate*, that this was a taonga work, the true purpose of which had been denigrated and abused through widespread commercial exploitation such as its use in an advertisement by the carmaker Fiat.[19] Under copyright law *Ka Mate* is in the public domain and this allows for a wide variety of uses. If one were to try and bring this taonga work and many others into a property system of protection one can see that potentially complex rules would be needed to settle issues of duration of protection, ownership, infringement and so on. Along similar lines, the flora and fauna of New Zealand also contain many taonga entities. How would a first duty rule for taonga flora be integrated with a public domain patent rule that places naturally occurring genes in the category of discovery? Public domain rules and indigenous peoples' intellectual property potentially create many conflict-of-rules scenarios.[20] It begins to look as if the rule-minded lawyer will end up ruling. Principles, followed by simple rules, seem to have to be followed by more complex rules in an evolution that leads us away from the virtues of simplicity, efficiency and certainty and back into vices of complexity, bureaucracy and uncertainty.

The argument for the inevitability of complex rule regulation assumes there is no other way to arrive at an understanding of what a combination of principles and simple rules is trying to achieve other than through the generation of more rules. But within general philosophy, explanations for what it means to follow a rule do not draw on yet more rules. Instead they look at the role played by inclinations, interpretive communities and conventions.[21] All rules, whether simple or complex, ultimately depend

---

[19] Waitangi Tribunal, *Ko Aotearoa tēnei: A Report into Claims Concerning New Zealand Law and Policy Affecting Māori Culture and Identity*, vol. 1 (Wellington, New Zealand, Legislation Direct, 2011), 66.

[20] For an analysis of the problems see S. Frankel and M. Richardson, 'Cultural Property and "the Public Domain": Case Studies from New Zealand and Australia' in Antons (ed.), *Traditional Knowledge*, 275.

[21] This literature has in part developed in response to the rule scepticism developed in S. A. Kripke, *Wittgenstein on Rules and Private Language* (Oxford: Basil Blackwell, 1982). For a response to Kripke see P. Pettit, 'The Reality of Rule-Following', *Mind*, 99 (1990), 433. For an argument that develops a conventionalist account of rule following in law see

on some background set of conventions that stabilize the rule for a rule follower. It is knowledge of the conventions that surround an apparently simple rule that stabilizes it and allows its user to decide when it is appropriate to apply it and when not.[22] The use of simple rules of politeness, for example, are not driven by long lists of complex rules, but by internalized conventions that confer an understanding of the rules, thereby allowing one to behave appropriately and use the rule in new situations. To understand a rule is to be able to apply it to new contexts.

When it comes to applying rules and principles to new situations, the regulatory prescription suggested by a conventionalist account of rule following is to look for means of convening through which a new understanding about the operation of the rule can be reached or an established understanding confirmed. Looking to support principles and simple rules for the protection of an indigenous knowledge system with a process of regulatory convening is a much better option than enacting complex legal rules. Convening in the sense of meeting together for a common purpose is a much more natural way of working for indigenous people than relying on formal adversarial court processes to settle the uncertainty of complex rules. In fact it is a more natural and less costly way of working for most people. Complex rules engender 'a structurally inegalitarian form of uncertainty'.[23] The cost of decoding complex law in order to understand it bars many people from understanding it.

The Waitangi Tribunal recommended the establishment of an expert multidisciplinary commission with adjudicative, facilitative and administrative functions in relation to taonga works, taonga-derived works, and mātauranga Maori.[24] The Tribunal's discussion of the proposed commission's functions suggests that a commission might tread a path of regulatory convening. According to the Tribunal, the facilitative function of the commission, which would involve the production of best-practice guidelines for the protection and use of Maori knowledge and works and consultation with the guardians of those works, might become the commission's most important function.[25] The Tribunal's discussion of the adjudicative function also suggests scope for a consultation phase between those with guardianship duties for taonga and those who might wish to use taonga works.

The Waitangi Tribunal's report is some of the most advanced thinking by any state on indigenous intellectual property. One challenge for a

---

P. Drahos and S. Parker, 'Rule Following, Rule Scepticism and Indeterminacy in Law: A Conventional Account', *Ratio Juris*, 5 (1992), 109.
[22] see Drahos and Parker, *ibid.*, 114–15.   [23] Braithwaite, 'Rules and Principles', 57.
[24] Waitangi Tribunal, *Ko Aotearoa tēnei*, 93–6.   [25] *Ibid.*, 95.

commission of the kind suggested by the Waitangi Tribunal is whether in fact it can become a forum in which to forge united understandings of a system of principles and simple rules for ancestral intellectual property. Ancestral systems are highly decentred systems of decision making. This much was clear from the Australian fieldwork. In any given Country, duties towards particular ancestral places, flora and fauna are dispersed amongst various individuals. The Waitangi Tribunal's report also makes clear that guardianship duties of many kinds are widely spread amongst Maori people. The existence of chiefs and elders should not blind us to the fact that ancestral systems are complex networks of decision making in which authority is mobile. Finding those individuals in an ancestral system who have genuine knowledge and the authority to make decisions under the system is extremely difficult for outsiders.

A recurring theme in our interviews was that there were not that many people with genuine knowledge left. In a variety of ways large companies have created markets in indigenous knowledge. Surveyors employed by mining companies want to work with indigenous people who have real knowledge of the land to be surveyed. Multinational perfume companies want exotic stories to accompany the ingredients they source from around the world from indigenous people. According to some of our interviewees in Western Australia this has led to problems of story stealing: 'indigenous people will steal stories from each other and pass it off as their own' (interview, 2008). The aim is to make money by being paid for the story or using it to authenticate one's status with a company in order to be hired for other services. Story stealing creates a spiral of distrust. There is more resort to secrecy and some old people take the view it is better not to pass on their knowledge: 'Stories must be told correctly. If they mean nothing, I'll take them with me' (interview, 2008).

At least in Australia, a national commission with responsibility for indigenous knowledge would be entering a landscape of fractured trust, ambiguity and rivalry over control of resources. Moreover, appointing high-profile indigenous leaders to such a commission might not be a solution in the Australian context. Authority in Australia's ancestral systems sets limits, or at least should, on what indigenous leaders can say on behalf of indigenous people. In a camp one night listening to an intense conversation about some proposed developments over which there was strong disagreement amongst various indigenous groups I heard one high-profile indigenous leader described as 'thinking like a whitefella'. Indigenous leaders from one territorial cosmos cannot speak for indigenous people from another territorial cosmos on issues affecting that latter cosmos any more than the British prime minister can speak for French people. Different indigenous groups do find ways to cooperate but in the end each group has responsibilities for its territorial cosmos. As we moved about Australia speaking to indigenous groups I began to realize how little representative authority indigenous leaders actually have. One young indigenous man captured it well – 'it's hard for us to think beyond the mob'. There is nothing surprising about this. Mob logic is a logic that local members of legislatures recognize and practise. This suggests that perhaps a national commission model for indigenous intellectual property is not the right model for Australia. A national commission would have to think hard about ways of encouraging direct participation in its processes as opposed to representative participation. This is challenging and has obvious resource implications.

The stresses on ancestral systems are real. Yet at the same time indigenous people do have ways of sorting out amongst themselves who has genuine knowledge and who does not. Indigenous people can call on other indigenous people to demonstrate their knowledge. They have ways of assessing who has and who does not have ancestral knowledge and accompanying duties. The Waitangi Tribunal also concluded that there were ways to test a claim that a certain species was a taonga species.[26] My impression was that the scrutiny of indigenous individuals claiming to hold knowledge by their peers could be a tough process. There are also deeper complexities. Colonization saw indigenous groups dispossessed and displaced from their traditional Countries. As a result many ended up living in towns, cities or reserves near towns, often a long way from the Countries of their origin. This in turn triggered new processes of group identity formation with indigenous groups drawing distinctions between 'bushies', 'townies' and those on reserves. With these labels can come harsh judgements by some indigenous people about the true expertise of other indigenous people. In one story we were told of an indigenous woman living in the bush who would introduce her sister as living in town, followed by the words 'she doesn't know anything'. But other indigenous people would talk about urban elders. Many indigenous people are highly mobile, moving between Country and urban environments. To live in a town does not necessarily mean one does not have knowledge of Country.

My discussion so far is intended to show that a number of variables affect the search for those with knowledge and authority to help resolve disputes over the use of indigenous intellectual property. However, I am not arguing that the work of a commission would be impossible. In order for a commission to be successful it would have to turn itself into a forum

---

[26] *Ibid.*, 114–15.

of convening. This means devoting a lot of its resources and time to searching for knowledgeable people and deferring any rule making or guideline issuance until it was clear that an understanding about those rules and guidelines had been reached. We have lots of evidence that indigenous groups had very extensive trading networks that covered tangible and intangible objects. Keen, for example, points out that the rights to the performance of ceremonies, the use of designs and songs could be transferred from one indigenous group or person to another.[27] In Howitt's work on Aboriginal tribes published in 1904 there is reference to 'an extensive system of inter-tribal communication and barter' as well as 'established trade centres at which the tribes meet on certain occasions for a regulated barter'.[28] Negotiating over the use of knowledge was a culturally familiar practice for indigenous groups. A commission that drew on culturally familiar practices for negotiating permissible uses of indigenous knowledge would probably win more trust and support than one that required indigenous people to become skilled in the ways of lawyerly design. Convening to barter, to negotiate, to settle differences, to establish boundaries are practices that are familiar to indigenous people and could become the basis of a system of convening for the protection and use of indigenous knowledge in Australia. The important thing is to move away from what comes naturally to lawyers – courts and tribunals with formal processes for managing witnesses, evidence and procedure aimed at the production of more rules. We have considerable evidence that the legal discourse structure in courts silences indigenous people in various ways, even when the court proceedings themselves are not adversarial and the lawyers and judges are trying to assist indigenous witnesses.[29] In the courtroom process legal language reaches its zenith of formality and simultaneously its greatest power to alienate (in the sense of separating itself from the lived experience of those before it).

Up to now I have been referring to a commission model, but it is not clear to me that a national commission is the right path for the Australian context. An alternative might be to consider the formation of regional networks to carry out the functions of adjudication, facilitation and administration that the Waitangi Tribunal has identified as being necessary. The strong desire for development by indigenous people in Australia's north is seeing the emergence of networks such as the North

---

[27] Keen, *Aboriginal Economy*, 355–6.   [28] Howitt, *The Native Tribes*, 714.

[29] See D. Eades, '*I Don't Think It's an Answer to the Question*: Silencing Aboriginal Witnesses in Court', *Language in Society*, 29 (2000), 161.

Australian Indigenous Experts Forum.[30] Where such regional networks emerge they might be better at finding those knowledgeable people who should be part of an assembly that creates new understandings around the principles and rules of indigenous intellectual property.

Obviously we cannot recreate those inter-tribal meetings described by Howitt. But we can try and capture something of the spirit of this approach to solving conflicts over the use of indigenous intellectual property.[31] This, as I have argued, involves a focus on convening. Convening should not involve court-style procedures although this does not mean that some of the outcomes of convening might not be recognized as law. A system of convening should recognize that under an ancestral system there are many possible conveners. For Australia regional networks rather than a central commission is probably a better way to bring together those who can speak with knowledge about a given problem. Whatever procedures are chosen they must not silence or interfere in storytelling. It is through stories and discussing stories that ancestral purpose for resources and knowledge comes to be understood.

One objection to a process of regulatory convening might be that it will slow down processes of commercialization. But for many indigenous people the issue of bypassing traditional decision-making structures is not an option to be considered in some process of trade-off: 'We have to [accept ancestral systems], it's in our souls. If you accept the land, you have to accept what comes with it.'

---

[30] North Australian Indigenous Experts Forum on Sustainable Economic Development, 'Towards Resilient Communities through Reliable Prosperity', First Forum Report, Mary River Park, Northern Territory, 19–21 June 2012 available at www.nailsma.org. au/hub/resources/publication/towards-resilient-communities-through-reliable-prosperity-first-indigenous.

[31] See L. Behrendt, *Aboriginal Dispute Resolution* (Sydney: Federation Press, 1995).

6   The Kimberley: big projects, little projects

6.1.   Big projects

The Kimberley region in Australia is a big place. Located in the northern part of Western Australia it is about three times the size of England. In tourist parlance it is usually described as one of the last great wildernesses. The increasing number of tourists to be found in its gorges, rivers and coastline means it is becoming one of the most visited last great wildernesses.

The Kimberley's remoteness has not stopped it from becoming a place of big projects. The latest of these is the proposal to build a liquefied natural gas precinct at James Price Point, about 60 kilometres north of Broome. To Australia's north, China's economy demands to be fed with hydrocarbons. Port infrastructure is desperately needed to service the Browse Basin gas fields. If a 30 billion dollar facility is built at James Price Point then the humpback whales, which come to the bays and inlets of the Kimberley to calve, will get the opportunity to mingle with gas tankers as they carry their cargo to its emissions destination in China.

There have been other big projects in the Kimberley. The Ord River Irrigation Scheme, which included building a dam across the Ord, produced in 1972 a huge artificial lake, Lake Argyle. The initial plans for a large-scale cotton industry based on irrigation did not quite work out and for a long time many saw the Ord River Scheme as Australia's best example of a great white elephant.[1] Cattle stations have been another large Kimberley project. The Western Australian government began granting pastoral leases of some 1,000,000 acres towards the end of the nineteenth century. The economics of open-range grazing in a remote area meant that many of the cattle stations were marginal operations, surviving only because the Aboriginal people who provided all the station labour did so under, what was in the beginning, a system of forced

---

[1] R. Symanski, 'Environmental Mismanagement in Australia's Far North', *The Geographical Review*, 86 (1996), 573, 575.

labour.[2] Station owners were given permits to work Aboriginal people on their stations.[3] Over the decades a tragedy of private property suzerainty played itself out as the pastoralists overstocked and overgrazed their stations leading to a deeply eroded landscape.[4] The earliest big project in the Kimberley was the pearling industry. European markets had been making increasing use of mother-of-pearlshell for decorative purposes. The discovery of vast quantities of pearlshell in the waters off northern Australia led to a boom that by the end of the nineteenth century saw Broome along with Thursday Island in the Torres Strait become the export conduits for an industry producing more than half the world's supply.[5]

6.2.   A little project

The big resource projects of settler capitalism in the Kimberley brought for Aboriginal people death, disease and dislocation. They were a source of forced labour. Over the last several decades as they have regained control of some land they have become much more active in resource management.[6] In this chapter I discuss the example of a Kimberley-based indigenous group that has taken out patents over compounds derived from a plant. It is a little project, but one in which the indigenous community had invested high hopes.

Generally when patents over plants and indigenous groups are discussed it is usually in the context of biopiracy. The term, generally attributed to the activist Pat Mooney, is a label for the non-consensual taking of biological knowledge and materials that have generative and customary links with local communities, most usually communities based in the states of the South.[7] As a rhetorical tool it has proved remarkably effective. During the 1980s the United States in particular was able to portray developing countries as 'pirates', arguing that they were stealing US

[2] On the problems facing the stations see Lord Rennell, 'The Kimberley Division of Western Australia', *The Geographical Journal*, 119 (1953), 306.
[3] For very personal accounts in their own words by Aboriginal stockmen see P. Marshall (ed.), *Raparapa Kularr Martuwarra; Stories from the Fitzroy Drovers* (Broome WA: Magabala Books, 1993).
[4] Symanski, 'Environmental Mismanagement', 578.
[5] J. Bach, 'The Political Economy of Pearlshelling', *The Economic History Review, New Series*, 14 (1961), 105, 106.
[6] For references to the literature see J. Holmes, 'Diversity and Change in Australia's Rangelands: A Post-Productivist Transition with a Difference?', *Transactions of the Institute of British Geographers, New Series*, 27 (2002), 362, 373.
[7] D. F. Robinson, *Confronting Biopiracy: Challenges, Cases and International Debates* (London: Earthscan, 2010), 14.

intellectual property. In the 1990s, the United States and its supporters like Australia and the EU found themselves on the receiving end of the same stigmatizing rhetoric. Confronted by examples of patents that clearly made use of indigenous knowledge and/or biological materials customarily linked to indigenous communities these countries had to explain and defend the operation of their patent systems.

One effect of the biopiracy discourse has been to focus much more attention on how certain actors have been able to appropriate the value of the stock of biodiversity created by countless rural local communities. At a practical level it has helped indigenous groups, which had very little bargaining power, to gain some negotiating leverage. The agents which have given the biopiracy frame some real-world coercive power have been non-governmental organizations (NGOs). In an internet-enabled world they have been able to shine global spotlights on the conduct of those bargaining commercially with indigenous people. When NGOs became involved in the negotiations between the Sans people of Southern Africa and actors from the pharmaceutical industry over a drug derived from the *Hoodia* plant, the negotiating dynamic changed in ways that gave the Sans some leverage.[8] The case discussed in this chapter goes the other way. An indigenous group is seeking through the patent system monopoly control over a biological resource, a resource that is part of its knowledge system.

6.3.   Trust and smoke

The smokebush story is one of those stories that has a wide commentary on the internet and is seen by many as yet another example of 'the great indigenous rip-off'.[9] The story starts in 1981 when the United States National Cancer Institute (NCI) acquired some samples of a plant belonging to the genus *Conospermum* (smokebush being the common name). The extract had been collected in the Gairdner Mountain Range in Western Australia as part of the world-wide programme run by the Natural Products Division of the NCI aimed at collecting plants that might be potentially useful for the treatment of cancer.[10] Collecting by

---

[8] R. Wynberg and R. Chennells, 'Green Diamonds of the South: An Overview of the San-Hoodia Case' in R. Wynberg, D. Schroeder and R. Chennells (eds.), *Indigenous Peoples, Consent and Benefit-Sharing: Lessons from the San-Hoodia Case* (Dordrecht, Springer, 2009), 89, 101.

[9] See, for example, T. Coyle, 'The Great Indigenous Rip-off', 11 June 2003 available at www.greatreporter.com/content/great-indigenous-rip.

[10] Information about the source of smokebush extract and its subsequent investigation can be found in US patent no. 5672607. The patent was filed on 29 January 1993 and granted on 30 September 1997.

the NCI goes back to 1960 with tens of thousands of plants having being collected from around the world and stored in a repository in Frederick, Maryland.[11] The smokebush sample lay in cold storage until in 1988 the NCI developed an anti-HIV screen. The sample was one of many thousands that were randomly tested against the screen. Signs of anti-viral activity led to further investigations and ultimately patent applications claiming isolated anti-viral compounds from the smokebush extract.

The NCI wanted more samples. The Western Australian government wanted a deal on any future royalties. The NCI's position was not helped when a collector was caught attempting to leave Australia with cases full of smokebush plants.[12] Eventually an Australian pharmaceutical company, AMRAD, acquired rights from the NCI to further develop these compounds. This led to research and development agreements between Western Australia and AMRAD. Western Australia managed to secure $1.65 million and $1.15 million under two separate agreements during the 1990s.[13] These sums were small compared to the $100 million in royalties that was being talked about as a possibility.[14] Royalties appear not to have flooded in, a not uncommon experience in the pharmaceutical business where few of many discoveries ever make it to blockbuster status. AMRAD ran into toxicity problems with the compound and ended up halting the research, although other research groups linked to the NCI continue to work on it.[15]

Not disputed is that the smokebush plant is known by indigenous people to have medicinal value. The events around the smokebush have come to be seen as a case of biopiracy.[16] For many indigenous people it is also part of a broader pattern, one in which, as one interviewee from the

---

[11] Details of the NCI's natural product collection activities can be found at www.meb.uni-bonn.de/cancernet/600733.html.

[12] T. Janke and R. Quiggin, *Indigenous Cultural and Intellectual Property and Customary Law*, Background paper 12 (Perth: Law Reform Commission of Western Australia, 2005), 487.

[13] The first amount is reported in a Ministerial Media Statement of 18 August 1995 (see www.mediastatements.wa.gov.au/Pages/default.aspx?ItemId=144854) and the second amount is reported in an answer to a question on notice in the Western Australian Legislative Assembly, Thursday 25 May 2000, p. 7318 available at www.parliament.wa.gov.au.

[14] This figure is reported in M. Blakeney, 'Bioprospecting and the Protection of Traditional Knowledge of Indigenous Peoples: An Australian Perspective', *European Intellectual Property Review*, 6 (1997), 298.

[15] The details are reported in C. J. Kavelin, 'The Protection of Indigenous Medical Knowledge: Towards the Transformation of Law to Engage Indigenous Spiritual Concerns', unpublished Ph.D. thesis, Macquarie University (2007), 99–100.

[16] See Janke and Quiggin, *Indigenous Cultural and Intellectual Property and Customary Law*, Background paper 12 (Perth: Law Reform Commission of Western Australia, 2005), 488.

Western Australian Department of Indigenous Affairs put it, indigenous people's 'knowledge is being mined – extracted and taken away' (interview, 2008).

The smokebush story and other stories that circulate about the lack of proper recognition for indigenous knowledge in Western Australia reinforce the low-trust environment that everybody operates in when it comes to any potential dealing, business or otherwise, involving indigenous knowledge. Events such as those surrounding the smokebush simply strengthen indigenous people's belief that they can expect to be ripped off if they reveal or share their knowledge with outsiders. In this particular case, however, we have no evidence of indigenous people sharing their knowledge about the smokebush plant with Richard Spjut, the person who collected the samples of the plant in 1981. Spjut's fieldwork report does show he had experience in the study of 'antitumor/medicinal-folkloric relationships', but there is no suggestion that he consulted with indigenous people during his fieldwork in Western Australia.[17] Rather, the report indicates the process was one of random sampling of plants. The report also reveals the extent to which the south-west region of Western Australia in which he was collecting represented a treasure house of biodiversity: 'A single trip to Western Australia yielded more new genra than all the field trips combined for all other (5) laboratory botanists during the last 5 years'.[18] In the last chapter I argue that this extraordinary diversity is best explored through high-trust networks in which indigenous people and scientists operate as epistemic equals rather than in relationships in which indigenous people are only seen as a source of useful tips.

Many of our interviews in Western Australia suggested that people saw themselves as operating in a low-trust environment when it came to the protection of indigenous knowledge. The Kimberley Land Council was full of stories about the difficulty of negotiating with Western Australian governmental officials about intellectual property. From the Land Council's perspective the government was keen to maximize the protection of its own intellectual property while at the same time not applying this protectionist philosophy to indigenous people's knowledge. The response of land councils to this government policy – 'Because they [government] won't give us the IP, we don't share with them'. Ironically, the smokebush incident made Western Australian officials sensitive to

---

[17] R. W. Spjut, Economic Botany Laboratory, United States Department of Agriculture, Foreign Travel Report: Western Australia and Tasmania, 20 August–8 November 1981, unpublished, available at www.worldbotanical.com/who-we-are.htm#usda.
[18] *Ibid.*

the potential costs to the State of not taking more interest in the mining of its genetic resources. In the words of one official describing the behaviour of bioprospectors: 'These guys would go in, scoop up things and you'd never hear from them again'.

The complaint of bodies like the Kimberley Land Council about the behaviour of the Western Australian government was exactly this – officials would come in, 'scoop up' knowledge from indigenous people and disappear. One important difference, however, is that the Western Australian government has an established property rights regime to help solve its problems (a combination of regulatory powers over flora and fauna, contract law and intellectual property law). Indigenous people operating under an ancestral system, however, struggle to make economic gains from knowledge they release as part of interactions with outsiders. In ancestral systems knowledge is encoded in a multilevel system of story-telling. Story-telling begins with the simplest, publicly known story. This simple story creates a connection that might grow. How much more is revealed to outsiders depends on how the relationship between the indigenous storyteller and the outsider develops. Officials interacting with indigenous people might listen to a knowledgeable indigenous elder talk about a fisheries resource. At some point they decide that they have heard enough to help them work out where they should place various fishing zones. As far as they are concerned the interaction is over. They move on to the next regulatory problem.

For the indigenous elder who has spent time with the people from fisheries, different expectations have arisen as he has continued to give more of his time and knowledge to the project. The storytelling becomes more like the performance of a service and he begins to look for reciprocities that signal respect for his knowledge and abilities. If the non-indigenous people find ways to repay the storyteller, trust begins to grow. For indigenous people these storytelling conversations are part of a process in which they have the chance to build a partnership that will help them manage their Country and bring them some extra resources for that purpose. Often it does not work out in this way. Their knowledge is used and they receive neither rewards of esteem, nor money. If there are non-indigenous consultants working on natural resource projects, their time will have been costed as part of the contract. They have status as consultants and financial rewards. Indigenous people who are experts under an ancestral system may not have this expertise recognized under a consultancy contract. One can, of course, improve the contracts and design protocols to guide contractual negotiations between indigenous and non-indigenous people. Bodies like the Kimberley Land Council do invest time in this kind of work. But in a world of limited funding and short-term contracts the risk is that it will be the indigenous person's knowledge that is not properly valued.

Whether they realize it or not, non-indigenous managers of resources in listening to stories are being given access to intellectual property under an ancestral system. They are being drawn into a world where reciprocation and an accounting for their use of the knowledge are expected.[19] An intellectual property lawyer might conclude that in many cases there is no copyright in the story or that confidentiality does not apply to the storytelling, that nothing the storyteller says makes it into any of the Australian state's property boxes. But this is irrelevant for indigenous people. The rules which define their intellectual property are the rules of the ancestral system.

For the people working in Western Australia's bureaucracy the issues around indigenous knowledge are, like smoke, hard to grasp. They are confronted by demands from indigenous leaders and activists that they do something to protect indigenous knowledge: 'There is a constant stream of demand for TK protection from the [X's] of the world' (interview, 2008) (I have omitted the names of the indigenous leaders). At the higher reaches of federal policymaking, papers circulate with Midas-like estimates of the billions of dollars to be made from biodiscovery, along with general recommendations about the need to achieve best practice on the recognition of indigenous knowledge.[20] But in the world of policy implementation, the middle-ranking bureaucrats struggle with the issue as do indigenous people who work in government:

'The whole TK area is in the too-hard basket. We all struggled and put it in the bottom drawer' (bureaucrat, 2008). 'Where do you start and where do you end?' (indigenous bureaucrat, 2009).

There is also the reality in Western Australia that bioprospecting has delivered very little in the way of revenue streams. The main game is another extractive industry – multi-billion dollar mining projects. In 2008 Western Australia received almost $3 billion in royalties from the mining companies with mining being worth almost $72 billion to the state economy.[21] In this royalty-based economy, the great fear of

---

[19] The link between things and services that appear to be freely given and reciprocity has been much discussed in the sociological and anthropological literature, much of it drawing on the ideas in M. Mauss, *The Gift: Forms and Functions of Exchange in Archaic Societies*, I. Gunnison tr. (London: Cohen and West, 1970).

[20] See Prime Minister's Science Engineering and Innovation Council, *Biodiscovery* (2005) available at www.innovation.gov.au/Science/PMSEIC/Documents/Biodiscovery.pdf.

[21] Figures obtained from the Western Australian Department of Mines and Petroleum www.dmp.wa.gov.au/documents/000194.jemma.williams.pdf.

indigenous people is that they will be cut out of or given very little of the royalty streams that are derived from mining or other income streams generated from the licensing of things such as water rights or the harvesting of trees. Competing with mining companies for water rights is not possible and so indigenous people have to argue for a reserve allocation (interview, 2008). With few other options on the table, indigenous groups negotiate with mining companies, securing the best deal they can. The sums of money on offer from mining companies dwarf everything else. A combination of factors has enabled some indigenous groups to secure better agreements with mining companies than were possible a few decades ago. These include the recognition of native title, improved environmental regulation and a realization by the mining industry that a social licence to operate is as important to their long-term operations as a formal licence.[22] Wise negotiation can find ways to secure protection for sites important to indigenous people, as well as create funding support for indigenous knowledge systems. The agreement that indigenous groups negotiated with Rio Tinto over its Argyll diamond mine sets up a trust that manages, amongst other things, a specific fund devoted to the long-term support of men and women's cultural practices.[23]

Whether or not the deals with mining companies will help indigenous groups achieve their ambitions to care for their Countries and bring them the development opportunities they so desperately seek, time will tell. The arrival of a large sum of money in a community is the beginning of a development opportunity with everything depending on the decision-making processes around that money.[24] Does the current biodiscovery business model have anything to offer indigenous communities? Should they be thinking about it as an option?

6.4.   A crocodile's bite

On 26 May 2010 a patent application on some analgesic compounds was accepted by Australia's patent office.[25] A patent application was first lodged on 27 November 2003, but the origins of the patent's invention

---

[22] For a discussion see B. Harvey and S. Nish, 'Rio Tinto and Indigenous Community Agreement Making in Australia', *Journal of Energy and Natural Resource Law*, 23 (2005), 499.
[23] *Ibid.*, 509.
[24] For a discussion of the hurdles that need to be overcome by an indigenous group see J. Altman, 'Benefit Sharing is No Solution to Development: Experiences from Mining on Aboriginal Land in Australia' in Wynberg, Schroeder and Chennells (eds.), *Indigenous Peoples*, 285.
[25] The Australian patent number is 2004293125.

lie in a fishing trip some twenty years earlier in which one of the fishermen lost a finger to a crocodile.

John Watson is Nyikina man. He grew up working on stations in the Kimberley. In his own words:

'I was born into the pastoral country. I grew up working sheep, horses and cattle ... On the stations we had three feeds a day. We got no pay, but at the time we didn't worry about that.'[26]

Life on the stations was hard in many different ways:[27]

'I never got a chance to meet my two eldest brothers because they were taken away before I was born ... My parents had no say in that, it was government policy ... So, whenever a police party came out to Mt Anderson they sent us off into the bush ...'.

One of the recurring themes of our interviews with indigenous people was the desire they expressed to find independent sources of income. Material poverty and then welfare dependence have stalked Aboriginal people since colonization. Most white Australians had very little idea of what Aboriginal poverty was truly like. Australian television simply did not broadcast the images. When an Australian current affairs programme finally did so, the images of communities living without running water 'came as a terrible shock to us because in 1961, let's face it, news crews from television stations didn't go anywhere near Aboriginal settlements. I mean there wasn't any story there'.[28]

The big projects of settler capitalism contributed to the dislocation of clan groups from their traditional lands. Many indigenous people became refugees, seeking protection and work in new Countries. Those in the cattle industry had the best chance of staying close to their traditional Countries, but after equal wages for Aboriginal stockmen came into operation in 1968 many lost their jobs: 'When the equal wage decision was handed down by the courts twenty-odd years ago, the Aboriginal people were forced off the stations. ... Hundreds of people were forced to leave the stations they'd grown up on, and to live under appalling conditions in town reserves.'[29] This dislocation complicated the capacity of immigrant indigenous groups to carry out the ceremonies that were fundamental to maintaining their

---

[26] J. Watson, 'We Know This Country' in Marshall (ed.), *Raparapa Kularr Martuwarra*, 207, 209.
[27] *Ibid.*, 220.
[28] Excerpt from transcript of 'Four Corners Celebrates 50 Years on ABC TV' 22 August 2011 available at www.abc.net.au/4corners/stories/2011/08/22/3284239.htm#transcript.
[29] Watson, 'We Know This Country', 208.

continuity as a group and important to their traditional rights over land.[30] Immigrant groups in their new locations had to find ways to cooperate with traditional owner groups.

Our fieldwork in the Kimberley suggested that the distinction between owner and immigrant groups remains a source of instability in contexts where there is competition for use of resources. For example, at one Aboriginal corporation we were told about a large order that had been placed for the picking of Gubinge, one of several local Aboriginal names for a fruit that has been classified as *Terminalia ferdinandiana* (also referred to as Kakadu Plum or Bush Plum). With some 250 species in the world *Terminalia* is not unique to Australia, but most of the thirty species found in Australia are not found elsewhere. The fruit is renowned for its very high vitamin C content. It has become something of a target for companies interested in Australian bushfoods, ending up in exotic products promising to save our immune systems from the ravages of free radicals. The US company Mannatech uses Kakadu Plum in one of its antioxidant capsule product lines. Like many companies in this field Mannatech uses patents to protect its dietary supplement products, including those in which Kakadu Plum is used.[31] Using the Patent Cooperation Treaty system, patent applications involving Australia's native plants can be easily spread around the world.[32] Mannatech is not the only company that has filed for patents relating to Kakadu Plum.[33]

When Mannatech placed orders for Kakadu Plum it created a demand in tonnes whereas previously demand had been measured in kilos. Many of the indigenous people doing the picking saw an improvement to their income. To the outside eye the sums of money appear small. We were told that pickers were getting about $10 a kilo, and this rate was generating enough income to make a noticeable difference to people. In the words of interviewees from the Aboriginal Corporation that had been involved in setting up the supply chain (interview, 2008): 'First time in living memory there were no food vouchers, no payments from

---

[30] For a case study see K. Palmer, 'Religious Knowledge and the Politics of Continuity and Change' in C. Anderson (ed.), *Politics of the Secret*, Oceania Monograph 45 (University of Sydney, 1995), 15.

[31] See, for example, Australian patent application no. 2005/328670, A1 'Methods and compositions for modified release of nutritional supplements', filed on 3 March 2005.

[32] By way of example see Mannatech's applications under the Patent Cooperation Treaty, WO 2006/096161/A1 and WO 2006/112958/A2 'Methods and compositions for modified release of nutritional supplements'.

[33] See, for example, Mary Kay's application WO 2007/084998/A2, 'Compositions comprising Kakadu Plum extract or Acai Berry extract' filed on 19 January 2007 and Amway's granted US patent no. 7,175,862, 'Method of Preparing Kakadu Plum Powder' (13 February 2007).

Centrelink, no school vouchers, kids had bicycles, extra dollar over Christmas.' '99% of our members are CDEP.[34] Everybody blows it [CDEP money] over Christmas. Picking [Kakadu Plum] was a way of earning a few dollars over Christmas and helping people over the break.' But there were also problems: 'I remember some of the fights around town [Broome] – you can't pick here. It was a load of crap.'

Our interview with Coradji, the company that had a contract to supply Gubinge to Mannatech confirmed this picture. Coradji itself had applied for a patent that claimed 'a method of removing at least the majority of the seed from the fruit of the tree *Terminalia ferdinandiana*', not because it was keen on patents but because of pressure from Mannatech (interview).[35] In any case the only people in this particular supply chain without patent applications were the indigenous pickers.

When Coradji began buying Gubinge, it resulted in a 'massive injection of cash into the Broome economy' but it also led to 'Gubinge wars – people were jumping over fences, cutting off tree limbs with chainsaws. We had to put out guidelines not to go onto private property'. Picking on the golf club was discouraged, as was picking on the rifle range. Pickers were told to steer away from areas that had been sprayed with chemicals. Some of the conflicts stemmed from the fact that some of the people doing the picking around Broome were not part of the group that had traditionally occupied the Broome area – 'you people aren't Yawuru'.[36] The order from Mannatech thus became something of a mixed blessing as it offered economic opportunity, but triggered conflicts over who had the right to pick Gubinge from which trees. Our interviewees suggested that these problems were eventually settled. Some groups went elsewhere to pick in order to 'pacify' other groups and customary law seems to have played its part: 'It's an unwritten rule, you have certain rights over the local vegetation' (interview).

Poverty is the broader context for what non-indigenous Australians like to refer to as Aboriginal politics, a phrase we heard often enough during the course of our fieldwork. The implication is that but for a failure of cooperation amongst indigenous people things would be much better for indigenous Australians. What this tends to overlook is that when people are poor and living in social conditions where they are the 'out group' on more than one level, the politics of cooperation is a hard thing to pull off.

[34] Community Development Employment Projects in remote communities funded by the Australian government.
[35] See AU 2004/203276/A1 entitled 'Fruit Processing Device', filed on 20 July 2004.
[36] The Yawuru people have been recognized as holding native title around the Broome area. See *Rubibi Community v State of Western Australia (No. 7)* [2006] FCA 459.

Instead people tend to fight to gain resources for those they care about the most, their families, their kin. In the words of one indigenous interviewee,

'People think too locally, not regionally, not nationally. Most local communities are concerned with looking after what little they have left, there's a fear of taking on change.'

Of course, protecting one's family at the expense of contributing to a collective good is a phenomenon that is hardly peculiar to indigenous Australians.

Potentially good business bush food enterprises have to operate in landscapes of dislocation in which groups of people have had to make new Countries their home, deal with different layers of in group and out group distinctions and cope with poverty. Indigenous politics is often the politics of poor people thrown together by circumstance rather than choice, competing for a few extra resources and dollars:

'At the end of the day you've got to survive. If you want to look after your mob and culture you maybe have to lock others out – won't be popular on the ground' (interview 2008).

These are not ideal conditions for starting small business enterprises.

Whether in spite of or because of these circumstances some indigenous people are still prepared to start small business ventures. This brings us back to the story of the patent application that began this section. John Watson and his brother were trying to catch a crocodile. Lifting his hand out of the water John saw that his finger had been bitten off. Knowing he was a few days away from seeing a doctor he resorted to a well-known remedy that Aboriginal people had been using along the Fitzroy River to deal with the pain from injuries, such as those arising from being spiked by a catfish. The remedy consisted of chewing a piece of bark from the Marjala tree and applying it to the wound. The doctor who treated John a few days later expressed amazement at the analgesic power of the treatment. From here and with the assistance of Paul Marshall, who had been the Administrator of the Kimberley Land Council, John Watson and other members of the Jarlmadangah Aboriginal Corporation embarked on a path of commercializing a product from the Marjarla tree using the patent system. How things have worked out is the subject of the next section.

6.5.   Once bitten twice shy

The costs of starting a patent application are comparatively low. One can pay a patent attorney to draft and lodge a provisional application in Australia to get the ball rolling. Costs depend on complexity, but they are in the order of $5,000 to $6,000. In effect this simply buys the patent applicant some more thinking and planning time. Things get serious when a patent applicant decides to seek patent protection in other countries. In the case of pharmaceuticals the big markets are Europe, Japan and the United States. Emerging markets such as China and India also have to be factored into a global strategy. Once one goes down this path the costs begin to mount because applicants end up having to obtain national applications in each jurisdiction in which they want a patent (this may involve using a regional patent system such as the European patent system). There are ways to delay the cost by using the Patent Cooperation Treaty, but eventually if one wants patents in other countries one has to pay the patent offices and patent lawyers in those countries. That means bills stretching past $100,000 and perhaps way past that figure depending on how many of the countries of the world one wants to cover with patents, the complexity of the application and how many problems one encounters in the application process.

The cost of developing a global patenting strategy is generally not within the means of indigenous communities in Australia. This is hardly a problem unique to indigenous communities. In the case of smaller companies or universities in the biotech or pharmaceutical sector in Australia the game is to gain a patent over the technology and then sell or license it for commercial development to a large player.[37] This is especially true for product development in the pharmaceutical sector.

John Watson is part of the Jarlmadangah Burru Aboriginal Community (the Jarlmadangah Community). This community owns the pastoral lease to the Mount Anderson cattle station. It did not have $100,000 to gamble on a patent application over a plant-based medical product. The infrastructure demands of a 330,000 acre property are huge. These pastoral leases came up for acquisition because the former owners decided that the costs of investment needed to keep the stations going were too high.

In the absence of capital to fund the patent application process and lacking experience with the patent system, the senior members of the Jarlmadangah Community began to look around for suitable partners. Through Paul Marshall's searching they found Griffith University and this eventually led to talks that in turn matured into a legal agreement between the university and the Jarlmadangah Community. What followed were several patent applications and eventually an international

[37] On this point see D. Nicol and J. Nielsen, 'Patents and Medical Biotechnology: An Empirical Analysis of Issues Facing the Australian Industry' (Centre for Law and Genetics, Occasional Paper No. 6, 2003), 208–9. Available at www.ipria.org/publications/reports/BiotechReportFinal.pdf.

application under the Patent Cooperation Treaty.[38] This application has entered the national phase of processing in a number of countries, including the United States where the patent has been granted.

The owners of the Australian patent are Griffith University and the Jarlmadangah Community. The inventors are Ron Quinn and Clive Mills. Ron Quinn is professor at Griffith University with a deep know-ledge of the chemistry of natural products and a long experience of working with large pharmaceutical companies. This particular case has received a lot of publicity. It is in many ways the quintessential good news story in which an indigenous group has taken a chance and become the co-owner of a patent. Australia's patent office advertises the case on its website as part of its Dreams Shield project suggesting that a 'host of commercial opportunities' have followed the grant of the patent.[39] Grif-fith University's website also draws attention to its partnership with Jarlmadangah, pointing to the commercial potential of the discovered compounds.[40]

So, how have things worked out? We first spoke to the members of the Jarlmadangah Community about the patent in 2008 and then over the course of the study stayed in touch with them about developments. At the time of our first interview in 2008 the senior members of the community were negotiating with Griffith University about a commer-cialization strategy. This eventually took the form of an agreement between Griffith and Jarlmadangah and Avexis, a small biotech com-pany set up in 2008 to develop products based on the patented com-pounds. Small companies with very few employees chasing a commercialization opportunity are not unusual in Australia's biotech scene. In Avexis' case it managed to win a $70,000 grant from the Commonwealth in 2009 to help cover some of the costs of developing a business strategy, clinical trials, obtaining regulatory approvals and so on.

In general terms a company in this kind of situation has to decide whether to use the discovered compounds to develop a product that meets all the regulatory standards of a registered medicine (amongst other things, this means full-scale human trials) or whether to aim for a complementary medicine where the standards are much less onerous. The regulation of complementary medicines in Australia has been

---

[38] The International Application Number is PCT/AU2004/001660, 'Novel Analgesic Compounds, Extracts Containing Same and Methods of Preparation'.

[39] See http://ipaustralia.gov.au/understanding-intellectual-property/ip-for-business/indigenous-business/dream-shield/.

[40] See http://studylink.blogs.com/virtual-research-week/2009/04/ancient-australian-remedy-as-novel-pain-killing-drugs.html.

described as a light touch model.[41] Using the complementary medicines pathway a product such as an ointment can be on the market in three to five years, considerably faster than the ten to twelve years it takes to put a new prescription medicine on the market. The size of this complementary medicines market in Australia is estimated to be about $1.2 billion and growing.[42]

Raising finance for biopharmaceutical projects in Australia's venture capital market faces the problem that only about 20 per cent of this capital is concentrated in the health and biotechnology, communications and information technology sectors.[43] Australian biotechnology firms have adapted to this by looking to foreign capital and finance.[44] In much the same way that nineteenth-century British financial capitalism shaped Australia's wool industry, so US, and to a lesser extent European and Japanese, financing deeply affect the commercial fate of the genes and compounds that are extracted from Australia's mega-diverse flora and fauna.

The year of 2008, a peak year in the global financial crisis, was not a good year in which to try and persuade people to risk capital. Even under better global circumstances it was always going to be difficult for Avexis to raise the needed equity. As the milestones went by it became clear to all that Avexis was not on a road to finance. Under the terms of the licence Avexis lost its rights and Griffith University and the Jarlmadangah group were left with the task of product development, this responsibility falling to the commercial arm of the university.

Griffith University continued to research the compound, discovering that it was highly complex and therefore making it too costly to synthesize in commercial quantities in the laboratory (interview, 2011). This in turn meant extracting the compound from the bark of the tree, raising questions about the quantities of the bark and trees that would be needed in order to run a sustainable harvest operation. The search for capital has turned in the direction of philanthropic sources (interview, 2011).

Avexis' story is hardly unusual. All small biotech companies operate at the pointy end of risk. What makes it a different story is the participation of an indigenous group. When we spoke to one of the people from the

---

[41] See K. J. Harvey *et al.*, 'Commercialism, Choice and Consumer Protection: Regulation of Complementary Medicines in Australia', *Medical Journal of Australia*, 188 (2008), 21.

[42] Australian National Audit Office, *Therapeutic Goods Regulation: Complementary Medicines* (Commonwealth of Australia, 2011), 34.

[43] D. Regan and G. Tunny, 'Venture Capital in Australia' (unpublished, 2008), 1, 6, available at http://cprs.treasury.gov.au/documents/1352/PDF/combined.pdf#page=5.

[44] Productivity Commission, *Public Support for Science and Innovation* (Canberra: Commonwealth of Australia, 2007), 312.

Jarlmadangah Community, who had primary carriage of the project, we were lucky enough to be able to listen to some quiet reflection about the experience of the commercialization process. Next time, our interviewee suggested, the community would hire the university as a subcontractor to do the chemical analysis of the plant rather than part with a 50 per cent ownership share of the patent as payment for the university's work.

But would there be a next time? In the words of our interviewee: 'I wouldn't put any other medicine on the market based on our experience.'

It is easy enough to understand the disappointment of the Jarlmadangah Community with the slow pace of the project. Some thought that the university should have done more. However, using universities as a route to commercialization does face difficulties and even where a university is experienced in the commercialization process this kind of venture is high risk.[45] There are also problems of a structural kind to do with the global pharmaceutical system and Australia's place in it (something I discuss in more detail in the next chapter). Where countries do not have deep venture capital markets they will likely struggle to capture the benefits of whatever inventions they produce and they will be more likely to lose a significant portion of their best inventions to foreign equity. One can turn to philanthropic funding sources, as this project has, but again there are limits to what can be expected from these sources in the Australian context.

Perhaps the project may yet bear fruit in the form of a marketable complementary medicine. For the time being there is some disappointment on the part of the indigenous people involved in the project. It has been a costly exercise for the Jarlmadangah community. At the time of our interview in 2008 its share of the patent fees had amounted to about $80,000 with another $30,000 about to fall due. Jarlmadangah is an exceptionally well-led and organized indigenous community. Meeting these kinds of costs would be beyond many Aboriginal communities.

6.6.   Patents, territory and Country

One of the interesting features of the use of the patent system by Aboriginal people is the way in which the territorial nature of the system interacts with the Country-based nature of indigenous innovation. The compounds were derived from plants of the *Barringtonia* species. As the patent specification makes clear these are widely distributed through Asia

---

[45] On the problems facing universities see Productivity Commission, *Public Support for Science and Innovation*, xxii.

and the Pacific with four species occurring in northern Australia.[46] The patent specification also contains a useful description of the many traditional medical and non-medical uses that local people have made of the various species over time. Certainly this is not a plant the knowledge of which is confined to the Jarlmadangah Community. Our interview data is consistent with what is described in the patent specification. Species of the tree, we were told, grow along the Fitzroy River and many indigenous communities know about the healing properties of the plant. Worth noting also is that although the compounds were derived from the bark of the *Barringtonia acutangula*, the compounds being claimed could also be extracted from other plants of the genus *Barringtonia*.

The effect of a grant of a patent is to create a set of exclusive exploitation rights for the owners of the patent in the territory of the granting office. In the case of a patent over the compounds from the *Barringtonia* tree, the two applicants own the patent rights in the Australian territory, as well as in the territories of the other patent offices that have granted a patent. The Jarlmadangah Burru community is located south-east of Derby in the Kimberley region. The *Barringtonia acutangula* species is the most widely distributed of the *Barringtonia* species in Australia, stretching from northern Western Australia to northern Queensland. In other words, many indigenous communities in Australia would know the plant.

The grant of a patent would not interfere with traditional uses of the plant by other indigenous groups. The patent claims are over the compounds with analgesic properties derived from the plant and the use of these compounds in methods of treatment. Traditional methods of using the plant, which, for example, involve its use as a fish poison or chewing the bark and applying it to a wound, would not infringe the patent.

What is affected by the granted patent is the capacity of other indigenous groups to patent the same compounds. Under patent rules there are no prizes for finishing second. Why would this matter to indigenous groups? The ancestral systems of indigenous groups decentred control of resources. Different groups in different Countries could co-evolve with plants of the same species. The use rights of an indigenous group based in, for example, the Kimberly did not interfere with the use rights of one based in northern Queensland. The concept of territory in patent law overrides these Country boundaries. The ownership rights in a class of compounds derived from trees of the *Barringtonia* species is now held exclusively by the Jarlmadangah Burru community and Griffith

---

[46] See PCT/AU2004/001660, 'Novel Analgesic Compounds, Extracts Containing Same and Methods of Preparation'.

University. The patent claims include a Markush claim, a specialized form of chemical claiming that enables a patent applicant to cover functional equivalents of elements in a chemical structure, thereby generating a claim over a class of compounds with millions of possible members. The territorial exclusivity of the patent system contrasts strongly with an ancestral system in which many groups could have rights over the same resource. The patent system does not allow for independent co-extensive ownership of a resource.

In this particular case this has turned out not to matter because the Jarlmadangah patent has thus far not generated commercial returns. Interestingly, our interviews suggested that if the patent had led to commercial success there might have been some questions asked by other indigenous communities in the Kimberley about how the Jarlmadangah Burru community was able to claim monopoly rights in the compounds derived from the widespread *Barringtonia* trees. Other indigenous groups were aware of the patent and were watching with interest. Would success have disrupted relations amongst indigenous groups along the Fitzroy River? In answer to my question one interviewee replied:

No, if we give other local people opportunities to share the benefits, collect the harvest – it's just like the acqua culture project – we didn't see that as just for us. If it [Marjala] is growing more at Fitzroy Crossing it makes sense to bring them into an arrangement. It's hard – we can't just run with the plant and lock out someone from Fitzroy Crossing who has just as much right to this plant as we have.

Senior people from Jarlmadangah had obviously given some thought to these issues. They were contemplating involving other communities in the tree plantations that would have been needed for the purposes of extracting the compounds.

The situation of many indigenous groups knowing about the medicinal or utilitarian uses of a plant is not uncommon. Wynberg and Chennells, for example, point to the wide distribution and knowledge by various indigenous groups of the *Hoodia* species in southern Africa and the conflicts between and within indigenous groups triggered by the arrival of benefits from the patent system.[47] As we saw earlier in the discussion of the Gubinge wars, the prospect of just a few extra dollars from plant collection can trigger fights in poor communities over who has rights to those plants. There are many in group–out group distinctions that affect cooperation in indigenous groups, some of which have come into play because of the way in which colonization has impacted on the movement

---

[47] Wynberg and Chennells, 'Green Diamonds of the South', 89.

and resettlement of indigenous groups. These groups have had few assets under their control and have had to fight, including amongst themselves, so that their group might be better off. The patenting strategy of the Jarlmadangah Community is an example of Aboriginal people's pragmatism in a landscape where colonization has drawn many of the lines and boundaries that make up the property system with which they now have to work. The patent system allows for a centralized control of assets in ways that an ancestral system does not. Looking after one's mob may mean taking advantage of this centralized control. But at the same time there are destabilizing dangers – there are unwritten rules about plants that the property fences of the colonists have not erased. Indigenous leaders will need wisdom and generosity when it comes to handling any benefits that the patent system delivers. Without wise leadership the pay-off from the patent system may include the poison that comes from angry, divided communities.

7   Secret plants

7.1.   Keeping quiet

The practice of secrecy is fundamental to Aboriginal religions.[1] Knowledge about the power of sacred sites and objects, the function of symbols and of the times of day and places where things happen in the ancestral world varies amongst individuals within indigenous groups. An individual's level of knowledge is affected by many things, including whether they are young or old, male or female, their level of initiation and the judgements of elders about whether they are fitting persons to have secrets revealed to them. It is a world permeated by degrees of secrecy ranging from open secrets to those so closed and sacred that almost none qualify to be their guardian.

There is a straightforward functional explanation for this elevation of secrecy. Aboriginal religions are, as we have seen, place-time cosmologies in which knowledge about ancestral places and forces in the landscape is central. Control over religious knowledge brings with it power, including power over land. Being able to demonstrate knowledge about land or to cross-examine others about it is a way of showing who is a rightful custodian of land. Elaborate rituals for the distribution and transmission of secrets reduce the diffusion of secrets and create an aura that increases demand for them, at the same as they reinforce hierarchies of older men over younger men, of older women over younger women, and of men over entire groups.[2] Within Aboriginal society indigenous people do not see ancestral forces as figments serving some social function of power and/or stability. Rather they believe in the existence of ancestors. Ancestral forces can be potentially dangerous.[3] Individuals who are not trained or who are not ready should not be exposed to

---

[1] See the collection of essays in Anderson (ed.), *Politics of the Secret*.
[2] E. Kolig, 'Darrugu – Secret Objects in a Changing World' in Anderson (ed.), *Politics of the Secret*, 27, 35.
[3] Palmer, 'Religious Knowledge', 15, 16.

knowledge about them, any more than one would allow an untrained person to fiddle with the controls to a nuclear powerplant.

The practice of secrecy in Aboriginal groups extends to the knowledge of plants. Knowledge about the benefits of some plants is widespread. For example, the health benefits of eating Gubinge are widely known, as might be expected of a plant that grows in both the Kimberley and the Northern Territory and has probably been used by indigenous people for hundreds or possibly thousands of years. But then there are other plants. In some cases the plant might be well known, but it may have secret uses that are revealed only to those who are thought ready to receive the knowledge. These are cases of hidden uses. There are, we were told, cases of hidden plants. These are powerful plants, the locations of which are kept secret, especially from visiting university researchers.

The scale and complexity of the natural plant world means that secrecy is an especially effective tool when it comes to controlling access to powerful plants. On a continent as vast as Australia it is easy to see why hidden plants are likely to stay hidden if the indigenous people who know about these plants do not want others to know about them. One may be in the bush only metres from such a plant, but, not knowing it is there, simply walk past it, more concerned about keeping an eye out for snakes than plants. (Keeping an eye out for snakes is quite natural if one is alarmed into alertness by indigenous companions given to making the occasional hissing sound.) The discipline of ethnobotany is founded on the practical fact that we need cooperation from people who have traditional knowledge about the uses of plants if we want to advance our knowledge of plants. Ethnobotanists who have been in the game a long time understand how much knowledge they do not receive: 'We're only getting the public story, a bunch of nouns, a slice of utilitarian knowledge' (interview, 2008).

How productive the relationship between ethnobotanists or other researchers and indigenous people will be significantly depends on the measure of trust that develops between them. People are not likely to reveal secrets or share information with those they deem untrustworthy, or someone they judge to be unfit to receive a secret. The experience of the Jarlmadangah Community with the patent system has led to a reluctance to share information with university researchers. In the words of one senior member:

'The universities are sneaking up here. I advised communities to stay quiet and not give information out. I've sent universities back to the drawing board.'

The consequences of this loss of trust are clear. As we saw in chapter 6 the senior people from Jarlmadangah would not put any more plant medicines on the market. When we were told this we followed up with the obvious question – how many more plants do you have like the Marjala tree? 'About twenty,' came back the answer. Of course, we do not know whether this claim is true.

7.2. Smart plays and losing games

With the Marjala tree, members of the Jarlmadangah Community set in train events that brought a class of analgesic compounds to the attention of the scientific community. As the patent specification states, 'it is surprising that the chemical nature of the bioactive constituents has attracted little attention'.[4] But as we saw in the last section the Community has become sceptical about the benefits of working with universities. The smart play for communities like Jarlmadangah is not to reveal what they know. This smart play comes with costs.

Jarlmadangah's use of secrecy to protect its plants is a defensive strategy that cuts the Jarlmadangah Community off from those who possess the commercialization skills needed to turn knowledge about plants such as the Marjala tree into products. Putting a medicine on the shelf of pharmacies was one of the goals that the Jarlmadangah Community had for this project. For the state, this defensive strategy also carries costs, nicely articulated by one of our interviewees from Jarlmadangah: 'The State Government [Western Australia] owns flora and fauna, but they don't have the knowledge about that flora and fauna.' The point being made by our interviewee is not that the Western Australian government lacks any knowledge about its flora and fauna, but rather that it is ignorant in important respects about the uses and potential of that flora and fauna. A defensive strategy of secrecy, widely adopted by indigenous groups, would mean that the state would continue to remain ignorant about the potential of its plant assets.

We encountered indigenous groups in Broome, Queensland and South Australia that were using defensive secrecy, but we do not know how many others have decided to follow a similarly shrouded path. Some of the government officials we interviewed had also come to the conclusion that suspicion and lack of trust was driving many indigenous groups into secrecy. Stories of rip-offs and biopiracy such as the smokebush incident circulate widely, as one might expect in a culture with deep roots in oral storytelling. That much was clear from our interviews. If we assume for a moment that the circulation of these stories is reinforcing what is already a low-trust environment then defensive secrecy may well

---

[4] See PCT/AU2004/001660, 'Novel Analgesic Compounds, Extracts Containing Same and Methods of Preparation'. 3.

be a common practice. Many indigenous groups may have decided to let the Australian bush cover their plant secrets. The Voumard Inquiry of 2000, which laid the foundations for the federal government's access regime, did report a view from its submissions and hearings that indigenous people's knowledge along with their culture and spirit 'had been taken from them'.[5] Our interview data suggests that a decade or so on this view has not changed much amongst indigenous people. As one official put it many indigenous families take the view that 'They [companies, consultants] suck us dry' when it comes to using indigenous knowledge for commercial benefit.

Should we be concerned about the possible social cost of this defensive use of secrecy? There are different lines of argument here, none of them with a certain conclusion. We are driven to conjecture when it comes to assessing the social cost of lost opportunities to work on secret plants. Some scientists think the cost is probably low. What is it that indigenous people were treating with their traditional techniques in pre-colonial times, one interviewee asked. His point was that the average life expectancy of indigenous people in pre-colonial times was likely to be shorter than those to be found in today's developed countries.[6] Medical science and the pharmaceutical industry are investing heavily in finding cures to aging-associated diseases such as arthritis, cancer and Alzheimer's. The probabilities of finding leads to treatments for diseases of aging in settings where indigenous people were on average not living long enough to experience those diseases are low. This is not an argument against natural product discovery processes, but rather an argument about the likely additional value of indigenous knowledge to the success of those processes.

Another line of argument that suggests we should not be concerned by the social costs of defensive secrecy is based on the idea that there are better paths to pharmaceutical discoveries than those based on the investigation of plants. Perhaps methods such as combinatorial chemistry that have come with the synthesis of biology, chemistry and computing will deliver the treatments we need for the diseases found in today's societies. Combinatorial chemistry came onto the drug discovery scene in a

---

[5] See J. Voumard, Inquiry Chair, *Access to Biological Resources in Commonwealth Areas* (2000), para. 6.64, www.environment.gov.au/resource/commonwealth-public-inquiry-access-biological-resources-commonwealth-areas.

[6] Estimating this is difficult, but some evidence suggests a range of 25 to 35 years. See J. H. Bodley, *Cultural Anthropology: Tribes, States, And The Global System* (Plymouth: AltaMira Press, 2011), 171–3. For a critical assessment of this range see G. Blyton, 'Healthier Times?: Revisiting Indigenous Australian Health History', *Health and History*, 11 (2009), 116.

significant way in the early 1990s. A decade later the evidence seemed to suggest that its methods were not delivering more leads than traditional synthetic chemistry.[7] Moreover, a study comparing compounds drawn from natural products, known drugs and combinatorial synthesis concluded that there would be advantages in drawing on some of the structural features of natural compounds in the combinatorial process.[8] A review of the sources of new chemical entities in the drug field over a twenty-five-year period revealed the deep importance of natural products. For example, of all the anti-cancer drugs available in Western countries and Japan, 73 per cent have had their origins linked to natural products.[9]

The evidence around drug discovery suggests two things. First, it would be premature for pharmaceutical firms to abandon the investigation of natural products. Second, in developing and using combinatorial methodologies science should pay close attention to the structures of natural compounds. However, this does not cast much light on what the social cost of defensive secrecy by indigenous people might be. There are claims that indigenous people may improve the chances of success for a bioprospector by up to 400 per cent.[10] Success here may simply mean finding potentially interesting plant leads, but even after such leads are found the chances of these being converted commercially into a major new compound remain low. The social cost of defensive secrecy could be seen as the higher probability of success that society forgoes when it fails to gain the cooperation of indigenous people in the search for new medicines. Quantifying this increase in probability in a robust way is difficult. In the United States in the 1950s and 1960s, the pharmaceutical industry did not use indigenous peoples' knowledge in its plant-based research. The disappointing results saw the industry largely pull out of funding this type of research by 1980.[11] In 1981 the US National Cancer Institute (NCI) terminated its plant and animal screening programme

---

[7] See M. Feher and J. M. Schmidt, 'Property Distribution Differences between Drugs, Natural Products, and Molecules from Combinatorial Chemistry', *Journal of Chemical Information Computing Science*, 43 (2003), 218. In their review of the sources of new drugs covering some 25 years (1981 to 2006) Newman and Cragg found only one new chemical entity that had been combinatorially discovered. See D. J. Newman and G. M. Cragg, 'Natural Products as Sources of New Drugs Over the Last 25 Years', *Journal of Natural Products*, 70 (2007), 461.

[8] Feher and Schmidt, 'Property Distribution Differences', 218.

[9] Newman and Cragg, 'Natural Products', 469.

[10] P. G. Sampath, *Regulating Bioprospecting: Institutions for Drug Research, Access, and Benefit-Sharing* (Tokyo: United Nations University Press, 2005), 25.

[11] J. R. Axt, M. L. Corn, M. Lee and D. M. Ackerman, *Biotechnology, Indigenous Peoples and Intellectual Property Rights* (Congressional Research Service Report for Congress, 1993), 9.

because of its limited success, but then reintroduced the programme later in the decade, including a strong focus on plants known to have traditional uses as medicines.[12] One study that looked back at the NCI's screening of more than 114,000 samples concluded that the NCI could have doubled its success rate of 4.3 per cent in finding biological activity if it had also used folklore.[13]

How we assess the social cost of indigenous peoples' defensive secrecy depends very much on our assumptions about the search process for new discoveries using biodiversity. Assume for a moment we are looking for a highly skilled medical specialist in a mega city that has no street names and numbers. We enter the city at some random point and begin asking locals for directions. Our success is poor and weeks later we are still looking. Imagine now that we enter the city not at some random point but with prior knowledge as to the area of the city in which the skilled medical specialist is to be found. Our chances of finding locals who know the streets and perhaps the actual street in which the medical specialist lives improve. Our prior knowledge of where to enter the city makes the knowledge of the locals much more valuable to us. In a similar way, as we learn more about the world's biodiversity we can enter nature's cities of biodiversity aiming for its 'hot spots'. In these spots indigenous peoples' knowledge may turn out to be crucial to the success of our search.

We can make the assumption that indigenous peoples' knowledge makes no difference to the probability of discovering a species that will yield a therapeutically significant product, instead assuming that this probability depends on the scientific procedures that we apply to a species selected at random. If we apply this assumption to a unitized view of biodiversity and ask what additional value an extra unit of biodiversity brings to discovery, we are led on marginalist assumptions to conclude that an extra unit adds little extra value in the case where we already have a large number of units.[14] Markets will not generate enough willingness to pay to preserve marginal units of biodiversity, even under a favourable property rights regime. This marginalist approach to biodiversity is very different to the connectionist approach described in chapter 2 in which there are overall duties to maintain healthy Country. By changing the assumption about information and allowing for the

[12] Ibid., 10–11.
[13] P. P. Principe, 'Valuing the Biodiversity of Medicinal Plants' in O. Akerele, V. Heywood and H. Synge (eds.), The Conservation of Medicinal Plants (Cambridge University Press, 1991), 79, 92.
[14] For a model to this effect see R. D. Simpson, R. A. Sedjo and J. W. Reid, 'Valuing Biodiversity for Use in Pharmaceutical Research', Journal of Political Economy, 104 (1996), 163.

possibility of a selection of a class of promising units for analysis based on special knowledge about those units we arrive at the conclusion that some markets in biodiversity might be possible.[15] If indigenous people are to benefit from whatever markets in biodiversity do emerge they will need stronger rules of protection for their indigenous knowledge assets. These stronger rules should, as chapter 5 argued, take the form of simple veto rules over transactions that are made using indigenous peoples' knowledge assets without their permission. Providing indigenous people with simple veto rules is something the state has been reluctant to do. The probable cost of this will be higher levels of defensive secrecy.

As a matter of general principle a society should try to discourage the use of defensive secrecy and encourage individuals to release information that will contribute to innovation. A lifetime of defensive secrecy means valuable knowledge ends up being buried with its discoverer, the worst possible social outcome. Patents and trade secrets can both be seen as providing incentives to avoid the problem of defensive secrecy when it comes to the social diffusion of knowledge. The lure of patents for an inventor is a set period of strong exclusive protection, including protection against independent origination. Trade secret protection also aims to discourage defensive secrecy by offering an indefinite period of protection, but one that does not include protection against independent origination. Trade secret protection is a subtle diffusion mechanism since it encourages a person to switch out of defensive secrecy into commercial activity using the secret. Commercial activity increases the chances of the loss of the secret in some way such as employees talking or competitors uncovering it through reverse engineering or independent experimentation. Many trade secrets in mature industries are in fact widely known.

The resort to defensive secrecy by the Jarlmadangah Community is based on a disappointing outcome with the patent-based system of drug discovery, a system they only came to understand over time and through experience. Members of the Community took pride in the fact that their knowledge of the plant had led to the discovery of a significant class of compounds that had potential in pain treatment. The scientific analysis of the compounds does indicate that they are significant.[16] But in today's patent-regulated markets for medicines a number of factors affect

[15] For the detail of this approach see G. C. Rausser and A. A. Small, 'Valuing Research Leads: Bioprospecting and the Conservation of Genetic Resources', *Journal of Political Economy*, 108 (2000), 173.

[16] The chemical analysis of the compounds is presented in C. Mills, A. R. Carroll and R. J. Quinn, 'Acutangulosides A-F, Monodesmosidic Saponins from the Bark of *Barringtonia acutangula*', *Journal of Natural Products*, 68 (2005), 311.

whether a therapeutically significant discovery will become a commercially available medicine. A large pharmaceutical company's preparedness to invest in the development of a new analgesic depends on a number of factors, including the projected global demand for pain management therapies, the patent status of existing treatments and the number of new compounds already being evaluated. There is also an element of business dictatorship in the system. The CEO of a large pharmaceutical company will not hesitate to kill a project in which millions of dollars have been invested if the maths of market share do not favour his company. With its patent, the Jarlmadangah Community bought itself an entry ticket to the lower decks of a global pharmaceutical system. On these lower decks there are the small players such as the biotech start-ups, the universities, private research institutes, public research bodies and so on, all trying to attract the attention of venture capitalists and ultimately the captains of the system, the pharmaceutical multinationals. The chances of a winning ticket are small.

One explanation for the use of defensive secrecy by indigenous people is that they do not trust or have lost trust in the property system that underpins the commercialization process. Yet formally, the position of indigenous people to make gains from the use of their knowledge in biodiscovery projects appears to have improved. After joining the Convention on Biological Diversity in 1993, and going through a period of policy development, the federal government in 2005 created an access regime for biological resources in Commonwealth areas.[17] One of the express purposes of the access regulations is to recognize the 'special knowledge' held by indigenous people about biological resources.[18] A person must have a permit to access biological resources and in the case of access for commercial purposes that person must have entered into a benefit-sharing agreement with the access provider.[19] Indigenous people can be access providers if they are owners of land or native title

---

[17] The access regime took the form of a new Part 8A (Access to biological resources in Commonwealth Areas) that was inserted into the Environment Protection and Biodiversity Conservation Regulations 2000. Part 8A commenced operation on 1 December 2005. This access regime was enacted after a Commonwealth public inquiry. See Voumard, *Access to Biological Resources*. For a comprehensive discussion see G. Burton, 'Australian ABS Law and Administration – A Model Law and Approach?' in E. C. Kamau and G. Winter (eds.), *Genetic Resources, Traditional Knowledge and the Law: Solutions for Access and Benefit-Sharing* (London: Earthscan, 2009), 271.

[18] See paragraph 8A.01(c) Environment Protection and Biodiversity Conservation Regulations 2000.

[19] See subregulation 8A.06(1) and subregulation 8A.07(1).

holders.[20] If an applicant is using indigenous knowledge, the benefit-sharing agreement has to protect that knowledge, indicating how it will be used, the benefits being given for that use and providing evidence of the terms of agreement concerning the use of the indigenous knowledge.[21] The access regulations allow for the possibility that the source of the indigenous knowledge might be the public domain or another indigenous group. If the access provider is the owner of indigenous land or a native title holder then they must have given informed consent to the benefit-sharing agreement.[22] The Minister also has to come to a judgement about whether informed consent has really been given using a number of criteria.[23] The access regulations also deal with access for non-commercial purposes. In this case the permit application requires an applicant to stipulate the use to be made of indigenous people's knowledge, along with any agreements reached concerning that use.[24]

Aside from this federal regime, the Northern Territory and Queensland also passed laws to cover bioprospecting.[25] How things have worked out for indigenous people under Queensland's Biodiscovery Act of 2004 is discussed in the next chapter. The federal, state and territory governments of Australia also came to an agreement on a set of principles to help promote amongst themselves a consistent approach to issues of access to biological resources.[26] These principles were expressly based on the Bonn Guidelines.

In chapter 4, I argued that the international regime for indigenous knowledge delivers symbolic recognition while preserving the sovereignty of states over their property orders. Australia's implementation of this international regime has largely followed this path of symbolic recognition. Australia's regime for access to its biological resources does not disturb its intellectual property system. Not altering existing intellectual property law is one of the stated elements of Australia's approach to achieving nationally consistent access regimes.[27] The Voumard Inquiry came to the conclusion that the best way to protect indigenous

---

[20] See paragraphs 8A.04(1)(c) and (i).   [21] See paragraphs 8A.08(h) (i) and (j).
[22] See subregulation 8A.10(1).   [23] See subregulation 8A.10(2).
[24] See paragraph 17.02(2)(ga).
[25] Queensland enacted the Biodiscovery Act of 2004 and the Northern Territory the Biological Resources Act of 2006. For a comparative analysis of Australia's biodiscovery regimes see N. P. Stoianoff, 'The Recognition of Traditional Knowledge under Australian Biodiscovery Regimes: Why Bother with Intellectual Property Rights?' in Antons (ed.), *Traditional Knowledge*, 293.
[26] See *Nationally consistent approach for access to and the utilisation of Australia's native genetic and biochemical resources*, endorsed by the Natural Resource Management Ministerial Council on 11 October 2002, www.environment.gov.au.
[27] See *ibid.*, 3(e).

knowledge and resources was to use the existing property order and freedom of contract. It based itself on the principle that indigenous people as owners of land could prevent bioprospectors from accessing their land and where they decided to grant access they could negotiate a contract to protect their interests.[28] The federal access regime operationalizes this freedom of contract value. On this approach protection for indigenous knowledge becomes a contingent affair. For an indigenous group it depends on whether or not they hold a title that enables them to be recognized as owners of the land, as well as their capacity to negotiate a contract to protect their interests.

A deeper issue is whether Australia's strategy of using the existing property order and freedom of contract will do much to cause indigenous groups to move away from defensive secrecy. In a high-trust environment indigenous people might be happy to engage in a deeper dialogue about their plant knowledge. But in a low-trust environment they will keep quiet and use whatever power they have over their land to make access more difficult. Recovering trust is extraordinarily difficult. Writing more rules into a system in which people have no trust is unlikely to bring trust back. Trust in a system depends much more on people being able to use the system to protect those things they truly value.

Before we move on to discuss Queensland's biodiscovery regime in the next chapter it is worth asking how the Commonwealth regime fares when it comes to a test of simplicity. Chapter 5 argued that simple rules of property should be part of a system of protection for indigenous knowledge. Earlier in this chapter I suggested that a veto rule would be a very useful tool to help overcome the problem of defensive secrecy. Using the indicators of complexity mentioned in chapter 5 (uncertainty, density, technicality, differentiation) one can plausibly say these access regulations are an example of complex rule making. Missing from the access regulations is a simple rule that gives indigenous people a veto right over the use of their knowledge. The access regulations certainly provide an incentive for an applicant for access to come to an agreement with indigenous people. If indigenous people are unhappy with the applicant's proposed use of their knowledge or they wish to stop access to biological materials they could presumably withhold their consent to a benefit-sharing agreement and this would make it difficult for a minister to issue a permit for access.[29] Without a permit access to biological resources in a Commonwealth area is prohibited. However, the failure

[28] See Voumard, *Access to Biological Resources*, para. 6.66.
[29] See paragraph 17.03(1)(a) and subregulation 17.03A(6) Environment Protection and Biodiversity Conservation Regulations 2000.

to issue a permit would not necessarily stop an applicant from making use of indigenous people's knowledge. The only other clear consequence of a failure to issue a permit is that the benefit-sharing agreements relating to the access do not take effect.[30] This can become potentially messy where more than one indigenous group is involved. The rights of the applicant over this knowledge would be determined by reference to existing laws for the protection of knowledge (for example, was the knowledge in the public domain, was there a contract, or was it subject to an obligation of confidence?). The general thrust of the Commonwealth scheme is to encourage indigenous people to negotiate over the use of their knowledge against the background of the settler state's property order.

---

[30] See Regulation 8A.11.

8   Paying peanuts for biodiversity

8.1.   Law, ethical codes and instructions to applicants

Biodiversity conservation has not had a long tradition in Queensland. In the 1950s one of its former premiers, Joh Bjekle-Peterson, pioneered a method of land clearing in which a massive chain was dragged through the bush between two tractors. By 2000 Queensland was ripping out enough of its vegetation to put it sixth in the world in terms of land clearing.[1] In 2003 the premier of Queensland announced at a US bio-technology conference that the Biodiscovery Bill would be passed. Providing raw material such as wool, wheat and coal to the states of the north has been a traditional feature of the Australian settler economy. The Biodiscovery Act of 2004 continues this tradition.

During the discussions and consultations surrounding Queensland's proposed biodiscovery law, indigenous communities did get involved in the indigenous knowledge issues: 'Indigenous communities thought they had these rights of ownership of plants' (bureaucrat, interview, 2010). A submission by a number of traditional owner groups heavily criticized the draft law.[2]

When the Biodiscovery Act became law in 2004 the words of recognition and protection that indigenous groups had asked for were not to be found. Queensland's bureaucrats had in part been reluctant to deal with indigenous intellectual property because of the federal government's legislative power over intellectual property. This objection to dealing with the issues of indigenous knowledge in the Biodiscovery

---

[1] For the history see www.wilderness.org.au.
[2] A submission was made and endorsed by the following organizations and traditional owner groups: The SW Qld Traditional Owners Natural Resource & Cultural Heritage Management Association, The Southern Qld Traditional Owners Federation, The Balonne Indigenous Progress Group, The NSW Traditional Owners Federation, Phil Duncan, Traditional Owner – Terry Hie Hie, Moree, Wayne Wharton, Traditional Owner – Kooma, Cunnamulla, Kym Wiseman, Traditional Owner – Kamilaroi, St George, Bob Munns, Traditional Owner – Gunggarry, Mitchell. The submission is available at http://sqtof.bioregion.org/.

Act is much less significant than first appears. The intellectual property power in Australia's constitution is a concurrent power and historically, state copyright laws, for example, had operated concurrently with a federal copyright law.[3] Moreover Queensland, like other states, had more than enough constitutional power to pass legislation recognizing indigenous customary rights and cultural heritage. Queensland had in fact in 2003 passed legislation on indigenous cultural heritage containing principles that recognized the indivisibility of Aboriginal law, Country, innovation and knowledge in Aboriginal people's cultural heritage.[4] This constructive approach to cultural heritage could have been incorporated into the Biodiscovery Act. There was also nothing to stop the Queensland government from including provisions in the Biodiscovery Act to regulate bioprospecting contracts dealing with indigenous knowledge. Regulating contracts was well within its constitutional powers. The Biodiscovery Act is intended to give effect to contractual benefit-sharing arrangements contemplated by Article 15 of the CBD.[5] In short, the explanation for the rules of the Biodiscovery Act has little to do with Queensland's constitutional capacity. As we will see it has everything to do with the state's perceptions about the biotechnology industry and the prevailing property order.

Article 15 of the CBD contains a set of core principles for states to follow when it comes to determining access to genetic resources. These principles, if properly implemented, would place states as providers of resources in a close regulatory partnership with those states where use was being made of the resources. Under Article 15 access has to be on mutually agreed terms and subject to prior informed consent. Research on the resources should take place with the full participation of the provider state. A state in its role as a user of genetic resources is obliged to have in place a regulatory scheme that shares with the provider state in a fair and equitable way the results of research and development along with any commercial and non-commercial benefits coming from uses of the accessed genetic resources. The benefit-sharing obligations in Article 15 serve one of the goals of the CBD. Where there are benefits from the utilization of indigenous peoples' knowledge and innovation, states under Article 8(j) should find ways to equitably share them. Queensland also had the benefit of the Bonn Guidelines, unanimously

---

[3] S. Ricketson, *The Law of Intellectual Property* (Sydney: Law Book Company, 1984), 49.
[4] See section 5 of the Aboriginal Cultural Heritage Act 2003 and section 5 of the Torres Strait Islander Cultural Heritage Act 2003.
[5] See subsection 4(4) of the Biodiscovery Act.

adopted by the members of the CBD in 2002.[6] The Bonn Guidelines set out best-practice elements for designing a regulatory system for access and benefit sharing that corresponds with the principles and obligations of the CBD, including Article 8(j). Hardly surprisingly, an objective of the Bonn Guidelines is to prod states in the direction of developing access and benefit-sharing regimes that recognize the protection of indigenous knowledge.[7] Part III of the Bonn Guidelines deals with the participation of stakeholders in access and benefit-sharing arrangements, expressly recognizing indigenous communities as stakeholders who should be part of any consultative arrangements. Obtaining the consent of indigenous communities is a basic principle of a prior informed consent system.[8] On the issue of mutually agreed terms, the Bonn Guidelines recommend that the contracts regulating the use of the resources reflect the ethical concerns of indigenous communities.[9] This would obviously matter to ancestral systems in which plants were regarded as ancestors.

The Bonn Guidelines represent a decent first step towards recognizing the interests of indigenous communities in access and benefit-sharing regimes. Probably not much more could have been expected from Westphalian states bent on the sovereign enclosure of their resources, especially from those in conflict with their indigenous communities. The Guidelines can be seen as an opportunity to build a governance partnership with indigenous communities when it comes to managing the benefits of genetic resources. Done well, such a partnership could be about much more than a simple commerce in genes. It could be about shifting indigenous groups out of defensive secrecy and into having the confidence to descend into deeper levels of storytelling about their plants. The Biodiscovery Act could have represented a starting point in building the trust that is needed to make any governance arrangement for the sharing of knowledge work. Things did not work out this way. The sections of the Biodiscovery Act make no reference to the protection of indigenous knowledge or the involvement of indigenous groups in its regulatory framework.[10]

---

[6] Bonn Guidelines on Access to Genetic Resources and Fair and Equitable Sharing of the Benefits Arising out of their Utilization, 2002. Adopted by CBD COP 6 Decision VI/24.
[7] See Guideline 11(j).   [8] See Guidelines 26(d) and 31 of the Bonn Guidelines.
[9] See Guidelines 43(a) and 44(g).
[10] There is a Compliance Code (Taking Native Biological Material Under a Collection Authority) established by executive authority under section 44 of the Biodiscovery Act. It provides detailed standards for the collection of samples, including standards to cover cases where collecting is taking place near an indigenous cultural heritage place such as a burial site or ceremonial place.

The bureaucrats I interviewed saw the Biodiscovery Act as a success. Western Australian bureaucrats saw Queensland as being ahead of the game in dealing with indigenous knowledge. Those interested in defending the Biodiscovery Act would argue that it provides industry with some certainty while the interests of indigenous people are recognized. Under the Act, a Minister cannot enter into a benefit-sharing agreement unless an applicant has an approved biodiscovery plan.[11] There are guidelines for the preparation of biodiscovery plans and these stipulate that an applicant has to provide details of any use of indigenous knowledge and any related benefit-sharing arrangements.[12] There is also the Queensland Biotechnology Code of Ethics (the Code) (first released in 2001).[13] Within the Code there are guidelines requiring those in the biodiscovery business to negotiate benefit-sharing arrangements with indigenous people in cases where they have used their traditional knowledge.[14] There is also a guideline prohibiting biopiracy or assisting a third party to commit biopiracy. The Code is mandatory for Queensland government organizations, organizations receiving biotechnology funding from the government or research organizations that have government officials as part of their membership. Other organizations can sign up for the Code by means of a Statement of Intent. There is a simple complaints procedure that can lead to a review of a biotechnology organization by a panel made up of representatives from a number of Queensland government departments. The principal sanction for an organization failing to comply with the Code is a review of its government funding. A public register lists the organizations that are covered by the Code.[15] The number of biotechnology organizations covered is fewer than thirty. This does not mean there is a massive non-compliance problem because the Code is only mandatory for some organizations. Rather the explanation for this small number that was suggested by my interviews is that there are only a relatively small number of small players in Queensland's

---

[11] See subsection 33(2). Section 37 stipulates in general terms the content of a biodiscovery plan.

[12] See Guidelines for preparing a biodiversity plan, Department of Science, Information Technology, Innovation and the Arts, www.business.qld.gov.au/__data/assets/pdf_file/0007/9628/guidelines-biodiscovery-plan.pdf – 28 March 2013.

[13] Queensland Biotechnology Code of Ethics: Update of the Code of Ethical practice for Biotechnology in Queensland (2006), http://www.science.qld.gov.au/dsdweb/v4/apps/web/content.cfm?id=16795.

[14] See Guideline 10 of the Code.

[15] The Register is available at http://www.science.qld.gov.au/dsdweb/v4/apps/web/content.cfm?id=16795.

biotechnology scene.[16] The principal function of these players is to contribute to the research links of global pharmaceutical value chains of production.[17]

The aim of the Code and the Biodiscovery Act was to encourage more investment in Queensland by large industry players. Policy makers were hoping that Queensland's smaller players would do more 'value-adding' and not 'licence out too early', a practice that is seen as a problem (interviews). Together the Code and Biodiscovery Act helped Queensland to project an image of a CBD-compliant environment in which biotechnology companies, large and small, could work. At the same time the access and benefit-sharing regime could not depart too radically from the business model with which the global biotechnology industry was comfortable, one that placed freedom of contract at the centre. Involving indigenous people in the Act's regulatory process had to be weighed against how the global biotechnology industry might see this, especially its implications for their patents. So protection of indigenous people's interests was not made a part of the provisions of the Biodiscovery Act. This was seen as being fraught with risk: 'the state was not going there' (interview, 2009). It would have unsettled industry players and have raised the expectations of indigenous groups.

The Code and the Biodiscovery Act together implement a regulatory scheme that allows the smaller biotech players to assure the larger global players that there will be no reputational or legal surprises for them in doing business in Queensland. The Biodiscovery Act applies to collecting biological material from state land and Queensland waters. Collecting on private land is not covered. A review of the Biodisovery Act in 2009 recommended against extending the Act to private land. Collecting on private land is covered by the Code.[18] The Code states obligations towards indigenous people in sparse form. Where indigenous knowledge is used there is an obligation to 'negotiate reasonable benefit sharing

[16] Details of the companies can be obtained from the Queensland Biotechnology Directory available at www.sd.qld.gov.au/dsdweb/v3/guis/templates/webapps/biotech/gui_biotech_search.cfm. According to the Directory there are 90 companies and 68 biotechnology-related research institutes and centres.

[17] See, Queensland Department of State Development and Innovation in conjunction with PricewaterhouseCoopers, *Queensland Pharmaceutical Industry Profile: Springboard for Opportunities* (2004), 7.

[18] This was accepted by the Queensland government. See *A Response to the Review of the Biodiscovery Act 2004 (Qld)* (Queensland: Department of Employment, Economic Development and Innovation, 2010), www.cabinet.qld.gov.au/documents/2010/aug/response%20to%20review%20of%20the%20biodiscovery%20act/Attachments/Qld_Gov_Response_2009_Biodiscovery_Review.pdf.

arrangements'. There is not much here that would displease a supporter of freedom of contract.

Summing up, industry players have the benefit of certainty that comes with Australia's intellectual property order and the Biodiscovery Act's rules. Indigenous people have the benefit of an ethical code and instructions to bioprospectors in application forms. As I argued in chapter 4, the soft imperative form of the CBD leaves states with lots of discretion when it comes to implementation.

Not a lot of collecting had taken place under the Biodiscovery Act when I visited Queensland's Biotechnology Office at the end of 2009. The Office did not give me exact numbers, but said that fewer than ten benefit-sharing contracts had been approved. The Department of Environment and Resource Management told me one permit had been issued under the Act. So where is the collecting taking place? At an interview at the law firm that had carried out the independent review of the Biodiscovery Act, I was told that 'lots of companies' had entered into benefit-sharing agreements with private land owners (interview, 2009). Again, I was not given numbers, but 'lots' is more than one and probably more than nine.

A chance to forge a deeper partnership with indigenous people in the biodiscovery process has been missed. According to one of my interviewees they either do not know or do not care about the Biodiscovery Act. Perhaps this is right. Or perhaps they recognize symbolic regulation and game playing when they see it.

8.2. Collectors and peanuts

The decade or so preceding Queensland's Biodiscovery Act is worth a brief stop for two reasons. First it reveals a little of how the benefits from biodiscovery are divided. Second it shows how the rules around biodiscovery just don't seem to work out in indigenous people's favour.

Premier Beattie in a speech in the Queensland Parliament in 1999 outlined a strategy for turning Queensland into a biotechnology powerhouse.[19] By 2003 Queensland's plans to turn itself into a biotech leader were largely in place. The Queensland Bioscience Precinct, which was located at the University of Queensland, was launched. The building cost of some $105 million had been met by the Queensland government, the federal government, Queensland University, the Commonwealth Scientific and Industrial Research Organization and the Atlantic

---

[19] The text of the speech is available at Hansard, 24 March 1999, Legislative Assembly, 705–6.

Philanthropies, with the Queensland government committing itself to more than \$77.5 million to help with the first ten years of running costs.[20] As we saw in the previous section, a biodiscovery regime was put in place in 2004.

Queensland's biodiscovery regime has helped to create a competitive market in biodiscovery. Private landowners can compete with each other and the Queensland state as well as other Australian states in granting access. The obvious consequence of this is to drive down the cost of access. Vogel argues that states rich in biodiversity are faced with high opportunity costs of maintaining biodiversity assets, but users of samples of that biodiversity face low costs of accessing those assets.[21] Under market conditions states will not recoup the investment costs of maintaining biodiversity. This is consistent with the argument in chapter 7 that when biodiversity is unitized and the units treated as being of equal discovery value the marginal value of the units fails to provide an incentive to preserve them. It may in fact be rational for a state to convert its biological resources to other uses.[22] The solution is for all states to cooperate in the creation of a public cartel that would fix royalty rates at a level that would allow states to maintain biodiversity assets. The cartel would in effect fund a global public good by arresting the decline of biodiversity and fund its maintenance. The consequences of competitive markets in biodiversity access are clear. Vogel argues that the Queensland government's royalty scheme under its biodiscovery regime sees it getting a real rate of 0.3 per cent.[23]

As low as this rate of return is, it is probably better than what Queensland was receiving in the 1990s for access to its biodiversity. Back in 1993 Ron Quinn of Griffith University forged what was to become a long partnership with the pharmaceutical company AstraZeneca (then simply Astra). With a background in natural product chemistry and time with Roche's Research Institute of Marine Pharmacology, Ron Quinn understood better than most the potential asset that Queensland's naturally occurring plant chemicals represented for drug discovery. Over a period lasting from 1993 to 2007 AstraZeneca invested more than \$100

---

[20] See the speech by Peter Beattie in Hansard, 27 May 2003, Legislative Assembly, 2037.
[21] J. H. Vogel, 'Sovereignty as a Trojan Horse: How the Convention on Biological Diversity Morphs Biopiracy into Biofraud' in B. A. Hocking (ed.), *Unfinished Constitutional Business? Rethinking Indigenous Self-determination* (Canberra: Aboriginal Studies Press, 2005), 228.
[22] This is something than can be debated, but for the economic argument see T. Swanson and S. Johnson, *Global Environmental Problems and International Environmental Agreements* (Cheltenham: Edward Elgar, 1999), ch. 3.
[23] Vogel, 'Sovereignty as a Trojan Horse', 231.

million in a project that led to the development of the 'AstraZeneca-Griffith University collection asset'.[24]

The earth is estimated to hold somewhere between 5 and 100 million species with bacteria and arthropods making up about 90 per cent of this diversity.[25] Looking for molecular leads amongst this scale of diversity is like looking for a needle in tens of thousands of haystacks. During the 1990s a set of technological developments, referred to as high-throughput screening, increased the scale and rapidity with which this diversity could be investigated. The drug discovery process using high-throughput screening involves testing a material that has a function of some kind in a disease (for example, a protein linked to heart disease) against a library of extracts drawn from collected biological materials. The aim is to identify a naturally occurring compound that reacts with the target function in some significant way. The compound then becomes the basis for further structural and analytical work. Modern techniques of miniaturization, robotics and data management allow targets of interest to be tested in a variety of ways against large extract libraries in a short space of time. During the 1990s, Ron Quinn's laboratory became a node of world excellence in high-throughput screening. From 1994 until 1997 continuous screening was used, allowing about 20,000 extracts to be evaluated against target screens over a period of two years. In 1997 the laboratory shifted into campaign screening with 30,000 extracts being tested in four weeks. By 2000 the first 100,000 campaign was completed.[26]

Fundamental to the success of this approach is a large extract library. The more extracts there are the more opportunities there are to find something that might react with the target. AstraZeneca-Griffith University's collection asset tripled in size between 1997 and 2000. Two public bodies, the Queensland Museum and the Queensland Herbarium were central to the effort of collecting the thousands of samples that formed the basis of the extract library (interviews with Queensland Museum and Herbarium, 2009). At first, collecting in relatively small areas reaped rich results, as one might expect in a region of high biodiversity. But over time the collectors from these institutions found that

---

[24] See R. J. Quinn, P. A. Leone, G. Guymeyer and J. N. A. Hooper, 'Australian Biodiversity Via its Plants and Marine Organisms. A High-throughput Screening Approach to Drug Discovery', *Pure Applied Chemistry*, 74 (2002), 519. The figure of $100 million is from S. Laird, C. Monagle and S. Johnston, *Queensland Biodiversity Collaboration, The Griffith University Partnership for National Product Discovery: An Access & Benefit Sharing Case Study* (Japan: United Nations University Institute of Advanced Studies, 2008), 20.
[25] Quinn, Leone, Guymeyer and Hooper, 'Australian Biodiversity'.   [26] *Ibid.*, 520.

they were travelling further and getting less and less (interview at Queensland Herbarium).

The overall collecting strategy was coordinated by the researchers at Griffith University. Instructions would be given, for example, to collect all the grasses, or to collect more eucalypts and so on (interview at Queensland Herbarium). The participation of the Queensland Museum and Herbarium was also important for the purposes of re-collecting. If particular extracts turned out to produce interesting results they could go back to the area to collect more material for further testing.

For all the organizations involved there were important scientific benefits such as the discovery of new species and increased knowledge about Queensland's biodiversity. Moreover funds to cover the costs of collecting were coming from AstraZeneca. The Queensland government would not have funded collecting on this scale. This was a case where a significant public good (the increase in scientific knowledge) was being generated with private money. The Bonn Guidelines list a number of possible non-monetary benefits that should be considered in benefit-sharing arrangements, including sharing of research and development results, collaboration in scientific research programmes and training, technology transfer on concessional terms to the provider state, institutional capacity building, contributions to the local economy and so on.[27] Many of these benefits did emerge from the Griffith–AstraZeneca partnership.

Griffith University was able to build a laboratory of world excellence (now part of the Eskitis Institute at the university). The extract library is a major scientific asset, which makes Griffith University an attractive partner for other major pharmaceutical companies. One benefit, expressly mentioned by the Bonn Guidelines, is joint ownership of intellectual property rights. Details of the contractual arrangement between Griffith and AstraZeneca are not available, but it has been reported that AstraZeneca owns any intellectual property coming out of the period of its exclusive partnership with Griffith University.[28] It would be surprising if a multinational pharmaceutical company negotiated anything other than this on intellectual property.

The benefit of owning the intellectual property, as well as gaining access to one of the world's most biodiverse regions came at a comparatively low cost for AstraZeneca. Over the fourteen years of the partnership AstraZeneca was paying something over seven million dollars per year in nominal terms. In real terms it would have been considerably less.

---

[27] See Appendix II.
[28] Laird, Monagle and Johnston, *Queensland Biodiversity Collaboration*, 30.

The partnership contributed to AstraZeneca's entry into the federal government's Factor f scheme. This scheme was designed to compensate pharmaceutical companies for the price effects of Australia's Pharmaceutical Benefits Scheme.[29] Under Phase II of Factor f, companies in order to be eligible had to show, amongst other things, an increase in their level of R&D spending. However, this did not prevent companies from taking advantage of tax concessions such as the 150 per cent concession for R&D expenditure (although it affected the level of payment under Factor f) or other industry development initiatives.[30] In fact over-compensation of companies under Factor f was one of the main reasons why the Industry Commission recommended that the scheme be discontinued.[31] While the scheme finished in 1999 it is not implausible to suppose that AstraZeneca's lawyers would have continued to exploit other tax advantages that arose by virtue of its R&D relationship with an educational institution. On top of that the Queensland government began spending large amounts of public money on the biotechnology industry, spending that had reached $3 billion by 2007.[32] All in all, the price that AstraZeneca paid for access to Queensland's biodiversity and the ownership of any intellectual property arising from that biodiversity amounted to peanuts. Vogel's argument that governments are failing their publics when it comes to correctly pricing access to biodiversity seems right.

At the beginning of this section I indicated that this case also reveals how things just do not quite seem to work out for indigenous people when it comes to the formulation of rules around bioprospecting. Consider the following sequence of events:

1992 CBD opens for signature.
1993 Australia ratifies the CBD.
1993 Griffith University-AstraZeneca partnership begins.
2001 Queensland publishes its *Biotechnology Code of Ethics*.
2004 Queensland's Biodiscovery Act comes into operation.
2005 Commonwealth access regime comes into operation.
2007 Exclusive partnership between Griffith University and AstraZeneca ends.

---

[29] Industry Commission, *The Pharmaceutical Industry*, Volume 1, Report No. 51 (Melbourne: Australian Government Publishing Service, 1996), 95.

[30] In the case of the R&D, a company was entitled to 50% of the increase in after-tax expenditure or 25% of the increase in total expenditure, whichever was the lesser. See Industry Commission, *The Pharmaceutical Industry*, 118.

[31] Industry Commission, *The Pharmaceutical Industry*, Volume 1, Report No. 51 (Melbourne: Australian Government Publishing Service, 1996), 463.

[32] Laird, Monagle and Johnston, *Queensland Biodiversity Collaboration*, 20.

Collecting, as we have noted, was particularly intense in the late 1990s when the size of the extract library tripled. For most of the Griffith–AstraZeneca partnership collecting took place in the absence of specific access and benefit-sharing legislation. It does not follow, however, that it took place in the absence of social norms.

As chapter 4 showed, the international community through a series of treaties had committed to a basic norm of recognition of the importance of indigenous knowledge systems. The CBD linked this recognition norm to a principle of sharing equitably the benefits flowing from the use of indigenous knowledge, innovations and practices linked to bio-diversity. One of the interesting features of the 1990s was how rapidly the principle of equitable benefit sharing came to be accepted by states and private parties, with the real disagreements being over issues of regulatory implementation. The United States, which is often depicted as one of the world's biggest biopiracy havens, accepts the principle of benefit sharing but argues that the principle is best implemented through freedom of contract and does not require reforms to the intellectual property order.

The soft imperative form of the CBD means that states can take a narrow technical view of their obligations or they can take an expansive view and work towards the design of systems that enable indigenous people to share in the true value of the biodiversity assets that are linked to their innovation systems. On an expansive view one would not confine an obligation of equitable sharing to the benefits flowing from the use of indigenous knowledge. Rather one would read that obligation to include the benefits flowing from indigenous people's innovation and practices (as expressly mentioned by Article 8(j) of the CBD). Indigenous people's systems of innovation produced techniques, most obviously fire technologies (see chapter 2), for managing ecological systems. The sharp distinction that we see between the natural product world and the manufactured product world does not have much resonance within the indigenous cosmologies I described in chapter 2. In these cosmologies indigenous people see themselves as being made by Country and participating in its remaking, guided by duties to ancestors. For indigenous people the natural samples being extracted from biodiverse regions are not natural products, but products of the remaking of Country. They are part of the benefits of their innovation systems.

In Queensland the narrow technical view of equitable benefit sharing rather than the expansive view has prevailed. Under the Code, bioprospectors should negotiate a benefit-sharing agreement where they use indigenous knowledge obtained from indigenous persons. According to a case study of the Griffith–AstraZeneca partnership indigenous knowledge was not obtained from indigenous people and collecting did not take place on indigenous land.[33] Instead it took place in national parks and on Crown land. If the obligation to indigenous people to negotiate a benefit-sharing agreement is confined to only those cases where knowledge is obtained from indigenous people then this reduces the likelihood of such agreements being negotiated where a natural product drug discovery programme based on high-throughput screening is being used. Under this approach the goal is to collect, for example, as many grasses as possible, rather than a small set of grasses in consultation with indigenous people (the ethnobotanical approach). On this narrow approach, biodiversity assets that are the products of indigenous innovation systems are seen as 'natural products' that do not trigger benefit-sharing obligations. In the case of the Griffith–AstraZeneca partnership, according to one of my interviewees, a great deal of care was taken by the collectors not to work with indigenous people. Why this care was taken is readily understandable. Pharmaceutical companies have many competing projects and will end up pulling those that are uncertain in some way, such as those complicated legally by claims of the use of indigenous knowledge (interview, Griffith University, 2009).

What of the claim that no collecting took place on indigenous land? Queensland's Code makes clear that collectors have to seek the informed consent of landowners and negotiate a benefit-sharing agreement if they take samples. In my interviews the question of where collecting took place was settled by reference to categories of settler property law – nationals parks, state land, Crown land, native title etc. Since both the CBD and the Nagoya Protocol on Access to Genetic Resources and the Fair and Equitable Sharing of Benefits Arising from their Utilization to the Convention on Biological Diversity make various provisions concerning indigenous people subject to domestic law (see chapter 4), appealing to settler law to settle the matter of benefit-sharing obligations seems allowable. Still indigenous people might object to this, pointing out that it is a little like settling the question of who is free in a slave society by reference to the rules of slavery.

Even under settler law what was or was not Aboriginal land was in a state of flux during the 1990s. The High Court had recognized native title in the 1992 *Mabo* decision. This was followed by the federal government's Native Title Act of 1993. In the case of Queensland, applications for native title determinations rose rapidly in 1996 and peaked at over 200 per year in 1999.[34] Thereafter they dropped a little and plateaued until 2004 from where they went into a slow decline. One possibility,

---

[33] *Ibid.*, 25–6.
[34] This information is available at www.nntt.gov.au/au/Pages/default.aspx.

therefore, is that some collecting did take place on land over which native title was eventually determined to exist. According to one of my interviewees the organizations involved in the collecting hammered land that was under native title claim. They were stripping the country clean.[35]

If one goes back to the sequence of events I outlined earlier one can see it as a sequence of steps leading to higher levels of rule complexity, rules that did not work in favour of indigenous people. A bioprospecting regime was not in place in Queensland before 2004 and when it did arrive care was taken not to involve indigenous people in its regulatory framework. In any case most of the collecting took place well before 2004. As one interviewee put it, 'most people got what they wanted before the legislation kicked in'. Collecting did not take place on Aboriginal land as defined by the settler state and the collectors were careful not to use indigenous knowledge. Everything was done by the rules of an evolving rulebook. The upshot was that there was no obligation to enter into a benefit-sharing agreement with indigenous people. AstraZeneca, as noted, walked away with the ownership of any intellectual property rights. What this cost it after the tax benefits and any benefits it received from the public spending on the biotechnology industry are taken into account is likely to be a very small amount. The cynic might contemplate the possibility that the Queensland state incurred a net loss over the deal. Finding this out would be difficult because one would have to find out the tax gains to AstraZeneca of its investment. We can be confident that the public will never know the true costs to it of the deals that were done.

As for the benefit-sharing arrangements, the principal beneficiary is Griffith University. It would receive a royalty return from AstraZeneca from any commercial products coming out of their partnership.[36] The two collecting organizations, the Queensland Herbarium and the Queensland Museum, would receive a share of Griffith University's royalties, reported to be 15 per cent of whatever fraction Griffith might receive.[37] Indigenous people appear to have received nothing from this set of deals even though all those involved in the process agreed that indigenous people had legitimate interests in bioprospecting activities.

[35] One of the areas identified by my informant was Umpila Country, including areas near the town of Coen. Umpila refers to the language of Cape York Peninsula. Indigenous people have extensive landholdings in Cape York under a variety of tenures, including native title. See P. Memmott and S. McDougall, *Holding Title and Managing Land in Cape York: Indigenous Land Management and Native Title* (Perth, WA: National Native Title Tribunal, 2003), 5–6.
[36] See the interview with Ron Quinn in 'Plundering the Plants', ABC, Background Briefing, 13 October 2002, www.abc.net.au/radionational/programs/backgroundbriefing/plundering-the-plants/3526718#transcript.
[37] Laird, Monagle and Johnston, *Queensland Biodiversity Collaboration*, 30.

This is not the only case where those in the biodiscovery business have put their efforts into playing by the rules rather than the spirit of principle. For example, AMRAD (Australian Medical Research and Development Corporation) entered into an agreement with the Northern Territory government in which employees of the Northern Territory Herbarium during the 1990s supplied plant samples for screening. A few botanists spent a lot of time in four-wheel-drives combing the state looking for new plants. There were scientific benefits in the form of the discovery of new species, but part of the strategy was to try and collect as many samples as possible without entering onto Aboriginal land (interview, 2009). In order to gain access to some places in the Northern Territory AMRAD negotiated agreements with two Aboriginal organizations, the Northern Land Council and the Tiwi Land Council. At this time there was no biodiscovery regime in place in the Northern Territory.

The Northern Territory did establish an access regime for biological resources in 2006.[38] Under the legislation indigenous people can be 'resource access providers', but as mentioned in chapter 1, the legislation also extinguishes knowledge as an indigenous person's knowledge if it is in the public domain.[39] The effect of this is to remove the obligation to detail any use of this public indigenous knowledge in a benefit-sharing agreement. At the time of our interviews in 2008 there seemed to be some bioprospecting taking place in the Northern Territory. We were told that some fifty-five benefit-sharing agreements had been concluded with the department responsible for administering the legislation. This suggests that it was the Northern Territory government that was the resource access provider. More recent government annual reports reveal that only a small number of benefit-sharing agreements are being con-cluded – two were concluded in 2010–2011 and one in 2009–2010.[40] In any case it seems that, as under the Queensland access regime, the chances of indigenous people being able to benefit from their knowledge in the context of bioprospecting are slim. Success under the rules of access regimes, which these days are full of care and concern for their interests, remains elusive.

For indigenous people the loss of an opportunity to benefit commer-cially from plants is keenly felt. In the words of one indigenous man, 'Plants are a natural resource for us. The only resource we have. Other resources are harder for us to control.' Things tend not to work out for

---

[38] Biological Resources Act.   [39] See subsections 6(1) and 29(2).
[40] The annual reports of the Northern Territory Department of Business and Employment are available at www.dob.nt.gov.au.

indigenous people in the complex rule systems devised by the state because the state's priority is multinational investment capital. It is all about doing deals with big research engines such as the US National Cancer Institute or large companies such as Johnson and Johnson. In order to attract this kind of research and capital the Australian state signals in various ways its compliance with a global intellectual property order that has been shaped by multinationals. Queensland's politicians spent large sums of public money chasing the idea of a biotech Silicon Valley. The measure of success was not milestone payments under a contract, but the growth of investment and a value-adding industry. Whether this plan will work out remains to be seen. Political elites sometimes fail to grasp that in a global intellectual property regime multinationals will shift production to wherever best suits their production chains. The critical thing in the end is who owns the intellectual property rights. Perhaps some politicians do grasp this and count on entering a world of personal benefits through a revolving door.

One question is whether indigenous people in Queensland will ever receive significant benefits from biodiscovery. The extract library that Griffith acquired through the efforts of the Herbarium and the Museum is a hugely valuable scientific asset. It is also an asset that is free of complicating claims about the use of indigenous knowledge. Pharmaceutical companies wishing to go down the path of natural product drug discovery know that the screens they send to Griffith University will be tested against one of the best compound libraries in the world. The problem for companies will not be a lack of leads: 'They [Griffith] develop so many hits that they can't chase all of them' (interview at Queensland Museum, 2009). For pharmaceutical companies the problem will be more one of deciding which of the leads offered to them to choose for development.

The incentives for pharmaceutical companies to fund large-scale collecting of the kind that AstraZeneca did have probably declined. The regulatory regime has become more complex with the passage of biodiscovery regimes in Australia, a complexity that is likely to increase as states like Australia begin to implement the Nagoya Protocol. More and more land has also been returned to indigenous people, placing them in a better bargaining position over access. Civil society groups track and report cases of biopiracy.[41] Through treaties such as the CBD, states have crystallized a principle of equitable sharing of benefits with indigenous people, but it is civil society networks that provide the social sanctioning power for the principle's enforcement. Reputational shaming

---

[41] For cases in which civil society has been involved see Robinson, *Confronting Biopiracy*.

in the form of awards such as the Capitan Hook Awards for Outstanding Achievements in BioPiracy seem amusing, unless one is on the receiving end of one.

So, one possibility is that less collecting will take place in Queensland, with companies preferring to make use of Griffith University's extract library or similar libraries in other parts of the world. Some indigenous people might be able to come to benefit-sharing arrangements if collecting takes place on their land. It may also be that more collecting might take place in the oceans. Organisms in the sea are older and the sea is potentially richer in the toxic compounds that are of particular interest to collectors of natural molecules. The sea is also seen as offering a simpler regulatory environment when it comes to indigenous interests. Not many sea products were used as medicines by indigenous communities (interview at Queensland Museum, 2009). Collecting microorganisms in Australia's oceans is a less complicated exercise than terrestrial collecting where one may have to negotiate with groups of traditional owners. Bioprospecting may turn out to be a more convenient enterprise in the ocean.

9 Gentle on Country, gentle on people

9.1. The network option

Australia is an example of a wealthy state that has been a non-developmental state for its indigenous people. A principal argument of this book is that the non-developmental features of the Australian state have their roots in an extractive property order. Once indigenous people lost ownership of their land they became largely excluded from participating in cycles of income, savings and investment upon which economic growth in a capitalist economy rests. Their other major asset, knowledge, was either not recognized by the state's economy or treated as a free input. In short indigenous people's assets were taken away, not recognized or the subject of freeriding. Where the rules surrounding assets either expressly or indirectly prevent or hinder the re-acquisition of one's traditional assets means that participation in the productive life of the economy takes a long, long time. Indigenous people also faced a special kind of indivisibility problem. Land and knowledge assets were inextricably linked and so the loss of land was more than just the loss of land. It was the loss of a territorial cosmos.

As chapter 4 showed, states through various treaties have granted symbolic recognition to the value of indigenous peoples' knowledge. But at the same time, as my discussion of biodiscovery in chapters 6, 7 and 8 showed, this treaty symbolism leaves a state with potentially many ways in which to devise rules that limit the extent to which indigenous people can control their ancestral knowledge as property assets in a state's property order. So, while one can point to various ways in which the position of indigenous people in Australia has improved in terms of their control of property assets, the state continues to maintain property rules that are extractive for indigenous people.

Faced by an extractive property order what options do indigenous people have? They can continue to push for a reform of the property order that better recognizes their interests. This they will undoubtedly do. In the next section, using the example of India, I show how difficult it is for indigenous people to change the extractive approach of states. I choose India because it is an example of a state that has taken steps to prevent the misappropriation of traditional knowledge (TK) (the term it prefers to indigenous knowledge). But as we will see, the rules it has used to protect TK do not necessarily line up with the development interests of indigenous people in India. The example of India serves to illustrate a more general proposition: the state acting as a rational egoist will always prioritize its own development agenda in setting new rules of property.[1] We saw another example of this in chapter 8. Queensland carefully kept indigenous people out of its biodiscovery framework in order to ensure that it sent the correct signals to the global pharmaceutical industry when it came to investing in Queensland's biotechnology industry. The power imbalance between the state's political elites and multinational capital on the one hand, and indigenous people on the other, sets a feasibility constraint on the degree to which indigenous people can bring a state's property order into line with their own development interests and goals.

Faced by the developmental egoism and power of the state, another track for indigenous groups is to look for ways to adaptively manage the state's property system for their own ends. Exploring such a track does not prevent them from campaigning for a reform of property rules. The Australian fieldwork suggests that some indigenous groups are forging developmental networks in order to use existing intellectual property tools to manage their knowledge assets. The case of the Jarlmadangah Community discussed in chapter 6 is one example of an indigenous developmental network. Another example is the Chuulangun Aboriginal Corporation chaired by David Claudie. The Chuulangun Corporation represents a group of families from the Kuuku I'yu Northern Kaanju people who live on their homelands in the upper Wenlock and Pascoe Rivers in Central Cape York Peninsula in Queensland. Like the Jarlmadangah Community, the families from the Kuuku I'yu have found a way back to Country and, through the Chuulangun Corporation, are using intellectual property rights as part of a plan to exploit their knowledge of plants.[2] Both these indigenous groups have a clear development focus. In essence they want to create enterprises around their knowledge assets that will lead to further investment, as well as employment and education

---

[1] On states as rational egoists see R. O. Keohane, *After Hegemony: Cooperation and Discord in the World Political Economy* (Princeton University Press, 1984).

[2] For details see D. J. Claudie, S. J. Semple, N. M. Smith and B. S. Simpson, 'Ancient but New: Developing Locally Driven Enterprises Based on Traditional Medicines in Kuuku I'yu Northern Kaanju Homelands, Cape York, Queensland, Australia' in Drahos and Frankel (eds.), *Indigenous Peoples' Innovation*, 29.

opportunities, especially for their children. Everywhere we went in Australia, indigenous people spoke about their hopes for a better future for their children. It is an overriding concern:

We envisage that culturally appropriate development of medicinal plant products will contribute to improved opportunities for Kuuku I'yu people to live and work on homelands. This will also allow younger people to engage with and learn about natural resources on their homelands, and provide an alternative to life in centralised townships.[3]

The creation of developmental networks by some indigenous groups is a pragmatic response to the property order of the non-developmental state. Indigenous groups are practised in the art of survival pragmatism, finding ways to reclaim Country and overcome the assimilationist and centralizing strategies of the state. Using the patent system to turn their plant knowledge into an asset is a practical first step by both these groups. It is a case of moving to obtain potential benefits from an imperfect system rather than waiting for the day when a better system might arrive. It is an example of regulatory bricolage, a concept explained in more detail in the last section of this chapter. For reasons explained in chapter 6, the chances of a blockbuster pay-off under the patent system are slim, but as we will see in chapter 10, the more important development experience in this case lies in the creation of trusted networks with scientists. These trusted networks are at least as important as obtaining property rule reform from the state. As the next section shows, obtaining property rules that are optimal for indigenous peoples' development is very difficult, even from states that might on the surface seem to be more disposed to protect indigenous knowledge.

9.2.   Where have the neem trees gone?

India has been very active in the formulation of rules to regulate the interaction of national patent systems and its TK systems. In response to European patent claims relating to the neem tree and US patent claims concerning turmeric, the Indian government set up a taskforce in 2000 to track the extent of misappropriation of Indian traditional medicinal knowledge.[4] The taskforce studied the patent databases of the major patent offices and produced numbers suggesting that tens of thousands

---

[3] *Ibid.*, 30.
[4] A brief description of the history of the taskforce as well as the data produced by it can be found at the website of the Indian Department of Ayurveda, Yoga & Naturopathy, Unani, Siddha and Homoeopathy in a document entitled 'Traditional Knowledge Digital Library' available at www.indianmedicine.nic.in/showfile.asp?lid=316.

of patents were being granted over materials with medicinal uses that had been known for a long time in Indian knowledge systems such as Ayurveda, Unani and Siddha. Documents detailing these traditional uses of plants were available in Sanskrit, Hindi, Arabic, Urdu and Tamil. However, the patent offices of the world basically had no way of searching or understanding these documents, even if they had known of their existence. These documents became the basis of the Traditional Knowledge Digital Library (TKDL), a database containing some 38 million documents searchable in English, French, German, Japanese and Spanish. India was also able to push for reforms of the International Patent Classification (IPC) system, the system of hieroglyphic complexity used by patent offices to classify inventions. Amongst other things, India designed a traditional knowledge resource classification system that shares structural similarities with the IPC. As a result of all this India's traditional knowledge systems are much better integrated into the patent searching systems used by the world's major patent offices.[5]

The TKDL is a proprietary database that the Indian government makes available to other patent offices on the condition that these offices use it only for patent searching and they only disclose so much as is essential as part of their reporting processes for dealing with patent applications.[6] The TKDL is a regulatory tool that is being used in a defensive strategy to stop the foreign patenting of medicines related to TK and uses of plants originating from India. There is some evidence that the TKDL is being used by patent offices in decisions about the grant of a patent as well as by applicants to modify their claims.[7] The TKDL does not necessarily stop the grant of a patent related to the traditional use of a plant. It may instead improve the quality of the claims over the invention and produce a stronger patent.[8]

One possible interpretation of India's non-disclosure strategy for TKDL is that it does not want to make the contents of the database

---

[5] For a description of the cooperation between WIPO and India on the TKDL see www.wipo.int/pressroom/en/articles/2011/article_0008.html.
[6] A copy of the agreement allowing the European Patent Office access to the TKDL is available at www.spicyip.com/docs/TKDL-EPO.pdf.
[7] For a list of patent applications at the European Patent Office involving the TKDL see www.wipo.int/meetings/en/2011/wipo_tkdl_del_11/epo_examples.html.
[8] An example of where this occurred is a patent granted by the European Patent Office to Livzon Pharmaceutical Group, a Chinese pharmaceutical company (see patent EP 1849473). The invention concerned a traditional medicine composition for the treatment of avian influenza. The Council of Scientific and Industrial Research, which administers the TKDL in India, filed relevant prior art under the third party observation procedure at the EPO. This led to an amendment of some of the claims. All the relevant documents are available at https://register.epo.org/espacenet/application?number=EP07001215&lng=en&tab=doclist.

globally public for fear it will provide too many interesting leads for the foreign pharmaceutical sector. The TKDL is likely to be used to invalidate patent claims to plant extracts in combination with other material for therapeutic use. But it would not stop claims to compounds derived from plant materials meeting the novelty requirement of the patent system. The TKDL is full of useful information about which plant samples might be included in large-scale screening assays. Amongst other things, the TKDL contains about 240,000 medicinal formulations.[9] It also contains a large database of tribal knowledge gathered from various states within India Jammu and Kashmir, Uttarakhand, Himachal Pradesh, Odisha, Maharashtra, Andhra Pradesh, Tamil Nadu, West Bengal, Assam and Chattisgarh.[10]

While third parties cannot gain access to the TKDL, or only restricted access if they are patent offices, one reasonable supposition is that the Council of Scientific and Industrial Research, the state body that administers the TKDL, does have access to it for research purposes. Worth noting is that the Council is also one of India's largest patent filers, obtaining patents in a range of fields, including pharmaceuticals, plant and herbal treatments.[11]

It is easy enough to see how the TKDL fits in with the Indian state's interests. But how do these kinds of knowledge-recording initiatives fit in with the interests of indigenous people? We saw in chapter 2 that Aboriginal knowledge systems are living systems that rely on memory, storytelling and ritual for their regeneration and growth. Initiatives like the TKDL are attempts to codify electronically these living systems. In many cases knowledge about plants is held by indigenous women and communicated to their children in the course of picking and using the plants. Children find themselves in an open-air laboratory in which they listen to stories at the same time as they learn what to look for in a plant and how to use it. Databases cannot substitute for these socially intimate processes of telling, showing and doing things with plants. These are the experiences that build connections with kin and Country at many levels. Knowledge about plants becomes embedded in the memory of children through multiple experiences – the taste of the plant's berries, a story about the ancestors of the place, a joke, the laughter of the group, a successful day.

[9] See Council of Scientific and Industrial Research, *Annual Report 2010–11*, New Delhi, xi, www.csir.res.in/External/heads/aboutcsir/Annual_report/AnnualReport_1011.pdf.
[10] *Ibid.*
[11] A list of patents is contained in Council of Scientific and Industrial Research, *Annual Report 2010–11*, New Delhi, Annexure-IIA, //www.csir.res.in/External/heads/aboutcsir/Annual_report/AnnualReport_1011.pdf.

One standard defence of recording initiatives is that indigenous peoples' knowledge will be lost if it is not recorded. In cases where what is being recorded is an indigenous language where there are only one or two speakers left, this argument has weight. In Australia some indigenous people are keen on the recording of language in these circumstances. The loss of indigenous languages was seen by some of our interviewees as a very real problem and that time was running out. In the words of one ethnobotanist who was being asked by indigenous people to help them record language: 'People are dying quicker than I can keep up with them.'

But what of the case where there is no danger of the loss of language and the recording initiative is aimed at capturing knowledge represented by the language? Here the matter is more complex. If an indigenous group is given a choice by the state between a recording initiative and no recording it may well choose the recording initiative. But the group may also want the freedom to choose other options. A group should not be driven to a recording initiative because it is the only option on the table. In the end older indigenous people with knowledge to pass on would like to pass it on as personal communication and teaching and not as a database. It is the former that turns knowledge into a living and growing system that connects or reconnects their young people to a territorial cosmos. They are sometimes driven to the latter because they see no other choice and they prefer that at least some of their knowledge survive them. For states, recording initiatives are convenient. They allow them to talk about preserving some slice of indigenous knowledge such as traditional ecological knowledge for which they see utilitarian value while not talking about the property implications of the fusion between land and knowledge in indigenous cosmologies.

India's claim that its TKDL is protecting its traditional knowledge from misappropriation is a good example of the danger for indigenous people of treaty regimes that create partitions between indigenous peoples' knowledge systems and their land (see chapter 4). These partitions enable the political elites of states and multinational capital to place much less weight on maintaining indigenous peoples' knowledge as living systems in cases where the land rights implications of that maintenance would compromise the economic growth agendas of these elites. The case of the state of Orissa in India provides an example of how the developmental egoism of state elites cuts across the developmental goals of indigenous groups.

Historically, Orissa has been one of India's poorer states, something that did not change much during the 1990s when India began its deregulatory initiatives.[12] Orissa is a state rich in tribal populations and natural resources such as water and forests. It also has minerals. Mining multinationals come from all quarters of the globe to carry out projects in Orissa. One of its minerals is bauxite, the high quality of which leads to lower refining costs. In the south, where this better grade of bauxite is to be found, live tribes such as the Kondhs, for whom the mountainous hills are the sacred centrepiece of their cosmological scheme. Some of the confrontations in Orissa between indigenous people and the police over mining have resulted in the deaths of indigenous people. Money has become the weapon of choice in these conflicts; money to pay officials to sign the necessary environmental permits and money to pay individual indigenous families to relocate. Some families accept and others fight on. Those who sell end up sliding into poverty, ill health and despair.[13] When miners buy land from indigenous people they often end up taking much more than the land.

Some mining projects such as Vedanta's proposed bauxite mine in the Niyamgiri ranges have been delayed.[14] The highest hill peak, covered by the mining lease, is the home of the Niyam Raja (the giver of law), a sacred being worshipped by a local tribe living in the ranges, the Dongaria Kondh. The mining would lower the topography of the area by ten to fifteen metres.[15] Niyam Raja is the pinnacle of an animistic system in which the ranges and forests look after the Dongaria Kondh and they look after the ranges and forests. Like Aboriginal people in Australia, the Dongaria Kondh have used fire over the generations to cultivate a habitat rich in biodiversity.[16] There is a deep knowledge of plant medicines to treat a range of things including 'scorpion and snake bites, stomach disorders, arthritis, tuberculosis, paralysis, cholera, acidity, eczema, tumours, menstrual disorders, wounds and sores, diarrhoea, dysentery, bone fractures, rheumatism, asthma, malaria'.[17]

---

[12] See M. Panda, ' Did Orissa Benefit from the Reforms?' in R. K. Panda (ed.), *Reviving Orissa Economy: Opportunities and Areas of Action* (New Delhi: S. B. Nangia, A. P. H. Publications Corporation, 2004), 167.

[13] See *Report of the Four Member Committee for Investigation into the Proposals Submitted by the Orissa Mining Company for Bauxite Mining in Niyamgiri*, Submitted to the Ministry of Environment and Forests, Government of India (New Delhi, 16 August 2010), 40–42, available at http://moef.nic.in/downloads/public-information/Saxena_Vedanta.pdf.

[14] Details of the project are available on Vedanta's website: http://lanjigarhproject.vedantaaluminium.com/lanjigarh-project.htm.

[15] *Report of the Four Member Committee for Investigation into the Proposals Submitted by the Orissa Mining Company for Bauxite Mining in Niyamgiri*, submitted to the Ministry of Environment and Forests, Government of India (New Delhi, 16 August 2010), 11, available at http://moef.nic.in/downloads/public-information/Saxena_Vedanta.pdf.

[16] *Ibid.*, 17.   [17] *Ibid.*, 18.

The Dongaria Kondh people are very clear about the greater destruction the mining of bauxite would bring:[18]

'We can never leave Niyamgiri. If the mountains are mined, the water will dry up. The crops won't ripen. The medicinal plants will disappear. The air will turn bad. Our gods will be angry. How will we live? We cannot leave Niyamgiri.'

The assessment of the Dongaria people about the effects of bauxite mining has scientific support. The independent committee which examined these effects pointed to the water-retention properties of bauxite soils. During the low-rainfall season the water which has been absorbed by these bauxite soils slowly seeps from the hilltops to supply the streams below. Mining the bauxite would damage the hydrological systems of the Niyamgiri ranges.

What will happen to the Dongaria Kondh if the bauxite mine goes ahead? As the anthropologist Felix Padel has documented, confrontations between tribal people and mining companies in India frequently turn tribal people into landless wanderers who disappear into India's long night of poverty.[19] Benefit-sharing obligations tend to drift away on the wind in these kinds of real-world situations. There is nobody with whom to sign a benefit-sharing agreement. One arrives at a mining site and not a thriving ecosystem. The landscape has been transformed beyond recognition. The top of the hill has disappeared. The giant neem trees have died. The indigenous people have vanished. Who had custody of this plant? Who was responsible for it? Nobody knows. There are just mining company roads, giant trucks, noise and a lot of dust.

Let us assume for a moment that some of the knowledge that the Dongaria Kondh have accumulated about plants makes it into India's TKDL. Whose interests, exactly, would this digital codification exercise serve? It would help to improve the accuracy of novelty searches by patent offices which have access to the TKDL. This would serve the defensive agenda of the Indian state. In fact the TKDL means that even if the Dongaria Kondh do not as a community survive Orissa's mining economy their knowledge can be recovered and mined at some future date.

The Dongaria Kondh people are not against the use of their land for economic purposes. In fact the evidence shows that they are thriving as independent farmers, cultivating small patches of the forest to grow crops such as banana and mango, as well as raising livestock, especially buffaloes. Their assets are the hills and the ecosystem that they have

[18] *Ibid.*, 34.
[19] F. Padel and S. Das, *Out of This Earth: East India Adivasis and the Aluminium Cartel* (New Delhi: Orient Black Swan, 2010).

maintained over many generations, along with their knowledge of plants. These assets are framed by a cosmological system that gives them economic agency and the freedom to make choices about how to spend their farming incomes. The cosmological system coheres to produce social relations, beliefs, actions (including customary use rights) that constitute the overall relationship that they have to the land on which they live. The cosmological system governs how a group approaches the forest, the limits it places on the use of the forest for economic purposes and who has use rights for given purposes.

A reframing of indigenous peoples' assets within the property order of the state is full of potential dangers, even if it is done in the name of protecting their assets. The developmental egoism of the state means that it will choose property rules that enclose assets in ways that prioritize its own development visions and goals. As we have seen, the TKDL is a tool that clearly serves India's development goals. But it also provides an example of the dangers for indigenous people that come with state-designed tools of intellectual property. The capture and codification of indigenous peoples' knowledge in a database renders them potentially redundant in the further exploitation of that knowledge. The database becomes a resource for players that have the necessary analytical, statistical and computing tools to exploit it. The electronic codification of indigenous knowledge makes it potentially mobile. A few keystrokes can send it down the internet's pathways.

My analysis of India's TKDL is not intended to suggest that indigenous groups should never become involved in state-sponsored recording initiatives of their knowledge, but clearly it is a step that requires the deepest discussion. States are recognizing the value of indigenous knowledge in various ways, but there is great danger for indigenous people in an approach that seeks to codify their knowledge. Codification may rob them of an asset. State-sponsored programmes such as Australia's 'Caring for our Country' resource management initiative in which indigenous people are paid to work on Country as rangers to help in biodiversity conservation is a step towards helping indigenous people to rebuild their innovation systems.[20] But it is only a step. Regenerating indigenous peoples' innovation systems will not help them to improve their economic autonomy unless a state looks to reform its intellectual and land property systems in integrated ways that become more developmental for indigenous people. The starting point for this reform lies, as

---

[20] *Caring For Our Country: Report on the Review of the Caring for our Country Initiative* (Canberra: Commonwealth of Australia, 2012).

I argued in chapter 5, in simple rules, principles and regulatory convening.

For the time being, as the first section of this chapter suggested, indigenous groups have to approach the state's intellectual property systems in the spirit of adaptive management. In Australia, this spirit of adaptive management is taking on a network form in which the indigenous leaders at the Jarlmadangah Community and those heading the Chuulangun Corporation have forged networks to help their groups move towards development goals that have been framed in terms of their land-centred cosmology. One can see these networks as developmental networks designed to make the best of a state property order that has been non-developmental for indigenous people. A distinctive feature of both these networks is the way in which they have enrolled expertise, in particular scientific expertise.

In the final chapter, I argue that indigenous futures in Australia have the potential to be helped by alliances with science. The collaboration between scientists and indigenous groups over methods of burning Country described in chapter 2 is another example of the benefits such an alliance might bring. When scientists join an indigenous developmental network they increase the capacity of a network to gain from the assets that it holds. Without the help of scientists neither the Jarlmadangah nor Chuulangun group could have turned their knowledge and plant assets into an invention for the purposes of the patent system. Whether the potential of an alliance between scientists and indigenous groups is realized depends heavily on whether indigenous developmental networks can create relationships of trust with scientists. Achieving this trust, as will become clear, is far from easy. Much of science today serves the economic growth agendas of states and the scaling logic of its industries that this implies. Today's intellectual property systems have also been designed to serve these agendas. Indigenous groups in Australia are certainly interested in economic growth opportunities, but their views of these opportunities are shaped by the cosmologies described in chapter 2. As the next section suggests their development choices will not necessarily follow the choices a non-indigenous person might make. On those occasions when studies of the cultural values and preferences of Aboriginal people have been done using techniques such as choice experiments, they reveal different preferences to those of non-indigenous Australians on matters such as the use and protection of rivers.[21] The

---

[21] K. K. Zander and A. Straton, 'An Economic Assessment of the Value of Tropical River Ecosystem Services: Heterogeneous Preferences Among Aboriginal and non-Aboriginal Australians', *Ecological Economics*, 69 (2010), 2417.

fieldwork suggests that business growth models aimed at a rapid scaling up of production will not necessarily be embraced by indigenous people if those models impact on Country in a deeply harmful way. Instead indigenous networks will be more likely to operate with the constraint of gentleness in mind.

9.3.   The constraint of gentleness

Schumacher's classic 1973 book *Small is Beautiful* is full of prescient analysis. In his opening chapter he argues that the problem of production has not been solved because of the failure to realize that modern production is consuming irreplaceable natural capital, in particular fossil fuel. His solutions look to placing production on a biologically sound footing, finding ways to change the scale of production and investigating more closely the possibilities of common ownership. These solutions would not seem radical to many indigenous people. Schumacher was deeply critical of large technological production systems: '[t]he technology of mass production is inherently violent, ecologically damaging, self-defeating in terms of non-renewable resources, and stultifying for the human person'.[22]

The scale of production did emerge as an issue in the course of the fieldwork. Australia has an enormous comparative advantage when it comes to its stock of native plants. For example, it has 18,000 vascular plant species of which about 90 per cent are unique to it, as well as some 1,500 species that yield essential oils.[23] With many of these plants in remote locations this does open the possibility of indigenous people being able to gain some benefits from the commercial exploitation of these plants. The potential of industries based on Australian native plants has been recognized, but for the time being these industries have not achieved significant commercial scale.[24] In 2006–07 native plant foods contributed about $7 million to a gross value of production of $940 million for Australia's most significant emerging plant and animal industries.[25] This latter figure represented some 2.6 per cent of Australia's

[22] E. F. Schumacher, *Small is Beautiful: Economics as if People Mattered* (New York: Harper and Row, 1973), 154.

[23] A. B. Cunningham, S. T. Garnett and J. Gorman, 'Policy Lessons From Practice: Australian Bush Products for Commercial Markets', *GeoJournal*, 74 (2009), 429, 431.

[24] See G. Mier, *Cultivation and Sustainable Wild Harvest of Bushfoods by Aboriginal Communities in Central Australia* (Canberra: Rural Industries Research and Development Corporation, 2003).

[25] M. Foster, *Emerging Animal and Plant Industries – Their Value to Australia* (Canberra: Rural Industries Research and Development Corporation, 2009), viii.

total value of farm production for the same period. In achieving commercial scale for industries based on native plants, Australia has had to compete with countries such as China, India and Brazil where labour and production costs are lower. China, for example, dominates the world production of Eucalyptus medicinal oil.[26]

One Australian native plant that has been identified as having considerable potential in the food, cosmetic and nutraceutical industries is *Terminalia ferdinandiana*.[27] More commonly known as Gubinge, Bush Plum and Kakadu Plum, its vitamin and antioxidant properties have seen it incorporated into products in the health and cosmetics market, as well as becoming the target of patent applications (see chapter 6). Whenever the commercial potential of a native plant is studied, a standard set of issues are addressed, including potential demand for the product, reliability of supply, cost of production, product specification, certification issues and marketing strategies. The end game is to turn something that is a cottage industry into large-scale industry that will generate jobs and export earnings. This way of thinking about Australian native plants follows an orthodox economic growth logic that would have few critics, except for the occasional heterodox Schumacher figure.

There is, as one of our interviewees observed, a tendency for 'whitefellas to start thinking big – cooperatives, supply chains'. Gubinge is an ingredient that could be used by global cosmetic multinationals such as Aveda, Estee Lauder and L'Oreal in their various products. For these companies the link with an ancient culture and a natural ingredient would create the right kind of mystique that helps to convince women around the world that the nightly ritual of applying cream really will hold back the demons of aging. But this would all require a dramatic transformation of the way in which the Gubinge business currently works in Western Australia. Cosmetic multinationals need a 'stable product with clearly defined qualities that are contained in a standard specification that industry can produce in mutually agreed volumes'.[28] The supply of Gubinge would have to be dramatically increased from present levels of somewhere between five to fifteen tonnes to 100 tonnes, product specification standards would have to be developed and certification standards created along with a unifying generic brand image so that consumers everywhere could recognize the product under one name.[29] Supply

---

[26] Cunningham, Garnett and Gorman, 'Policy Lessons', 433.
[27] S. Birkbeck, *Discussion Paper on the Australian Bush Plum (Terminalia Ferdinandiana) Industry: Market Opportunities and Key Objectives in the Cosmetic Sector* (Western Australia Department of Agriculture and Food, 2009).
[28] *Ibid.*, 3.   [29] For an overall strategy for scaling up see *ibid.*

chains would become more complex as companies specialized in sourcing ingredients for the global cosmetics industry would have to convert Gubinge into materials that met the industry's technical standards as well as the sanitary and phytosanitary standards of states. A lot of processing goes into products described as natural. At the moment the supply of Gubinge depends on wild harvest operations carried out by indigenous people as part of small family enterprises. Achieving significant increases in supply would eventually require plantations. But with plantations come systems, systems of plant breeding, pesticide control and mechanical harvesting. Once these are put in place, the goal of working on Country with the young to impart training and knowledge about traditional plants slips away.

This more industrial vision of Gubinge is very different to the family business model that we encountered in the Kimberley region. Do the indigenous people currently involved in these businesses want to turn the wild harvest of Gubinge into a large-scale industrial enterprise? Probably there will be different views amongst indigenous people about this. At least some of the indigenous people we spoke to saw virtues in their smaller-scale operations. Wild harvesting is a time for families to be out on Country. It is a different kind of experience to operating harvest machinery on a plantation. As one indigenous woman pointed out, large orders for Gubinge may bring more money but create other problems for family businesses. People have to be found to help with the picking. Time pressures might lead to trees being damaged in the process of picking, especially if the pickers are not experienced. What we want, she concluded, is something that is 'gentle on Country, gentle on people'.

Schumacher, who wanted to put people rather than systems at the centre of economic production, would have agreed with the constraint of gentleness. Our interview data supports what others have found when they have asked indigenous people about plant-based enterprises. Many indigenous people have a preference for small-scale enterprises that will serve cultural goals such as the inter-generational transfer of knowledge and respect for plants.[30] This preference is also based on experience of the past. The macadamia nut, tea tree and cut flower industries have followed the scaling logic of plantations and mechanical harvesting, but this has not seen Aboriginal people benefit from their knowledge about these plants.[31]

It is not that indigenous people do not think big, but rather that thinking big implies something else. It implies thinking about the

---

[30] P. J. Whitehead, J. Gorman, A. D. Griffiths, G. Wightman, H. Massarella and J. Altman, *Feasibility of Small Scale Commercial Native Plant Harvests by Indigenous Communities* (Canberra: Rural Industries Research and Development Corporation, 2006).
[31] Cunningham, Garnett and Gorman, 'Policy Lessons', 433.

maintenance of sets of relationships – relationships between young and old, between groups, between people and Country, between people and ancestors. Thinking big is about maintaining the health of Country so that it can provide what today are fashionably called ecological services. The aspiration, at least for some indigenous groups, is to run business enterprises at a scale that allows them to maintain all these relationships. It was a recurring wish expressed in our interviews, of wanting to find ways to fund the cost of living on Country and caring for it. The desire for a traditional life is not a desire to be free of the benefits of modern technology. Far from it – technologies that enable one to be mobile, to communicate, that supply energy cheaply are all highly valued by indigenous people. The desire for a traditional life has to do with the desire to anchor one's being in relationships of caring for and being cared about that stretch backwards and forwards in the place-time of Country.

But there is also a cold logic of economic scale that says small-scale enterprise in remote locations will probably not succeed. The profit from a day of picking Gubinge can be wiped out by having to replace a blown tyre on a four-wheel-drive vehicle, a common occurrence on the stony tracks of the Outback. At the time of our interviews in 2008 we were given different figures for what indigenous people received for picking Gubinge, the range being from A$10 to A$20 a kilo. How much a person can pick in a day of wild harvest will be affected by a variety of factors including the density of trees per hectare and how much fruit the trees are bearing that season (dependent on factors like drought). A day on which only ten kilos have been picked and a tyre is blown is a bad day. There are also limits to how many small-scale enterprises wild harvest can sustain if demand is high. The surge in demand for Gubinge in Broome in around 2003 led to picking practices that were seeing trees stripped and damaged. For the Western Australian Department of Conservation and Land Management this raised issues of sustainable resource management of tree populations already under stress.

There may be ways to help indigenous people to achieve the scale they wish. For example, enriched planting techniques for Gubinge in the wild, which rely on highly efficient drip irrigation technology, have been suggested as a way of helping Gubinge trees to survive periods of drought and increase the reliability of supply.[32] This kind of technology is an

---

[32] Kim Courtenay at the Kimberley College of TAFE, Broome, Western Australia has been important in leading the development of enrichment planting techniques that are gentle on Country and allow indigenous groups the chance to establish small-scale horticultural enterprises.

example of Schumacher's intermediate technology. Each indigenous group interested in supplying the Gubinge market could use enriched planting on their traditional Country.

Indigenous people's intellectual property may also play a role in helping some groups to create enterprises consistent with their cosmological goals. As chapter 1 explained, indigenous people hold intellectual property under ancestral systems. States have given symbolic recognition to this intellectual property at the treaty level, making the issue of property rights a matter of state discretion (see chapter 4). In some cases indigenous groups have been able to negotiate recognition of their ancestral intellectual property by the private sector. This negotiated recognition of ancestral intellectual property does not enter the state's property order as a right enforceable against third parties, but it can gain indigenous groups greater economic returns to help support the kinds of enterprises in which they are most interested. Negotiated recognition of ancestral intellectual property by sectors of multinational capital is an incremental, almost accidental process. In the words of one indigenous man, it depends on 'good people at the top – it is as simple as that'. It also depends, as we will see in the next section, on regulatory bricolage.

9.4.   Regulatory bricolage

A good example of negotiated recognition is the voluntary protocol created for sandalwood supplied by indigenous people in Western Australia to cosmetic companies such as Aveda. Western Australia had been a source of sandalwood oil for global markets in the late nineteenth and early twentieth century. By the 1960s, with some of the native sandalwood forests of Western Australia cleared for agriculture and competition from cheaper sources, the industry went into decline. In the 1990s the global cosmetics industry, like other industries, was caught up in markets in which consumers were expressing preferences for products that were 'natural', environmentally sustainable, produced under humane labour conditions, did not involve cruelty to animals and gave poor producers a fair return. Extractive capitalism and its property order were under pressure from the rise of the ethical consumer. Voluntary certification schemes were having an increasing influence in many industries. The success of companies like the Body Shop (now owned by L'Oreal) and Aveda (now owned by Estee Lauder) showed that these preferences could not be ignored. The large players in the industry increasingly found themselves under scrutiny on matters such as the use of chemicals, their treatment of indigenous people (where the biopiracy discourse was reframing moral perceptions of their conduct) and the nature of their supply chain.

The Western Australian sandalwood industry had a regulatory structure in the form of the Department of Environment and Conservation and the Forest Products Commission, a statutory authority set up to manage the state's native and plantation forests. Western Australia represented a reasonable supply option compared with countries such as India where investigations revealed the supply of sandalwood into Europe was being run in an unsustainable way, with links to 'criminal guerrilla groups' (interview, 2008). Sensing the opportunity for a better approach the head of Mount Romance, Stephen Birkbeck, and Richard Walley (a Noongar man) devised in 2002 a prototype standard that recognized indigenous people's intellectual property in their plants. Mount Romance was a private company producing sandalwood oil. Indigenous people had a comparatively minor involvement in the harvesting of sandalwood in Western Australia, accounting for about 15 per cent of the annual authorized harvest (interview, 2008). They faced practical obstacles in obtaining the necessary licences and qualifications (for example, to operate a chainsaw) required by the state regulator before a permit to harvest could be issued (interview, 2008). Generally indigenous people were collecting on state land under licences from the Forest Products Commission rather than their own private licences. The former licence generated payments in the order of $1,700 a tonne while the latter produced payments of around $8,000 a tonne (interview, 2008).

Aveda was looking for a source of supply of sandalwood oil that met its ethical criteria and this led to a partnership between it and Mount Romance. The two established a supply chain in which sandalwood collected by indigenous harvesters would see Aveda and Mount Romance paying a premium to indigenous harvesters. Certification systems generally have more credibility when there is an independent third party carrying out the certification. Aveda and Mount Romance helped to establish the Songman Circle of Wisdom, each company donating (US) $50,000 to the project.[33] Incorporated in 2004 as an Aboriginal Corporation, the Songman Circle of Wisdom administers the Indigenous Plant Certification Protocol. The sandalwood that is supplied to Mount Romance by indigenous groups and which it in turn supplies to Aveda is certified under this Protocol. The upshot is that the

---

[33] See www.atns.net.au/agreement.asp?EntityID=2882.

indigenous groups supplying to Mount Romance receive more money for the sandalwood they harvest and they gain access to expertise that increases their capacities to obtain private licences from the state regulator.[34]

A critical factor in this particular story was the role of Richard Walley. A charismatic and skilled negotiator, he was able to persuade Dominique Conseil, the CEO of Aveda, of the virtues of buying Western Australian sandalwood that had been harvested from the wild. In Walley's words, Western Australian sandalwood is 'beyond organic' (interview, 2008). That may be, but Indian sandalwood has a much higher santalol content than the native sandalwood species in Western Australia. Santalol is the compound that most affects the quality of sandalwood oil. Of course, the perfume industry is not just about science and molecules. What is marketed is not the molecular structure of a perfume's compounds but stories and mystique. Sandalwood sustainably harvested in wild remote locations by indigenous people from one of the world's oldest cultures offers perfume companies a treasure trove of marketing material.

The gains to the indigenous groups who are supplying sandalwood to Mount Romance look modest when one looks at the global value chains in which the greatest profits exist in the scented products sold by multinationals, products that are tightly controlled under intellectual property rights such as patents, trade secrets and trade marks. An indigenous group like the Kutkabubba Community based near Wiluna on the edge of the Western Desert gains access to a debarking machine to help clean the sandalwood they collect, as well as interest-free loans from a special capital fund to invest in community projects. But these modest returns are for indigenous groups part of a bigger picture. Indigenous people are simultaneously short- and long-term players. In the short term they need practical help to be able to establish themselves in the sandalwood industry as efficient suppliers. The debarking machine lowers their costs and helps them provide a clean product. Access to the capital fund, which comes from the extra royalties paid by companies for indigenous harvested sandalwood, helps an indigenous community make further investments in their on-Country sandalwood enterprise. It is a way of showing their young people that their knowledge can deliver practical economic benefits.

The long-term game is to make companies, the regulators and others understand the importance of Country and its ancestral cosmology. When a Richard Walley spends time with the CEO of a perfume

---

[34] For an account of the benefits see www.aveda.com.au/cms/discover_aveda/ingredients/popup_ingr_sandalwood.tmpl.

multinational showing him how to throw a boomerang it is a piece of showmanship designed to stimulate interest. The deeper aim is to create a loop between the indigenous people at the beginning of the supply chain and the company at the end of it. For indigenous people this loop is a first step in creating a longer-term relationship. Protocols like the Songman Protocol create a voluntary standard that generates better economic returns for indigenous groups. But the hope for indigenous people is that the standard in the Protocol becomes something more than a convenient piece of corporate business ethics for dissemination in glossy annual reports. The goal for indigenous groups is to build long-term relationships with multinational capital in which companies come to have genuine respect for Country and its intellectual property, even if these companies will never understand its cosmology. The intellectual property for which indigenous people seek respect does not have to do with trade marks, patents or any of the other commodity-based systems that are now integral to capitalism's markets. Indigenous people want respect and recognition for the achievements of their ancestors, the knowledge about Country that has been handed down from custodian to custodian. For indigenous groups, protocols are part of a regulatory bricolage in which they make use of those market and non-market tools that are to hand to build the long-term relationships they see as vital to their long-term survival on Country.[35] These tools have imperfections – for example, a protocol does not create an intellectual property right – but they allow their users to act on a problem. Regulatory bricolage is not about waiting for the day when the perfect tools arrive to solve a problem, but about taking action with the skills and standards one has to hand.

In their role as bricoleurs, indigenous groups are not giving up on their long-term goals, but simply taking pragmatic steps towards it. The loop which is created in the supply chain between indigenous groups and a multinational perfume company creates the possibility for others to become part of the loop. It creates the possibility for more conversations that identify common interests. The Songman Protocol crystallizes these conversations into an instrument that offers a practical way forward and creates yet more possibilities for conversations, relationship building and long-term commitment. In 2007 Givaudan, a multinational in the fragrance and flavour industry joined Aveda and Mount Romance in the Songman Protocol and began sourcing its sandalwood oil from Mount Romance under the Protocol.

---

[35] The concept of bricolage is discussed in C. Levi-Strauss, *The Savage Mind* (University of Chicago Press, 1967), 17–18.

Ever-widening conversational loops may also widen success. Using his networks in the perfume industry, Stephen Birkbeck was able to persuade a group of influential CEOs, Gilles Andrier (Givaudan) Christian Courten-Clarins (Clarins), Jacques Rocher (Yves Rocher) and Dominique Conseil (Aveda) to form in 2008 the Presidents' Circle. Richard Walley and Alessandro Carlucci, the CEO of Natura, also joined the Presidents' Circle. With leadership from the top for examining global supply chain issues Stephen Birkbeck and others were able to launch the Natural Resources Stewardship Circle (NRSC) in October 2008 in Grasse, France.[36] The membership of the NRSC increased, joined by other major players such as Christian Dior Parfums/L.V.M. H. CEOs saw the importance of taking collective action to improve their global supply chains when it came to the sustainable use of natural resources and fair dealing with the custodians of these resources. The resolution text of the NRSC committed its members to, amongst other things, the principles in the Convention on Biological Diversity and the UN Declaration on the Rights of Indigenous Peoples, principles that had been forged by many generations of indigenous activists.[37]

The regulatory tools employed by the companies joining the NRSC are soft tools in the form of best-practice guidelines and declarations of intent. But in signing their companies up to initiatives such as the NRSC, CEOs are publicly associating their companies with a set of ethical principles such as fair and equitable benefit sharing and sustainable use of resources, principles that are not unique to treaty discourse amongst states, but are part of broader social discourses affecting the preferences of informed consumers. The CEOs are signalling to the world that companies will be honest, fair and trustworthy in their dealings with indigenous people. By publicly endorsing these principles they deepen their responsibility for ensuring their global supply chains live up to these principles. For these companies this is no longer a matter of seeking a reputation for producing good products, but rather of seeking esteem for being good companies because they practise business according to ethical principles that set standards of conduct and judgement in many of the networks, markets and societies in which they do business.

The treaty regimes described in chapter 4 may not have delivered property rights for indigenous peoples but they have delivered principles that permeate the cosmopolitan networks in which these CEOs move.

---

[36] See www.nrsc.fr/.
[37] A copy of the text is available at www.nrsc.fr/wp-content/uploads/RESOLUTION-TEXT-20-NOV-083.pdf.

Many consumers might not know about the principles of the CBD, but the members of the Presidents' Circle, for example, would be aware of them through their participation in UN networks. The treaty principles of this networked cosmopolitanism connect directly to more abstract values such as honesty, fairness and respect, which are part of the societies and markets in which multinationals do business. Networked cosmopolitanism, along with values that are societally bound but increasingly generalized across societies through communication technologies and markets, provide multiple sources for standards relevant to the conferral of esteem or disesteem. Soft tools of regulation can draw companies into what Brennan and Pettit call the 'economy of esteem'.[38] The theory of responsive regulation has been refined to show how multiple non-state actors can be drawn into networked enforcement pyramids that operate across jurisdictions drawing on that which follows us everywhere – reputation.[39] In today's world, companies that do not live up to the principles they espouse can rapidly find themselves in the internet's hall of infamy, their conduct reported upon by the many watching eyes of NGOs that track corporate behaviour. Companies have to consider carefully whether they wish to risk internet-enabled forces of disesteem. Soft tools of regulation cannot solve every problem, something the theory of responsive regulation recognizes, but the potential for weak actors to create clever enforcement strategies has never been greater.[40]

The case of Aveda and the Songman Protocol shows that there may be ways in which indigenous groups can achieve a scale of enterprise that is gentle on Country and gentle on people. Clearly much will depend on context. Not every indigenous group will have access to a product that is 'beyond organic' or a showman with the persuasive powers of a Richard Walley. But the bricoleur's path is one of using what one finds on one's path. If multinational companies arrive in the place-time world of indigenous groups seeking to extract resources for many groups, it becomes a matter of working with these companies, taking action to achieve what one can. Perhaps the results will look modest to outsiders, but if it helps a group to create jobs on Country that is enough for the short term. The

---

[38] See G. Brennan and P. Pettit, 'The Hidden Economy of Esteem', *Economics and Philosophy*, 16 (2000), 77.
[39] See P. Drahos, 'A Networked Responsive Regulatory Approach to Protecting Traditional Knowledge' in D. Gervais (ed.), *Intellectual Property, Trade and Development: Strategies to Optimize Economic Development in a TRIPS Plus Era* (Oxford University Press, 2007), 385.
[40] See J. Braithwaite, 'Responsive Regulation and Developing Economies', *World Development*, 34 (2006), 884.

long-term aim is to build relationships with these companies that will give indigenous people the time to civilize them into a non-extractive way of working with resources and indigenous people. The first step in this civilizing mission is to help multinationals that have 'bad reputations with chemicals and biopiracy' and that are 'big machines and can churn products out to clean up their act' (indigenous interviewee, 2008).

There are risks of dependency for indigenous people in linking to a global supply chain. In difficult times companies may recalculate whether it is worth their paying a premium for products harvested in the wild. Even if they decide to stick with wild harvest they may reduce their demand for some products as new ones are found. Aveda's many plant specialists visit dozens of countries each year in search of indigenous partners and wild harvested plants.[41] Indigenous people may see their plants as unique but in the world of marketing, one exotic ingredient can be substituted for another. Changes in trends and fashions can potentially affect the demand for any one ingredient being supplied by an indigenous group. Any one indigenous group may find that the demand for its stories and plants, like scent, fades. Much, of course, depends on the strength of the relationship between a company and an indigenous group.

None of these kinds of risk are news to indigenous people who have survived colonialism and some of the worst phases of environmentally destructive capitalism. It is easy, as one senior indigenous man put it, 'for us to end up on the bones of our arse'. But when this happens indigenous people pick themselves up and resume their way along the bricoleur's path.

---

[41] This information was found on Aveda's website, www.esteelaudercareers.com/retail/aveda/index.html.

10   Protecting Country's cosmology

10.1.   Options

We have seen that some indigenous groups in Australia are forming into indigenous developmental networks in order to manage their assets within the rules of the state's property order, a property order that at best only partially recognizes their ancestral systems of decision making. The indigenous developmental networks we encountered were locally led entities. They were engaging in micro-economic development planning using the property rights available to them. This networked, decentralized approach by indigenous groups makes sense. Clearly, each indigenous group will know which assets can be used for economic purposes and under what circumstances. Each indigenous group will be situated within a local context with a different set of assets in terms of knowledge, land and leadership. For example, some indigenous groups will have to work in landscapes that have been highly degraded because of over-exploitation through farming practices, pollution, pest problems and so on, while other groups will have the advantage of less degraded landscapes. The level of knowledge assets will be different for each group, much depending on the extent to which their authority structures and methods of knowledge transmission have managed to withstand the long hard processes of colonization. Aside from local leadership another feature of indigenous developmental networks is leadership that is willing to take risks and adapt to the circumstances. The patent system is not a simple, user-friendly system. The leaders of the Jarlmadangah Community and the Kuuku I'yu group in deciding to use the patent system were experimenting with a complex system that only delivers pay-offs over time, if at all. However, not trying the patent system meant closing the door on a possible developmental opportunity.

This chapter looks at some of the options a developmental network has when it comes to protecting its knowledge assets. The last chapter focuses on how a developmental network can increase its capacity to utilize its assets for developmental purposes. The first issue we can think of as the strategic choice issue and the second as the network capacity issue. The two issues are related. The Jarlmadangah Community and the Kuuku I'yu group were only able to choose patent protection as an option because they had increased the capacity of their respective networks by enrolling scientists into them. To foreshadow the argument a little, collaboration between indigenous developmental networks and scientific networks is crucial to the development goals of indigenous people. Science can play a corroborative role when it comes to assessing the nutritional value of indigenous foods, the pharmacological properties of native plants and the ecological and biodiversity value of indigenous resource management techniques such as the use of fire. But in order for a collaboration to be successful a trust problem has to be overcome. As we will see there are real obstacles in overcoming this trust problem in the Australian context. When it comes to indigenous people's knowledge assets, the state is in a trust trap from which escape is very difficult.

One metaphor that has become popular in relation to intellectual property systems is the toolkit metaphor in which the holder of a knowledge asset has to choose the best intellectual property tools for protecting the asset in question. The kit is much bigger than it used to be. In addition to older forms of intellectual property such as patents, copyright, designs, trade marks and geographical indications, newer and generally more specific forms of intellectual property have emerged, either as independent systems (for example, plant variety rights and protection for integrated circuits) or as linked to existing systems (for example, copyright-related rights for subject matter such as films and sound recordings). These systems have different strengths and weaknesses.[1] The combination of options that best suit an indigenous developmental network will depend on the goals and circumstances of a network, but as the discussion in this chapter suggests, a combination of secrecy and trade mark protection forms a low-cost and natural starting point for indigenous groups.

10.2.   The secret of the Mars Bar

We saw in chapter 7 that there was some evidence of the practice of defensive secrecy in relation to plants. Secrecy is a culturally familiar form of protection for indigenous groups. They have long understood its commercial value. The trade in pituri by indigenous people in Australia,

---

[1] For a discussion see *WIPO Intellectual Property Handbook*, 2nd edn. (Geneva: WIPO, 2004).

which covered some 550,000 square kilometres, illustrates this.[2] Pituri is
a plant drug that is a source of nicotine. The plant from which the drug
was made, *Duboisia hopwoodii*, was found to grow widely in Australia's
arid interiors, but it was pituri made from plants growing around a river
system in the south-western part of Queensland that was the most highly
sought after. An important part of the explanation for this lies in the
curing techniques developed by the clans in this region. Members of
these clans had discovered that the strength of pituri varied with drying
time, with drying by means of the sun weakening the potency of the drug.
These clans developed an artificial method of drying the pituri by
cooking it in hot sand. The great secret lay in the cooking time, something that is consistent with scientific knowledge about the curing of
plant alkaloids.[3] This knowledge was tightly controlled:

The preparation and wholesale distribution of the narcotic *pituri* or pitcheri was
in the hands of the descendants of the man who first discovered its narcotic
properties. The preparation was a close monopoly and any child born to the
horde or tribe who belonged to the pitcheri Moora automatically succeeded to all
rights and privileges in the distribution.[4]

Whenever trade secret protection is being compared with patents, the
risk of trade secret protection is said to be that trade secrets do not
protect against the possibility of independent invention.[5] While this is a
risk, it is a risk that companies have learnt to manage. For example, the
Mars company limits knowledge of its recipes to as few employees as
possible and allows very few visitors to its factories.[6] Those who make it
past the gates have to sign ferocious-sounding confidentiality agreements. But anyone can buy a Mars product, read its ingredients on the
wrapper and subject the bar to a chemical analysis in order to learn about
it.[7] The calculation that Mars is making is that a competitor may learn a

---

[2] See P. Watson, *This Precious Foliage: a Study of the Aboriginal Psycho-active Drug Pituri*,
Oceania Monograph 26 (University of Sydney, 1983).
[3] *Ibid.*, 49.
[4] G. Aiston, 'The Aboriginal Narcotic Pitcheri', *Oceania*, 7 (1936/37), 372.
[5] See, for example, M. A. Gollin, *Driving Innovation: Intellectual Property Strategies For
A Dynamic World* (Cambridge University Press, 2008) 179; M. Risch, 'Trade Secret
Law and Information Development Incentives' in R. C. Dreyfuss and K. J. Standburg
(eds.), *The Law and Theory of Trade Secrecy: A Handbook of Contemporary Research*
(Cheltenham: Edward Elgar, 2011), 152, 168.
[6] For an account of secrecy in the chocolate world see J. G. Brenner, *The Emperors of
Chocolate: Inside the Secret World of Hershey and Mars* (New York: Random House, 1999).
For an analysis of trade secrets in the context of the candy industry see J. C. Fromer,
'Trade Secrecy in Willy Wonka's Chocolate Factory' in Dreyfuss and Standburg (eds.),
The Law and Theory of Trade Secrecy, 3.
[7] Fromer, *ibid.*, 10.

lot about the chocolate bar through analysis, but not everything. Studying the bar will not reveal the exact source of the cocoa beans, the grinding machinery and techniques employed to process the beans, other processes used on the other ingredients in the bar and so on.

Even if a competitor was able to produce a bar that a consumer in a blind taste test could not pick from the Mars Bar, the competitor could not use the Mars trademark and packaging to sell the bar. The combination of secrecy and the brand image of Mars, along with legal protection of these two things through trade secret law, trade mark law and jurisdiction-specific actions relating to unfair competition, form a hugely powerful legal shield for Mars' products.

The Hopi in the United States have been described as 'fanatically committed to secrecy', not allowing tourists the use of media equipment and sketch pads.[8] It is a fanaticism that large corporations like Mars understand and practise when it comes to protecting their most valuable secrets. Restricting access to land (just as Mars controls access to its factories) and practising secrecy are natural starting points in the protection of knowledge assets, a conclusion indigenous groups arrived at long ago.

10.3.   The plant variety rights option

Some indigenous groups, we have seen, have been prepared to experiment with the patent system. Another option in relation to plants is to apply for protection under Australia's law for protecting plant breeders.[9] Breeding a new variety can take place through the discovery and selective propagation of a plant.[10] Making selections from undiscovered source material and breeding a new registrable variety using traditional breeder's techniques might be one way in which indigenous groups could make use of the plant breeder's system. If an indigenous group goes down this path any secrecy attaching to the source variety is lost.

For indigenous people, the problems of using the plant breeder's system do not flow from the fact that plant ownership is an alien concept. We have some evidence of strong individual use rights over particular plants.[11] That said, when plants are located within an ancestral cosmology the concept of ownership does shift away from a simple exclusive-

---

[8] M. F. Brown, *Who Owns Native Culture?* (Cambridge, MA: Harvard University Press, 2003), 13.
[9] Plant Breeder's Rights Act 1994.   [10] See section 5(1).
[11] P. A. Clarke, *Aboriginal People and Their Plants* (Dural, NSW: Rosenberg Publishing, 2007), 17.

rights model over a good. Some plants for some indigenous groups may have the status of Dreaming Ancestors who transformed into plants.[12] In such cases the question is not so much who owns the plant, but rather who belongs to the plant. The status of plants varies. Not every plant will have totemic status and some plants may be seen as not being particularly useful by some groups. The status of a plant will affect who can give permission for a plant to be used for the purposes of breeding and if in fact it can be so used. As one interviewee put it: 'plants are ancestral beings – they can't just be thrown around'.

The ancestral status of plants leads to an issue of accountability. As we saw in chapter 1, indigenous people see themselves as links in chains of caring about plant ancestors that go back thousands of years. The duties that indigenous people owe to ancestors mean that they worry about the release of plants into systems in which third parties may be able to use the plants without accounting to indigenous people for that use. For example, under the plant breeder's system third parties have independent access for private, experimental or breeding purposes.[13] Indigenous people look for mechanisms of accountability in these systems because it helps them fulfil the duties that have been handed to them by previous generations.

Another potential complication arises in relation to what is seen as the same plant. Conventionally we think of two plants as being the same if they share some common characteristics that allow them to be grouped together and that are not shared by other groups of plants. In other words, we focus on properties of plants across space that allow us to group them independently of their particular place. In the place-time cosmology of indigenous groups (see chapter 2) what distinguishes a plant is its relationship to a place. What we might think of as being a plant of the same species whether it is found in Western Australia or Queensland might, on this more nominalistic approach, be two different plants because of their locations in different places. If two indigenous groups applied to register a plant variety that had been propagated by each of them independently using the same plant where sameness was conventionally defined, potentially only one group could be successful in registering the variety.[14] The role of place in the identity and function of a plant is of enormous importance to indigenous groups. Where we see

[12] For a discussion see *ibid.*, 23–4.
[13] See section 16 of the Plant Breeder's Rights Act 1994.
[14] See subsection 45(1). Section 45 allows for the possibility of two breeders being joint applicants but whether indigenous groups would accept this as a solution is another matter.

the same plant they do not. Their nominalistic approach is consistent with a decentred approach to the control of resources and a principle of non-interference in each other's exploitation of resources. It might be possible to genetically link plants to certain places.[15] This place-based understanding of a plant would lead to a greater emphasis on understanding how a plant interacts with its specific location. From a scientific point of view one might become more interested in the exchanges taking place between a plant and its microbial environment and how those exchanges distinguish a plant. But in any case this place-based understanding of plants is not part of the legal definition of a plant variety.

There may be cases in which an indigenous group using its ancestral system is able to decide to use the plant breeder's system. It also seems reasonably clear that indigenous groups would have to enlist a degree of technical help before they could use the plant breeder's system. For example, in order to be able to meet the requirements of distinctness, uniformity and stability, a test growing trial in Australia, run by a registered qualified person, must present evidence to the Plant Breeder's office that the new variety in fact satisfies these criteria.[16] So, for example, in order to establish distinctness there has to be evidence that the candidate variety has a characteristic that is not to be found in the parent or comparator varieties. The application process also requires an applicant to describe the breeding method. The application form itself recognizes a number of methods, including genetic manipulation, controlled pollination and induced mutation.[17] Generally, plant breeding methodologies have grown in scientific sophistication, often being applied to highly domesticated varieties of industrial importance to Australia such as barley and wheat. For an indigenous group seeking to develop a new variety, expert input on the most suitable methodology is going to be required.

Aside from needing to have access to the right levels of scientific expertise, indigenous groups would also have to enter a world of strategic games about the best form of protection for their plant variety. A registered variety itself can be accessed by other breeders for the development of other varieties.[18] Australian law allows the option of patent protection for a plant variety in addition to the protection available under the plant breeder's system. The choice of options will in part

---

[15] Claudie, Semple, Smith and Simpson, 'Ancient but New', 50.

[16] Information on carrying out a growing trial is available from www.ipaustralia.gov.au/get-the-right-ip/plant-breeders-rights/pbr-application-process/test-growing/.

[17] The application form is available from www.ipaustralia.gov.au/get-the-right-ip/plant-breeders-rights/plant-breeders-rights-forms/.

[18] See section 16(c) of the Plant Breeder's Rights Act 1994.

depend on the breeding method. If the new variety is the product of genetic manipulation then many patent attorneys will advise using the patent system since potentially broad claims might be granted over the various parts of the genetically engineered plant (as opposed to a single variety). The patentee's exclusive rights attach to a claimed invention and in the case of patent claims over a plant gene these rights would follow the gene on its travels into the progeny of the plant as well as products derived from the plant. While the trend in the use of patents to protect plant products and processes varies amongst jurisdictions, it is clear that patents have become more important to the propertization of plants. The trend is most pronounced in the United States where large-scale use of genetically modified crops has occurred.[19] In Australia the use of patents for plant inventions increased from 1995, but then declined from 2003, perhaps as a result of moratoria on the use of genetically modified organisms at state government level.[20] As these are lifted, one would expect more plant invention patents because multinational seed companies such as Monsanto base their business models on the patenting of the seed varieties they develop.[21]

It is not only plants that evolve. So do systems of intellectual property. In the case of plants these systems are evolving in the direction that suits the business models of multinationals and the high technology techniques they use to produce new plant innovation systems. Technological changes that allow for selections at the level of the genotype as opposed to the phenotype may, some have suggested, lead to the obsolescence of present plant breeders' systems.[22] States also have aspirations that these property systems will bring new industries and economic growth. In Australia the purpose of the plant breeder's system is 'to encourage the development of new varieties of plants for Australia's domestic industries and for export'.[23] The agricultural, horticultural and ornamental sectors all have industry supply chains in which plant breeder's rights play a significant role. For example, in the case of the wheat industry new varieties are developed by networks of organizational actors including

---

[19] S. Hubicki and J. Sanderson, *Recent Trends in the Patenting of Plants and Animals* (Canberra: Rural Industries Research and Development Corporation, 2009), 27.

[20] S. Hubicki and J. Sanderson, *Recent Trends in the Patenting of Plants and Animals* (Canberra: Rural Industries Research and Development Corporation, 2009), 29.

[21] Something made clear by Monsanto on its website. See www.monsanto.com/newsviews/ Pages/why-does-monsanto-sue-farmers-who-save-seeds.aspx.

[22] M. D. Janis and S. Smith, 'Technological Change and the Design of Plant Variety Protection Regimes', *Chicago-Kent Law Review*, 82 (2007), 1557.

[23] Advisory Council on Intellectual Property, *A Review of Enforcement of Plant Breeder's Rights: Final Report* (Commonwealth of Australia, 2010), 26, available at www.acip.gov.au.

universities, government research organizations and the private sector.[24] The Grains Research and Development Corporation, which is a statutory body funded by a levy on growers, covers a set of crops worth more than seven billion dollars in terms of farm production.[25]

When deciding whether to send one of its secret plants (see chapter 7) on a transformational journey through the patent or plant breeder's system, an indigenous developmental network has to decide whether this is likely to bring it the development benefits it seeks. A developmental network will have to have the capacity to manage systems shaped by the interests of the non-developmental state and business actors. It will also have to bring in scientific help if it is to have any chance of success under the rules of these systems. Going it alone in these systems is not an option for indigenous groups. In other words, indigenous developmental networks will have to have non-indigenous components. For these non-indigenous components to be able to assist a developmental network an indigenous group would have to reveal some of its knowledge assets and the related materials. Revealing such assets is an act of trust. In the end an indigenous developmental network that needs to enrol a scientific component has to confront the issue of trust. The economic benefits of trust are well known. In the absence of trust, parties will invest in ways to protect themselves from being treated unfairly with the result that the cost of transacting business rises or in the worst case business deals are not done.[26] Creating a trusted network poses a huge challenge for an indigenous network. The weight of Australia's non-developmental history for indigenous people is not on the side of encouraging indigenous people to extend trust. Distrust seems a more rational option for indigenous groups. The last chapter addresses this problem in more detail.

10.4.   Signs

The names of indigenous groups have ended up as registered trade marks. For example, there is the Navajo sport utility vehicle made by Mazda, the Cherokee sport utility vehicle made by Chrysler, the Mohawk Carpet Corporation and the Apache helicopter. How much value is tied up in trade marks based on indigenous names, symbols and images owned by non-indigenous companies is hard to say. Amongst other

---

[24] For a description of the industrial structure see Advisory Council on Intellectual Property, *A Review of Enforcement of Plant Breeder's Rights: Final Report* (Commonwealth of Australia, 2010), 20–5, available at www.acip.gov.au.

[25] See www.grdc.com.au/.

[26] S. Knack and P. Keefer, 'Does Social Capital Have An Economic Payoff? A Cross-Country Investigation', *Quarterly Journal of Economics*, 112 (1997), 1251, 1252–5.

things, one would have to search the trade mark registers of the world. One guesses it is a big number.

The use of trade mark law by non-indigenous companies to register the names and images of indigenous groups is a long-standing practice that has now come under critical discussion and scrutiny.[27] Generalizing, the signs of indigenous peoples are systematically and intimately linked to their place-time cosmologies in ways that are difficult for outsiders to understand. Even the use of place names in conversation may, in some indigenous groups, be regulated by social rules because the name does much more than just refer to a place. It is also the key to an ancestral system of the place, a key of special resonance that should not be used without permission.[28] Some signs, in other words, may have cosmological functions that link to ancestors.

It follows that indigenous groups have an interest in preventing commercial uses of their signs that contravene the permissions of their ancestral systems. Trade mark registration of signs of ancestral origin is possible because signs (for example, names or figures) in public circulation are potentially available for registration as a trade mark if they have in fact become distinctive of an enterprise's goods or services. As trade mark law has moved towards a greater recognition of the role of factual distinctiveness in eligibility for trade mark registration, it has increased the scope for signs in public circulation to fall into trade mark proprietorship and therefore into use as trade marks.

A simple rule giving indigenous groups the right to veto all uses of their ancestral signs for commercial purposes (whether registered as trade marks or not) would be one way to stop this practice. As we saw in chapter 5 there are good arguments for using simple rules to protect the intellectual property of indigenous people. Obviously this simple-rule approach would not be popular with the corporate owners of trade marks using ancestral signs. New Zealand has probably come closer than any state to allowing its indigenous people to exercise a right of veto over the registration of indigenous signs as trade marks. Its legislation requires the Trade Mark Commissioner not to register a trade mark that is 'likely to

---

[27] See, for example, Zografos, *Intellectual Property and Traditional Cultural Expressions*, ch. 3; Frankel and Richardson, 'Cultural Property', 275; S. Frankel, 'Trademarks and Traditional Knowledge and Cultural Intellectual Property Rights' in G. B. Dinwoodie and M. D. Janis (eds.), *Trademark Law and Theory: A Handbook of Contemporary Research* (Cheltenham: Edward Elgar, 2008), 433.

[28] For an example see J. H. Bradley and A. Kearney, 'Manankurra: What's in a Name? Placenames and Emotional Geographies' in H. Koch and L. Hercus (eds.), *Aboriginal Placenames: Naming and Re-Naming The Australian Landscape* (Canberra: ANU E Press, 2009), 463.

offend a significant section of the community, including Maori'.[29] A committee made up of people knowledgeable about the worldview, protocol and culture of the Maori provides advice to the Commissioner on the issue of whether a mark is likely to offend.[30] Although the role of the committee is advisory, in practice the Commissioner follows its recommendations.[31]

In the rest of this section I want to focus on the possible development benefits for indigenous groups of a trade mark system. Trade mark systems are lower-cost registration systems compared with patent and plant variety rights systems and they involve lower levels of technical expertise compared with these systems. Trade marks also deal with a subject matter that is familiar to all societies – signs. The concept of a sign lies at the heart of the definition of a trade mark.[32]

The traditional function of a trade mark has been to provide the purchaser of a good with information about its origin.[33] A related function has been to provide information about the attributes and quality of the goods. Trade marks have moved beyond this information function into psychological functions in which corporations are deeply interested.[34] The psychology of signs in the context of marketing and the building of brands is now a matter of systematic psychological and neurophysiological study.[35] Corporations are keen to know how brands affect brains. A brand represents a 'cluster of functional and emotional values that enables organizations to make a promise about a unique and welcomed experience'.[36] When, for example, the driver of a BMW turns the ignition key, he is not just about to drive but is also 'taking ownership of a symbol that signifies the core values of exclusivity, performance, quality and technical innovation'.[37] One can contrast this with turning

---

[29] See paragraph 17(1)(c) of the Trade Marks Act 2002.

[30] See sections 178 and 179 of the Trade Marks Act 2002.

[31] S. Frankel, 'A New Zealand Perspective on the Protection of Mātauranga Māori (Traditional Knowledge)' in Graber, Kuprecht and Lai (eds.), *International Trade*, 439, 447.

[32] See Article 15.1 of the Agreement on Trade-Related Aspects of Intellectual Property Rights (1994).

[33] Ricketson, *The Law of Intellectual Property*, 603.

[34] For a judicial recognition of this psychological function in Australia see *Campomar Sociedad Limitada v Nike International Ltd* (2000) 202 CLR 45, 67.

[35] See, for example, C. Yoon and B. Shiv (eds.), 'Brand Insights from Psychological and Neurophysiological Perspectives', special issue of *Journal of Consumer Psychology*, 22 (2012).

[36] L. de Chernatony, M. McDonald and E. Wallace, *Creating Powerful Brands*, 4th edn. (Oxford: Butterworth-Heinemann, 2011), 31.

[37] *Ibid.*, 27.

the ignition key of a Trabant, where there is only a rush of gratitude if one hears the engine start.

Most trade mark signs do not end up signalling brand status, but where there is a successful brand, one can be sure that there will be supporting trade mark registrations. In such cases the trade mark sign becomes the mark of brand status.

In Australia indigenous groups make more use of trade marks than they do of the patent system. There are examples of regional organizations using the trade marks system to promote the art of a region.[38] Artists of the Central Desert, for example, can draw on the certification mark of Desart, an Aboriginal corporation that represents more than thirty Aboriginal art centres. Art centres have also gone down the path of registering their own trade marks.

The idea that indigenous communities in remote locations with few resources can build brands is an idea that needs little discussion. Building brands means large investments in advertising and being able to overcome the problem of many brands all clamouring for a spot in the consumer's memory bank.[39] But the trade mark system also offers a state the chance to act developmentally for its indigenous people. An example of where this appears to have happened is in the case of the Inuit art market in Canada.

The Canadian government's support for Inuit art goes back to the 1950s. By the 1940s, the Inuit people under the impact of Canada's resettlement and re-education policies had entered a period of great hardship. Government bureaucrats saw in the art market opportunities to reduce the welfare dependency of the Inuit, as well as using this art to help forge a distinctive Canadian identity.[40] Important to this commercial emergence of Inuit art was James Houston, an artist who in 1948 travelled to northern Canada and encouraged the Inuit to make traditional carvings out of soapstone. A successful exhibition in Montreal led to government support for more carving. Within a decade the Inuit went from a situation of 'near starvation' to benefitting from a 'multimillion-dollar enterprise'.[41]

---

[38] T. Janke, *Minding Culture: Case Studies On Intellectual Property And Traditional Cultural Expressions* (Geneva: World Intellectual Property Organization, 2003), 147.

[39] On the difficulties see D. A. Aaker, *Managing Brand Equity: Capitalizing on the Value of a Brand Name* (New York: Free Press, 1991).

[40] See N. H. H. Graburn, 'Inuit Art and Canadian Nationalism: Why Eskimos? Why Canada?' *Inuit Art Quarterly*, 1(3) (1986), 5; L. S. Pupchek, 'True North: Inuit Art and the Canadian Imagination', *American Review of Canadian Studies*, 31 (2001), 191.

[41] Graburn, *ibid.*, 6.

From the 1950s the Canadian government seems for a few decades to have taken on a developmental role in the art field, assisting in the organization of village cooperatives, buying Inuit art when sales went through a low period and helping to organize international exhibitions to promote the art abroad. Success always attracts imitators. In the case of the Inuit art market the imitators mass-produced plastic igloos, polar bears and the like. The Canadian Department of Indian and Northern Affairs responded by registering in 1958 what is known in trade mark law as a certification mark. This type of trade mark allows an owner to certify that goods or services have certain characteristics (for example, that something is handmade by a particular person, comes from a particular geographical area, or has certain materials). The owner establishes a system of rules for identifying the characteristics and governing the conditions of use of the mark and then may approve others to use the certification mark. Referred to as the 'Igloo Tag', only Inuit artists and their marketing agencies could use the mark. The Department was responsible for authorizing the printing of labels for use by marketing agencies.[42]

Obviously trade marks cannot ward off failure, especially in art and craft markets, which are fickle. Over the years there have been warnings about the future of the Inuit art industry[43] but to the outside eye at least there are also impressive successes with networks of galleries, cooperatives, festivals and associations working in different ways to support Inuit art.[44] All parts of the Inuit art market, from artists to exhibitions and sales, grew until the recession of the 1980s.[45] This world of Inuit art production is very different from the struggling communities that James Houston visited in the summer of 1948 at Port Harrison in northern Quebec.

The lesson of this Canadian story is not so much about the importance of certification marks, but rather their usefulness in the hands of a developmental network that is working towards increasing the capacity of an indigenous group, in this case the capacity of the Inuit to commercialize their art.[46] Houston's energy and leadership played a vital role in the beginning. Amongst other things, he set up a payment system that worked. Also important were the promotion and lobbying

[42] For a brief description of the mark see 'The Igloo Tag', *Inuit Art Quarterly*, 5(4) (1990–91), 57.
[43] See 'The Support System for Inuit Artists', *Inuit Art Quarterly*, 19 (2004), 86.
[44] For a description see *ibid.*
[45] R. C. Crandall, *Inuit Art: A History* (North Carolina: McFarland & Company, 2000), 238.
[46] For a description of the network see Pupchek, 'True North', 200–3.

activities of the Canadian Handicrafts Guild (formerly the Women's Art Association of Montreal). The Canadian government, attracted by the success, increased the scale of success through an international public relations campaign and by sending arts and craft specialists to help the Inuit with the quality of production. No doubt some of these craft specialists made errors of judgement about quality; still, there is enough evidence to suggest that the Canadian state was trying to foster a cultural industry that would benefit the Inuit as a whole. The creation of the certification Igloo mark played a part in the rise of this art market, helping to create confidence amongst consumers. Its use continues today.

An example of where a national certification system has not worked for indigenous people is the Australian indigenous arts certification system developed by the National Indigenous Arts Advocacy Association (NIAAA) in the 1990s. Two certification marks were registered, the Label of Authenticity and the Collaboration Mark.[47] However, by 2002 the NIAAA, which was the owner of the certification marks, had closed.[48]

The decision to push for a national certification system had been taken in the 1990s because it seemed to various indigenous representatives on bodies like the Aboriginal and Torres Strait Islander Commission that a certification system would probably generate the greatest protection and rewards for indigenous arts and crafts. The single biggest problem turned out to be getting support from indigenous communities for one national certification mark (interview, 2008). As we continued our fieldwork over the subsequent years this lack of support for a single mark became more and more understandable. Prior to colonization Australia had been a series of Countries, with different languages, different geographies and different cultures. There was no Australia. Indigenous communities viewed the idea of a national authenticity label with suspicion and some began to refer to the labels as 'dog tags'.[49] Defining authenticity for the purposes of the label had turned out to be a little like running through a minefield blindfolded. Those indigenous groups who had developed their own marks raised questions about the effects of a national system, in particular that it might create the impression that those who did not use the system were not producing authentic art. Issues were raised about how representative the NIAAA was of broader indigenous interests and its capacity to administer properly the system of rules underpinning the use of the certification marks.

---

[47] See Janke, *Minding Culture*, 137–41.   [48] *Ibid.*, 148.   [49] *Ibid.*, 147.

There was an answer to these regional and local concerns according to one of our interviewees who had been involved in the bureaucratic planning of the scheme. Once the national scheme was running, different indigenous groups could have developed their own subsidiary marks.[50] Co-badging rather than conflict between the national and local systems was a possibility. But it never got that far. This was a national certification system built on the cheap. Much of the drafting of the system of rules needed to register the certification marks had been done on a pro bono basis by one lawyer (interview, 2008). The NIAAA was given the task of administering the scheme and persuading people to use it, but questions had been raised about the NIAAA's governance and performance, leading to a loss of funding.[51] While it reportedly received over two million dollars, this was spread over eight years.[52] Moreover, it is not clear how much of this was available to make the investments in the advertising needed to build brand status. According to one interviewee the advertising budget was far too small. In the end the Australian government's efforts look amateurish compared to the systematic way in which Canadian governments from the 1950s onwards promoted the Inuit art market both domestically and internationally.

In a famous paper, the economist Akerlof argues that markets will often not lead to efficient results where there are information asymmetries about the quality of goods being traded.[53] For example, buyer ignorance in the used car market potentially leads to good-quality used cars being removed from trading by sellers. One counteracting institution to this problem, Akerlof argues, is the brand name. Drawing on this analysis one can argue in the context of the indigenous art market that a highly visible national label, backed by an organization with the capacity to administer the label, is more likely to engender purchasing trust amongst consumers. In the absence of such a label, what might be the effects of a proliferation of labelling systems on the market? At the very high end of the art market purchasers will probably do the research needed to obtain accurate information, but in other segments of the market they might not. The greater uncertainty might lead to some

---

[50] For an outline of a scheme allowing for the use of derivative marks along with multilevel decision making concerning licensing, see T. Janke, *Our Culture: Our Future – Report On Australian Indigenous Cultural And Intellectual Property Rights* (Sydney: Michael Frankel & Company and Terri Janke, 1998), 204–7.

[51] The NIAAA's problems are discussed in M. Rimmer, 'Australian Icons: Authenticity Marks And Identity Politics', *Indigenous Law Journal*, 3 (2004), 139, 160–4.

[52] See Zografos, *Intellectual Property*, 128.

[53] G. A. Akerlof, 'The Market for "Lemons": Quality Uncertainty and the Market Mechanism', *Quarterly Journal of Economics*, 84 (1970), 488.

variant of Gresham's law occurring in which the bad drives out the good, bad being non-indigenous people finding ways to produce art that takes advantage of the uncertainty and good being fair rewards going to indigenous artists for art produced by them.

Some of our interviewees from Aboriginal organizations thought that a highly visible certification system would help in the indigenous art and craft market, where tourists do ask about authenticity.[54] There was also a suggestion that a national label might help to remove some of the worst exploitation of indigenous artists, which still occurs. In remote communities where cash is short and emergencies common (for example, broken cars, illness, the kinship obligation to help relatives in trouble), art has come to function as a form of currency. The need to convert an artwork quickly into cash has created opportunities for 'carpetbaggers' to purchase the art cheaply and resell it. The term carpetbagger describes phenomena ranging from the service of converting art into cash to bad behaviour that most purchasers of art would not support if they knew about it.[55] According to one of our interviewees, the behaviour of some carpetbaggers borders on the criminal. The families of talented indigenous artists are pressured to lure these artists into town where the carpetbagger extracts weeks of painting from them in situations of confinement. A certification system would probably not stop the worst exploitative practices that we heard about in our interviews. Complex problems are rarely solved with a one-shot regulatory solution.

A trade mark system offers indigenous people options. An individual or an organization may apply for a trade mark. Trade marks can be used to develop a regional approach to marketing. Indigenous networks can also pool their autonomy, as it were, and set up a national certification scheme. But this does mean having a national conversation about authenticity. These are difficult conversations to have. How many of us have had to define authenticity for something we have produced? Different social group identities rub up against each other, creating dividing lines amongst those living in the cities and those on Country, amongst young and old, those who speak language and those who do not and so on. The 'essence' of authenticity is, like a phantom, elusive and hard to grasp.

---

[54] Interestingly, a Senate Committee inquiry into indigenous art recommended that the government begin planning a new authenticity scheme. A number of submissions strongly supported such a move. See *Indigenous Art – Securing the Future: Australia's Indigenous Visual Arts and Craft Sector*, Senate, Standing Committee on Environment, Communications, Information Technology and the Arts, Commonwealth of Australia, Canberra, 2007, 127.

[55] For a discussion of the term see *ibid.*, 100–3.

We do know there will be costs to setting up a national authenticity label. One study of the Silver Hand authenticity trade mark in Alaska showed that some retailers avoided stocking handicraft items bearing the Silver Hand label because they feared the smear of inauthenticity for items that did not carry the label.[56] Some indigenous artists shared this concern. However, the Silver Hand scheme has seen large increases in the number of indigenous artists using the label and is generally viewed as a success.[57] There is enough experience with authenticity labels for indigenous developmental networks to be able to form a view about whether they are feasible in a given context. An important factor is whether there is enough investment in creating consumer awareness of an authenticity label. The success of the Igloo Tag was helped by a long-term commitment by the Canadian government in the 1950s and 1960s. In the case of the Silver Hand label, in 2002 federal and Alaskan state bodies launched a public relations campaign that saw, amongst other things, the release of almost a million brochures informing consumers about the label and how consumers might help to enforce it by reporting seemingly fraudulent uses of it.[58]

A national certification system, once established in the minds of consumers, is a club good that can help to overcome the effects of Gresham's law in art and craft markets. But for that to happen, the club good has to be properly funded. Indigenous artists in remote communities do not have the financial or organizational resources to create a club good. One option, as in the case of the Igloo and Silver Hand certification systems, is for governments to become directly involved. But if they decide not to or do it badly, another option for indigenous communities is to consider joining a certification system that has already established itself in the market. This possibility is discussed in the next section.

10.5.   Moral action at a distance

One way in which consumers can express their moral preferences is through ethical shopping. For example, a consumer in a Western country may be interested in purchasing a handmade rug, but not one made by a five-year-old girl forced to work fourteen hours a day, in conditions that will cause her physical deformity and shorten her life. When it comes to

---

[56] See J. Hollowell-Zimmer, 'Marked by the Silver Hand: Intellectual Property Protection and the Market in Alaska Native Arts and Crafts' in M. Riley (ed.), *Indigenous Intellectual Property Rights: Legal Obstacles and Innovative Solutions* (Walnut Creek, CA: AltaMira Press, 2004), 54.

[57] See Zografos, *Intellectual Property*, 118–19.

[58] Hollowell-Zimmer, 'Marked by the Silver Hand', 74.

circumstances of production some consumers want to see a fair wage being paid, safe conditions of work, the use of a production process that minimizes environmental damage and so on. The cost to each individual consumer of tracing a retailer's international supply chain to ascertain the truth about the circumstances of production is high. The individual consumer also faces a collective action problem. One individual making the decision not to purchase the rug will have little impact on the market. Many coordinated individual moral acts of consumption, when aggregated as demand in the market, may have considerable influence on the circumstances of production. The problem is how to meet the costs of organizing this coordination. Individual retailers, it should be noted, also face information and coordination problems. An individual retailer may want to source rugs not made using child labour, but has to find ways to communicate that to consumers, as well as competing with retailers that take no interest in who makes the rugs they sell.

One response to these coordination and information problems has been the rise of standard-setting bodies that create voluntary standard systems for businesses aimed at fulfilling economic, social or environmental goals. Two well-known examples are the Forest Steward-ship Council, which was born of a mix of social movements, activists and traders in the 1990s, and the Fairtrade Labelling Organizations International (FLO), also established in the 1990s by those who had long fought for better conditions and rewards for poor farmers in developing countries. Certification marks are one critical tool for these organizations. The growth and globalization of organizations designing these voluntary standard-setting systems has been rapid. They operate in all sectors of the economy – forestry, fisheries, manufacturing, retail and international trade.[59] The very process of designing standard systems is itself being standardized with the rise of meta-regulators such as the ISEAL Alliance developing standards for standard setting.[60]

The rise of this type of organization has helped to create a world of overlapping circuits of certification in which the certifiers are themselves certified by other certifiers and certifiers are potential competitors. So, for example, FLO-CERT, which is the independent company that certifies producer organizations using FLO standards, is itself certified under the ISO 65, the standard for product certification systems. FLO's standard-setting processes are managed using ISEAL's codes of practice for standard setting. FLO and GoodWeave both have certification

---

[59] For an analysis see M. Chon, 'Marks of Rectitude', *Fordham Law Review*, 77 (2009), 2311.
[60] On the work of the ISEAL Alliance see www.isealalliance.org/.

standards for rugs, but GoodWeave claims that its system of random inspection gives it a superior system of enforcement.[61]

Competition amongst standard-setting organizations raises possible problems.[62] The proliferation of competing standards may end up offering companies standards and labels of convenience. For example, many activists who campaigned against the labour practices in Nike's global supply chain saw its decision to join the Fair Labor Association rather than the Worker Rights Consortium as an example of a company moving to lower, corporate-friendly standards.[63] Too much competition amongst standards creates uncertainty, possibly triggering a 'spiral of distrust'[64] amongst consumers. The success of standards also brings an old danger of regulation in the form of capture, as powerful stakeholders, realizing the importance of the system, enter it and begin to exercise a disproportionate influence over the direction and philosophy of the standards-setting organization. Where an organization's income becomes too dependent upon the licence fees paid by large licensees of the certification mark (for example, large roasters like Nestle and Sara Lee in the coffee market) capture and dependency become potential problems.[65]

Aside from these general problems there are more specific issues for an indigenous developmental network to consider before entering one of these systems. For example, when it comes to distributive decisions in relation to the profits generated from participation in the FLO system, FLO standards would bump up against the obligations that individual members of kinship societies owe to others. The Fairtrade Premium is an amount paid to a producer organization for 'the realization of common goals'. These might include things like improving the literacy of workers and investing in machinery to improve production. How prescriptive should standards be when it comes to goals? What if, asked one interviewee, a group of senior men decided to invest in four-wheel-drives

---

[61] See www.goodweave.org.
[62] See generally L. Fransen, 'Why Do Private Governance Organizations Not Converge? A Political-Institutional Analysis of Transnational Labor Standards Regulation', *Governance: An International Journal of Policy, Administration, and Institutions*, 24 (2011), 359.
[63] W. L. Bennett and T. Lagos, 'Logo Logic: The Ups and Downs of Branded Political Communication', *Annals of the American Academy of Political and Social Science*, 611 (2007), 193, 200.
[64] M. Schneiberg, and T. Bartley, 'Organizations, Regulation, and Economic Behaviour: Regulatory Dynamics and Forms from the Nineteenth to the Twenty-First Century', *Annual Review of Law and Social Science*, 4 (2008), 31.
[65] See A. Hutchens, *Changing Big Business: The Globalisation of the Fair Trade Movement* (Cheltenham: Edward Elgar, 2009), ch. 5.

rather than building a school house because they thought moving about on Country was a bigger priority for the community? Like other certification systems, FLO has standards on child labour and protection. Where an indigenous family is running a wild harvest operation children may well be involved. For indigenous women wild harvest is a chance to spend time with young children, teaching them in their own language about plants and Country. How much time spent by children in wild harvest is consistent with the standard? FLO's environmental and biodiversity goals would probably be shared by many indigenous communities but whether FLO's standards constitute the right path for each community to follow is a separate question. A meta-study concluded that surprisingly little is known about the environmental impact of FLO's standards.[66]

These are not arguments against indigenous groups participating in these systems and nor are they examples of irresolvable issues. But because these systems come with audit and compliance obligations they are vectors of practical change. They have to be discussed and debated by indigenous groups.

For any voluntary standards system such as the one run by the FLO, there will always be a balance to manage between its principles and the diversity of the local contexts in which those principles have to function. But there is enough evidence to suggest that these voluntary systems can help to support indigenous business enterprises based on the use of indigenous knowledge assets. FLO, for example, states that 1.2 million workers and farmers in fifty-eight developing countries in Africa, Asia and Latin America participate in its system.[67]

One possibility worth considering is that an organization with experience in running a global standards system might help interested indigenous groups develop a set of standards for indigenous business enterprises that utilize indigenous knowledge systems. Locating such a discussion within an established fairtrade system has some advantages.[68] Three are worth mentioning. First, there is an obvious advantage for indigenous businesses in being able to gain access to an established global brand. The costs of building consumer recognition have been met. Secondly, organizations like FLO have a great deal of experience in running the complex multi-stakeholder processes from which standards are

---

[66] V. Nelson and B. Pound, 'The Last Ten Years: A Comprehensive Review of the Literature on the Impact of Fair Trade' (2009) available at www.fairtrade.net/fileadmin/user_upload/content/2009/about_us/2010_03_NRI_Full_Literature_Review.pdf.
[67] See www.fairtrade.net/faqs.html.
[68] M. Spencer and J. Hardie, *Indigenous Fair Trade in Australia* (Canberra: Rural Industries Research and Development Corporation, 2011), 41.

eventually agreed. Obtaining agreement on standards will not be easy and experienced hands are required to assist the process. Thirdly, organizations like FLO that have long experience with certification systems are in the best position to devise something that is financially feasible for indigenous businesses. Obviously the costs of voluntary certification systems should not drive out the very producers they are meant to assist.

The value of voluntary certification systems for indigenous groups is best understood in the context of the process of regulatory bricolage that I described in chapter 9. They constitute a set of resources and networks that may help some indigenous producers survive economically in the world. In the field of fair trade we have many studies pointing to fair trade being important to poor producers making economic and organizational capacity gains.[69] We also have studies where fair trade has not helped producers and other strategies such as direct marketing have proved to be more effective.[70] There are no guarantees with voluntary certification systems, but for a bricoleur a world in which they are an option is a better world.

10.6.   Place and products: geographical indications

Geographical Indications (GIs) may be protected by trade mark law or, as in many European countries, by a distinct system of law. As distinct systems GIs have their modern origin in the national schemes of European states of the early twentieth century, with the French appellations of origin scheme, in particular, making an important contribution to the international evolution of this form of protection.[71] A GI system allows for the registration of a name that identifies products as originating from a defined geographical area and having special characteristics by virtue of that origination. The process of origination, which stamps special qualities on a product, may include techniques of production. In some cases these techniques may have a dominant role in the investiture of specialness (for example, Bohemian crystal). This form of protection proceeds on the assumption that it is the place of production that invests a good with special qualities even if the same raw material and the same

[69] See A. Le Mare, 'The Impact of Fair Trade on Social and Economic Development: A Review of the Literature', *Geography Compass*, 2 (2008), 1922.
[70] See, for example, J. Smith, 'The Search for Sustainable Markets: The Promise and Failure of Fair Trade', *Culture & Agriculture*, 29 (2007), 89.
[71] For the history see W. van Caenegem, 'Registered Geographical Indications: Between Intellectual Property and Rural Policy – Part II', *Journal of World Intellectual Property*, 6 (2003), 861.

techniques are used by producers elsewhere (for example, the same grape variety, cows milk, the same olive variety).

If the special qualities of the product result in demand in consumer markets then control of the name becomes important for producers in the defined area. For producers, GIs follow a broader branding logic in which they aim to create a distinctive status for the product amongst consumers for which they can extract a premium price. From an economic perspective the protection of GIs has important functions on both the demand and supply sides of markets.[72] They provide consumers with information about a product and allow producers to prevent freeriding on the reputation their goods have acquired amongst consumers.

In part because of the inclusion of standards of protection for GIs in the Agreement on Trade-Related Aspects of Intellectual Property Rights 1994 (TRIPS Agreement) much more attention is being paid by states to GIs.[73] Within the World Trade Organization's Doha negotiations, the European Union is arguing for stronger protection for GIs.[74] Interestingly, within the European Union registration system for GIs, four countries – Italy, France, Spain and Portugal – account for 70 per cent of the registrations.[75] These four countries are amongst those with the longest-established national systems of GI protection. This suggests that for those countries without much experience of national systems of GIs, taking advantage of GIs within the trade system will take time. Moreover, care needs to be taken in what can be inferred from the success of some famous European GIs. Their journey to success took place in historical circumstances that are different in today's world of globally competitive markets, changing market structures, multiple advertising strategies and different patterns of consumer behaviour. Would producers in Burgundy and Champagne be as successful today using a GI scheme if they were unknown and starting out afresh? The inclusion of standards on GIs in the TRIPS Agreement has meant that states tend to assess their interests in GI schemes, perhaps disproportionately so, from the perspective of trade gains and losses. The problem of the state's developmental egoism

---

[72] For a survey of the economic literature see C. Bramley, E. Bienabe and J. Kirsten, 'The Economics of Geographical Indications: Towards a Conceptual Framework for Geographical Indication Research in Developing Countries' in *The Economics of Intellectual Property: Suggestions for Further Research in Developing Countries and Countries with Economies in Transition* (Geneva: WIPO, 2009), 109.

[73] See Articles 22, 23 and 24 of the TRIPS Agreement.

[74] A summary of the various negotiating positions is available at www.wto.org/english/tratop_e/trips_e/gi_background_e.htm#wines_spirits.

[75] G. E. Evans, 'The Comparative Advantages of Geographical Indications and Community Trade Marks for the Marketing of Agricultural Products in the European Union', *International Review of Intellectual Property and Competition Law*, 41 (2010), 645.

for indigenous people looms in this area of intellectual property as much as in any other area.

GI schemes recognize linkages between a defined place, a product, a producer group and its techniques, for an indefinite period of time. These features of place and time make GIs, much like secrecy, a seemingly natural form of protection for indigenous groups. But as will become clear, GI systems have administrative and organizational dimensions that render this characterization somewhat illusory. There is debate about the extent to which GIs can protect indigenous knowledge. What is registered and protected is a name and this does not, as has been pointed out, protect a product.[76] The producers in the Champagne region cannot stop others from using Chardonnay grapes to make sparkling wine. Others take a more expansive view of the protection available under GI schemes when it comes to protecting indigenous knowledge.[77] Whatever one's view of where the line of protection falls, it is clear that GIs, like other systems of intellectual property, cannot protect an ancestral cosmology of place. They were never designed for that purpose.

The issue of the scope of protection that a GI scheme might offer for indigenous knowledge needs to be separated from the issue of whether a GI scheme might be useful as a development tool for indigenous groups. This is also a separate issue from whether the state sees GI schemes as being in its interests. Australia, for example, may well decide that it has nothing to gain from European-style GI schemes but it does not follow that these schemes might not have development benefits for indigenous groups in Australia. Much also depends on the dynamics of various product markets in which GIs have potential application. For example, the Australian food industry is thought to have huge export potential in the Asian century.[78] Demand from Asian middle class consumers for quality and interesting food products may see the rise in importance of GIs in these markets. A country like Australia, which relies on a mix of legal tools such as trade marks and the action for passing off to protect GIs, may have to re-evaluate whether it might be in its interests to adopt a branding strategy based on a distinctive GI scheme for at least some parts of its food industry, such as the bush foods industry. The state's interests and the interests of indigenous groups may end up converging.

---

[76] S. Frankel, 'The Mismatch of Geographical Indications and Innovative Traditional Knowledge', *Prometheus*, 29 (2011), 253, 257.
[77] See D. Gervais, 'Traditional Innovation and the Ongoing Debate on the Protection of Geographical Indications' in Drahos and Frankel (eds.), *Indigenous Peoples' Innovation*, 121; and Blakeney, 'The Pacific Solution', 165.
[78] See *National Food Plan: Green Paper 2012* (Canberra: Department of Agriculture, Fisheries and Forestry, 2012).

Assessing whether or not a GI scheme would have development value for indigenous groups within a country depends ultimately on the design of the scheme and the role that the state is prepared to play in supporting the scheme. Perhaps the most important point to make about GIs is that they are a cooperation-intensive form of market regulation. To begin with producers of a product do have to unite as a producer group. GI schemes are more an expression of collective action from below than decree from above. This would mean indigenous groups having to form producer groups and associations to represent their interests. Producer organizations have been a vital factor in the long-term success of the Australian wine industry.[79] This kind of collective action amongst indigenous groups may be difficult where there are pre-existing tensions between, for example, different language groups in an area that might possibly be defined for the purposes of a GI scheme. Similarly, in cases where there is tension between indigenous groups over land title issues, the cooperation needed to develop a GI for an area is likely to founder.

We came across only one producer cooperative formed by indigenous people operating in the bush food sector in our interviews. The cooperative had drifted, it was conceded, and needed to become more active. Those indigenous people we spoke to who were harvesting bush foods in the Kimberley region seemed to have a preference for family operations. The more general point is that indigenous groups in Australia have not had much experience in the organization of an industry. They have had almost no participation in organizations like the Australian Native Food Industry (interviews). Even if a GI scheme is successful, how the benefits are to be distributed along the chain of production depends on the organizational structure of the market. In a sweeping study of the potential of GI schemes in nine African countries, Blakeney and Coulet found that the product markets they were studying (for example, cloves, cocoa, honey, yams) were characterized by small-scale producers with little market power and with benefits going to distributors and purchasers of these products.[80] Organizational capacity looms large as a variable if small and dispersed indigenous producers are to benefit from GI schemes. The preference of indigenous people in Australia for family

---

[79] See K. Anderson, 'Building an Internationally Competitive Australian Olive Industry: Lessons from the Wine Industry', Discussion Paper No. 0225 (Centre for International Economic Studies, Adelaide University, 2002).

[80] M. Blakeney and T. Coulet, 'The Protection of Geographical Indications (GI): Generating Empirical Evidence at Country and Product Level to Support African ACP Country Engagement in the Doha Round Negotiations' (2011), 11, available at www.acp.int.

operations stems at least in part from a historic lack of participation in industrial organizational decision making that shapes market structures.

Choosing the name of a GI might not be straightforward for indigenous groups. For indigenous people, place names link to cosmological knowledge and authority structures.[81] Finding agreement on an indigenous language place name for a GI amongst a number of indigenous groups each located in different Countries that might all be part of a proposed GI territory might be a matter of long negotiation. During our interviews it became clear that indigenous people had different views as to how best to refer to *Terminalia ferdinandiana* (Gubinge, Bush Plum, Kakadu Plum are some of the names that are used to refer to this plant). Indigenous people did not mind what other groups called it elsewhere but were insistent on what the correct name was in their Country. The naming of GIs has to engage properly with a network of indigenous place names stretching across Australia that has been in use for thousands of years.[82]

Settling the boundaries of a GI area may be a straightforward process or it can trigger a bitter dispute as it did in the case of the decade-long fight amongst non-indigenous producers over the boundaries of the Coonawarra wine region in south-eastern Australia.[83] For indigenous groups operating in settler states such as Australia, GI schemes would represent another set of boundary issues to be negotiated, both amongst themselves and with the state. Obviously a critical question for indigenous people would be how boundary disputes might be resolved.

Aside from achieving cooperation amongst themselves, indigenous groups would potentially have to negotiate with non-indigenous people who might also be producers and therefore affected by a GI scheme. The design of a GI scheme would raise many issues for negotiation. The French GI system of wine regulation is highly interventionist with rules controlling matters such as trellis height and pruning techniques.[84] One can devise a minimalist scheme of regulation as Australia has for its GI system for wines, but the basic point is that some standards have to be agreed by producer groups and administered by the state otherwise there

---

[81] For a discussion of these kinds of issues see the essays in H. Koch and L. Hercus (eds.), *Aboriginal Placenames: Naming and Re-Naming The Australian Landscape* (Canberra: ANU E Press, 2009).

[82] G. Windsor, 'The Recognition of Aboriginal Placenames in New South Wales' in *ibid.*, 71, 72.

[83] For an excellent account see G. Edmond, 'Disorder with Law: Determining the Geographical Indication for the Coonawarra Wine Region', *Adelaide Law Review*, 27 (2006), 59.

[84] *Ibid.*, 62.

is little chance that the GI will become a place-brand of quality. The extent to which a GI helps a group of producers to make price gains beyond what they might have made individually or collectively with some other labelling strategy depends on the extent to which the GI makes the transition to place-brand status. This requires investment in promotion. In the case of France's famous wine GIs, this investment cost was incurred long ago and spread over generations. Wine is an example of a product in which supplier networks around the world have invested in educating consumers. This enculturation process has created taste discrimination amongst consumers, which in turn has laid the foundation for price discrimination strategies based on branding. This has not been an overnight phenomenon. Even in this evolved market, GIs are no guarantee of success as some consumers remain price sensitive rather than brand sensitive and the proliferation of GIs has led to some uncertainty amongst consumers.[85]

In the case of relatively little-known bush food products coming from geographical areas not widely known to consumers, indigenous producers face rather massive future costs of promotion. Not many Australians would be familiar with the qualities of the Kakadu Plum or the Bush Tomato. The large supermarket chain, Coles, has for a number of years stocked a small range of products based on bush foods, but it sees this venture very much in philanthropic terms (interview, 2010). The high volumes needed by large supermarkets to make profits are simply not there in the case of Australian bush foods. In order for products to stay on Coles' shelves they have to meet a 'hurdle rate' on a weekly basis otherwise they are pulled. Olive oil is an example of a market in Australia where consumers have become willing to pay a premium for quality and supermarkets like Coles have responded by carrying more expensive varieties (interview, 2010). But this has required a long investment in processes of consumer enculturation. Obviously, indigenous groups have neither the money nor the expertise needed to turn relatively unknown products such as the Bush Tomato into GI place-brands. This means that the state would have to take on a developmental role and support a brand promotion strategy. For a GI scheme the motto has to be build it, promote it and (hopefully) they will come. Unless this promotion cost is met the price benefits of GIs will remain largely theoretical.

Despite these problems, GI schemes may be worth considering in a world where companies can use the cost structures and capacity of

---

[85] See, for example, F. Adinolfi, M. De Rosa and F. Trabalzi, 'Dedicated and Generic Marketing Strategies: The Disconnection Between Geographical Indications and Consumer Behavior in Italy', *British Food Journal*, 113 (2011), 419.

countries such as China and Brazil to dominate markets in products such as plant oils and other plant products by virtue of scale of production. Australia has a poor track record of taking advantage of its endemic plants.[86] As chapter 4 explained, the Convention on Biological Diversity has been crucial in stimulating the enclosure of biological resources by states, but ultimately there may still be many cases where multinationals may be able to legitimately obtain plant samples and commercialize these where the costs of production are the lowest. For example, the multi-national Amway, which has factories in Brazil, China and Mexico, was involved in an orchard consisting of thousands of Gubinge trees near Darwin and in 2004 exported tissue culture to its factory in Brazil.[87] Another export of Gubinge took place from the Northern Territory to India in 2008 (interview). For some of our interviewees these two exports were seen as potentially commercially damaging: 'Slipping Gubinge to India and Brazil will kill the industry in Australia'.

In these kinds of cases, working out who owns property rights in what things (the trees, genetic resources, the data, the knowledge etc.) can be difficult, and even if there is a benefit-sharing agreement in place indigenous people may not be beneficiaries. These two cases of export also took place well before the adoption of the Nagoya Protocol in 2010. Whether or not the Protocol would apply to a utilization of these resources that takes place after it comes into effect is a matter of interpretation because the Protocol is silent on the matter. In those cases where access and utilization take place before the Protocol comes into operation it becomes even harder to argue that its provisions apply. The Australian state should probably anticipate a certain amount of leakage of its plant genetic resources through legitimate and illegitimate means and invest in ways of differentiating the Australian commercialization of these resources from commercialization by other countries. Branding its biology may turn out to be a good long-term strategy.

Indigenous people could, with their sophisticated plant culture, make a huge contribution to the development of branding strategies. GIs offer one branding path, but they are a cooperation- and negotiation-intensive form of market regulation in which the state has to play an important role in the design, promotion and maintenance of the regulatory system. This is especially true if the system is to serve poor indigenous producer groups. A critical question in the Australian context is whether there is

---

[86] A. B. Cunningham, S. Garnett, J. Gorman, K. Courtenay and D. Boehme, 'Eco-Enterprises and *Terminalia ferdinandiana*: "Best Laid Plans" and Australian Policy Lessons', *Economic Botany*, 63 (2009), 16, 23.
[87] *Ibid.*, 24.

enough trust between indigenous people and the state to negotiate a GI system that really works developmentally for indigenous groups. Can indigenous producers trust Australia to become the developmental state? The next chapter argues that Australia is in a trust trap in its relations with indigenous people. If this is right then the potential benefits of GI schemes for indigenous producers will probably be difficult to realize.

11   Trust in networks

11.1.   Payment for ecosystem innovation: Waiting for Godot

The previous chapter showed the potential usefulness of trade secrets and trade marks for the protection of indigenous knowledge assets. However, intellectual property systems are likely to remain extractive for indigenous groups. The distinctive feature of indigenous peoples' innovation lies in their capacity to devise systems for the maintenance of ecological systems (see chapter 2). The maintenance of ecological systems has come to be recognized as important to the provisioning of what are called ecosystem services. The concept has broad and narrow versions, but the basic idea is that there are many complex functions of ecosystems that are drawn upon in various ways by humans for the purposes of their well-being such as the use of water and air, the use of soil, the pollination activities of insects and so on.[1] For reasons having to do with the commodity nature of capitalism, intellectual property rights are more suited to commodity-based forms of innovation (for example, an artistic work, an invention, a plant variety right, a semi-conductor chip).[2] Copyright, to take one example, does not recognize or protect a relationship an artist may have with the landscape, or the aesthetic value that comes from a landscape, but simply the artist's paintings of the landscape. The collective labour of groups of indigenous people using a system of fire burning to manage Country (and its ecological systems) does not in any obvious way produce a single commodity. While a method of fire burning might conceivably be the subject of a patent application, the effects it has on the complex functioning of an ecological system and the services that humans draw upon from the

---

[1] For a discussion of definitions see R. Greiner, I. Gordon and C. Cocklin, 'Ecosystem Services From Tropical Savannas: Economic Opportunities Through Payments for Environmental Services', *Rangeland Journal*, 31 (2009), 51, 52–3.

[2] Marx's theory of capitalism links it to the fetishism of commodities. See B. Fine, *Marx's Capital*, 2nd edn. (Houndmills: Macmillan, 1984), 25.

system's functions (for example, biodiversity services) cannot be patented.

In essence, indigenous people's innovation took place in a territorial cosmos and contributed to the increase of what under the rules of capitalist production is 'natural' capital. For the most part, natural capital has been available as a free input into systems of production. The role of exclusive property rights in systems of production has not been to preserve or increase natural capital, but to make a given system of production more efficient. The property solution to the tragedy of the commons is not about saving multifunctional ecological systems, but rather about making a commodity system such as cattle production more efficient so that the economies-of-scale logic can operate. Cattle grazing may be made more efficient through private property rights but that heightens rather than lessens its destructive impact on ecosystems. Parts of an ecosystem such as its trees can be commodified, but this captures only a very small part of the overall value of the system and can easily lead to a tragedy of commodification in which the exploitation of the commodity ends up destroying the ecosystem and the services it provides.

The voluntary certification systems discussed in chapter 10 help some indigenous groups to sell their products into consumer markets willing to pay a premium for ethical and sustainable production. What is being paid for by consumers is a commodity (coffee, timber, chocolate etc.), but the price of the commodity is unlikely to reflect the true value of the range of services being provided by the ecosystem from which the commodity is being extracted and the extractive process itself may not be sustainable. For example, we saw in chapter 9 that purchasers of perfume containing sandalwood oil that has been certified by the Songman Circle are helping to support the indigenous groups who harvest the sandalwood. Critics of capitalism would see this as an extension of a consumption model designed to create lucrative niche markets. Indigenous people are being drawn into an unsustainable exploitation of the last remaining wild stands of sandalwood, which, in the case of Western Australia, began about 150 years ago. The broader point is that capitalism's property rights systems are designed to serve those who can extract most value from resources rather than to protect relationships between the human and non-human world that sustain the world for all.

The standards of some certification organizations expressly recognize the role of indigenous knowledge in the maintenance of ecological systems.[3] For example, the Rainforest Alliance and its partner Imaflora

---

[3] Principle 3.4 of the Forest Stewardship Council's principles recognizes the rights of indigenous people and requires, amongst other things, that they be 'compensated for

validated in 2012 a forest carbon project led by the Paiter Suruí, an indigenous tribe in the Brazilian Amazon.[4] Amongst the standards used in this process were the Climate, Community and Biodiversity Standards, standards developed by an alliance of voluntary standards bodies, NGOs and private companies.[5] Under the standards, project developers must draw on the knowledge of indigenous groups when it comes to estimating the impacts of projects on natural resources and ecosystem services.[6]

As the example of the Paiter Suruí shows, models using certification services can be devised, which, to a limited extent, will support private investment in a function of an ecosystem. Linking the design of certification systems to local needs of indigenous groups is crucial if these systems are to have any prospect of long-term success.[7] But this model is still dependent on commodification, in this case carbon. We are still a long way from being able to value the uses of ecological systems,[8] but it also seems reasonably clear that the future of capitalism, at least in the context of ecosystems, lies less in Schumpeterian creative destruction and more in creative preservation. Over time we may be able to devise better regulatory models for maintaining ecological services.[9] A number of countries have moved towards purchasing defined environmental services that have an environmental goal such as the reduction of the pollution of land or the maintenance of biodiversity.[10] The payment by ConocoPhillips to indigenous people to carry out a fire burning regime in northern Australia in order to offset greenhouse gas emissions is an example of a payment for an environmental service (see chapter 2). The theory behind paying for environmental services is that the targeting of specific services will contribute to one or more functions of an

---

the application of their traditional knowledge regarding the use of forest species or management systems in forest operations'. The principle and criteria are available at www.fsc.org/principles-and-criteria.34.htm. See also principle 3 of the World Fair Trade Organization's ten principles of fair trade available at www.wfto.com/index.php?option=com_content&task=view&id=2&Itemid=14.

[4] www.rainforest-alliance.org/newsroom/news/surui-forest-carbon-project.

[5] See *Climate, Community & Biodiversity Project Design Standards*, 2nd edn. (Arlington, VA: CCBA, December, 2008).

[6] See *ibid.*, 25.

[7] See E. Boyd, M. Gutierrez and M. Chang, 'Small-Scale Forest Carbon Projects: Adapting CDM to Low-Income Communities', *Global Environmental Change*, 17 (2007), 250.

[8] N. Hanley and E. B. Barbier, *Pricing Nature: Cost-Benefit Analysis and Environmental Policy* (Cheltenham: Edward Elgar: 2009), 205.

[9] For an example of a major initiative see *The Economics of Ecosystems and Biodiversity: Mainstreaming the Economics of Nature: A synthesis of the approach, conclusions and recommendations of TEEB* (2010) available at www.unep.org/pdf/LinkClick.pdf.

[10] Greiner, Gordon and Cocklin, 'Ecosystem Services', 56.

ecosystem and thereby improve the provisioning of ecosystem services. But in political economies where commodification is the main game and exclusive property rights function to extract maximum value, as well as extractively (see chapter 1), the market in environmental services may not attract enough suppliers to make much difference in the long run to the degradation of ecosystems. For indigenous people the way to halt the slide in the viability of ecosystems is to recognize overriding duties to Country.

For indigenous people, emerging regulatory models around payment for environmental services and the provisioning of ecosystem services may offer greater opportunities to make gains from their knowledge assets. In this final chapter I argue that the realization of any such opportunities depends crucially upon an alliance between indigenous developmental networks and science. The case studies I have discussed all involve, in one way or another, scientists working with indigenous groups to find ways in which indigenous groups might realize some economic gain from their knowledge. It is clear that at least some indigenous leaders have concluded that an alliance with scientists is crucial to their developmental strategy. But, as I hope to make clear, this alliance holds the promise of more than just scientists helping indigenous groups turn their knowledge assets into a commodity form demanded by capitalism's extractive intellectual property systems. For scientists, cooperation with indigenous people carries with it the possibilities of de-routinization, of shifting away from servitude to commodity production and into innovation of services to ecological systems or what indigenous people would call 'healthy Country'. The need for this kind of innovation is, as the next section makes clear, well understood by scientific communities.

11.2.   The new voyage of the *Beagle*

Over the decades science has helped to reveal the importance of ecological systems and the services that they provide. Under the auspices of the United Nations an initiative known as the Millennium Ecosystem Assessment (MA) was launched in 2001.[11] Involving more than 1,360 scientists from ninety-five countries, it produced a series of technical studies and reports that give us the best understanding we have so far of changes in ecosystems and the likely consequences for human well-being. The picture that emerges from the MA is one in which our current

[11] See www.maweb.org/en/index.aspx.

state of development has been supported freely by streams of services in the form of clean water, food, disease control, climate regulation and many others emanating, often in hidden ways, from mountain, polar, inland water, coastal, marine, forest, desert and other ecosystems. Economic growth has impacted on these ecosystems to the point where some fifteen out of twenty-four of the services provided by these systems are in global decline.[12]

The MA and its sister global assessment project, the International Panel on Climate Change, are, much like Darwin's *Voyage of the Beagle* (1839), examples of scientific journeys. They are not the work of one scientist. They do, in the spirit of Darwin, sweep across the scientific disciplines, piecing together a picture of many ecosystems operating at different levels and with high degrees of integration. The interdisciplinary science behind the MA has in a sense caught up with a basic truth known to many indigenous people. In Australia this truth is captured in the phrase 'Caring for Country'.[13] For indigenous people it is a truth that should be stated as a categorical imperative – 'Care for Country'. But it also has a conditional form: If you want Country to Care for you then Care for Country. A truth known and lived locally by many indigenous groups now has a scientific macro-equivalent. If we are to continue to enjoy well-being we will have to care for the ecosystems on which we have depended for so long.

The global state of ecosystem crisis documented by the MA is also a time of opportunity for indigenous people. Behind the MA is a science that is more integrated and discursively open than perhaps at any time during its history. The smokestack capitalism of the nineteenth century began, as Marx correctly foresaw, the process of bending science to its industrial and military needs, culminating in the twentieth century in a science that laboured with some autonomy, but heeded the calls of its military and industrial paymasters.[14] The prospects of cooperation between what Thomas Kuhn called 'normal science', an inward-looking science in which its practitioners do not lift their head above the paradigm they have internalized, and indigenous people, are slim. The

---

[12] Millennium Ecosystem Assessment, *Ecosystems and Human Well-being: Synthesis* (Washington, DC: Island Press, 2005), 1.

[13] The Australian government funds natural resource management projects under its 'Caring for our Country' programme. See www.nrm.gov.au/about/caring/index.html. For indigenous people the phrase refers to specific duties and responsibilities they have towards particular places. See J. Gorman and S. Vemuri, 'Social Implications of Bridging the Gap Through "Caring for Country" in Remote Indigenous Communities of the Northern Territory, Australia', *The Rangeland Journal*, 34 (2012), 63, 66.

[14] P. Drahos, *A Philosophy of Intellectual Property* (Aldershot: Dartmouth, 1996), 112.

prospects are better now for deeper epistemic cooperation between science and indigenous people than at any other time. For example, the MA did involve a multi-stakeholder board, which included indigenous people and produced a report that examined how local and traditional knowledge systems could be incorporated into managing ecosystems.[15]

For indigenous people the benefit of cooperation with scientists lies in the global recognition that science can bring to the achievements of indigenous people in creating systems for managing ecosystems. Science's techniques for analysing, measuring and quantifying the role of ecological services are crucial to understanding the historical contribution that indigenous people have made to the maintenance of those services. Science, in other words, is needed in order for us to be able to understand fully the social value of indigenous peoples' innovation. But as I indicated in the previous section an alliance between science and indigenous people has the possibility of moving beyond a relationship in which science acts as an instrument of verification and commodification, and into one that aims to make both partners in the growth of knowledge. The next section, drawing on the concept of de-routinization, presents an analytical argument for this possibility.

11.3. De-routinization: irregular paths to knowledge

The twentieth-century debate over how science best makes progress was dominated by Kuhn and Popper.[16] Kuhn's core answer seemed to lie in the idea of an exhaustive and insular exploration of a paradigm that would generate enough anomalies for the paradigm to be toppled by another. For Popper it was a process of relentless bold conjecture supported by the rules of methodological falsificationism. Neither of these approaches seems to place much weight on the role of observations, especially by outsiders to science. The Kuhnian paradigm believer has to labour on minor puzzles until the day of scientific revolution arrives, hardly a recipe for cooperation with those from outside his discipline, let alone another knowledge system. Popper was dismissive of the idea that observational experience formed the path to bold conjecture,

---

[15] See W. V. Reid, F. Berkes, T. J. Wilbanks and D. Capistrano, 'Introduction' in W. V. Reid, F. Berkes, T. Wilbanks and D. Capistrano (eds.), *Bridging Scales and Knowledge Systems: Concepts and Applications in Ecosystem Assessment* (Washington DC: Island Press, 2006), 1, 3.

[16] For an excellent account see S. Fuller, *Kuhn vs. Popper: The Struggle for the Soul of Science* (New York: Columbia University Press, 2004).

arguing instead that the source of these conjectures lay in speculative and critical reason.[17]

Popper perhaps underestimates the role observational experience can play in generating hypotheses. Placing scientists into long-term working relationships with indigenous people and encouraging a process of respectful conversation and listening about the patterns in the environment that indigenous people have observed may actually be an important way in which both parties can increase their knowledge about the world. Through forming long-term partnerships with indigenous groups scientists may achieve two things. The first is that they take themselves away from the routines of normal science and the second is that they create the opportunity to listen to observations and conjectures outside of the scope of normal science. We saw in chapter 2 that the use by indigenous people of a fire system to manage the landscape was thought to be a destructive practice by the early colonizers. It was not until the last two or three decades of the twentieth century that systematic scientific study began to reveal the truth about the beneficial effects of the use of a fire system to manage ecological systems. One can imagine another history in which indigenous masters of the mosaic method of burning sit down with scientists and under conditions of mutual respect begin to discuss the patterns and connections they see released in the land through the systematized use of fire. In this world we arrive at an understanding of fire as a system and its relationship to ecological systems at a much earlier point in time than we actually have. We do not have to wait until the 1970s for some non-indigenous individuals to begin asking deeper questions about the effects of indigenous people's burning practices. Another example of where the connectionism of indigenous knowledge has helped scientists is in the field of water hydrology and wetlands where, it turns out, there is a deep knowledge by elders of the links between groundwater hydrology and the maintenance of wetlands.[18]

The translation of observational experience into bold conjecture is not inevitable. It is a matter of chance. But the chances may improve in the case of partnerships between indigenous people and scientists because scientists in interacting with indigenous people are more likely to experience a de-routinization of their practices and communication about problems. De-routinization is a process in which actors begin to

---

[17] See his essay 'Back to the Presocratics' in K. R. Popper, *The World Of Parmenides: Essays on the Presocratic Enlightenment* (London and New York: Routledge, 1998), 7, 8–11.

[18] See J. K. Weir, R. Stone and M. Mulardy Jr., 'Water Planning and Native Title: A Karajarri and Government Engagement in the West Kimberley' in J. K. Weir (ed.), *Country, Native Title and Ecology* (Canberra: ANU E Press, 2012), 81.

question their adherence to conventional routines of thought and behaviour.[19] Assumptions lose their privileged status and the door to bold conjecture quietly swings open.

But why should the chances of de-routinization increase when indigenous people and scientists come together? The explanation lies in a juxtaposition of two very different cosmologies in which the differences of belief cannot go unnoticed. When two people from the same tradition meet, routine is likely to dominate the encounter. When people from two very different traditions meet there is no joint routine to fall back upon. This opens up the possibility of questioning one's own assumptions. The norm of organized scepticism in science should commit it to a relentless quest for falsifying evidence of theories, but in reality this quest is constrained by conditions of Kuhnian normal science. The encounter with an indigenous cosmology has the potential to awaken organized scepticism or to release it in different directions.

This awakening potential of indigenous cosmology can be illustrated with an example from plant medicine. One standard way in which to think about plant medicines is the single active ingredient model in which the plant is screened for activity as part of a search for a single active molecule. In this model of discovery indigenous people's knowledge might be used to help identify a candidate plant, a plant that is then taken back to the laboratory for the purposes of identifying the active ingredient. Indigenous knowledge is seen as a tip, only deserving of a tipster's fee. There is, on this approach, little to be gained in terms of knowledge from developing a long-term relationship with indigenous people. They do not understand 'high' technology. Few can ascend to these commanding heights.

But the indigenous knowledge about the plant may represent a different kind of tip, the tip of an iceberg in which the specific information about the therapeutic use of the plant is but one part of much deeper knowledge of the whole plant and its uses. Traditional medicine often uses plants together when treating disease, something that poses challenges for clinical research into plant medicines.[20] The answers to treating some diseases may lie in understanding the causal efficacy of combinations of plant compounds and their pathways rather than in the pursuit of one molecule.

---

[19] The concept of de-routinization comes from Giddens. Routine features heavily in an explanation of the continuity of social reproduction. De-routinization helps to explain social change. A. Giddens, *Central Problems in Social Theory: Action, Structure and Contradiction in Social Analysis* (Berkeley: University of California Press, 1979), 219–21.

[20] R. R. Chaudhury, U. Thatte and J. Liu, 'Clinical Trial Methodology' in G. Bodeker and G. Burford (eds.), *Traditional, Complementary And Alternative Medicine: Policy and Public Health Perspectives* (London: Imperial College Press, 2007), 389, 391.

Developing testable models of synergistic causality is difficult, but then this strengthens rather than weakens the case for investigating it.[21] There can hardly be a more foundational area of inquiry than causation. There is mounting scientific evidence that studying whole plants along with their traditional methods of preparation will lead to models of synergistic causality in drug development.[22] Such models may prove to be of enormous importance for the treatment of diseases like malaria where resistance to existing drugs such as chloroquine has developed.

The principle of synergistic causality may also help to explain why some indigenous people we met were confident that a plant taken from their Country without their permission would not work therapeutically off Country. If one thinks in terms of the single active ingredient model for the treatment of disease then the search for that active ingredient while difficult is not impossible. The high-throughput screening methods discussed in chapter 6 will produce some hits. However, if the causal power of the plant as a treatment lies in a combination of agents and methods of preparation that remain undisclosed to the searchers, their task of understanding how the plant medicine works drifts into the realm of impossibility. Williams, for example, points out that if synergistic causality is at work then a bio-assay led search for the single compound 'is doomed to failure'.[23]

This knowledge, knowledge of what is hidden below the surface, has the potential to trigger de-routinization in scientists and this may trigger the kind of bold conjectures that Popper thought were crucial to scientific progress. It is worth repeating that de-routinization followed by bold conjecture is not an inevitable outcome of a partnership between indigenous people and scientists. I have merely advanced some reasons for why I believe the chances of such a sequence occurring improve.

11.4. Beyond instrumental trust

My argument so far has been that a partnership between indigenous people and scientists may trigger de-routinization that sets those scientists along the path of proposing and testing bold conjectures. However, partnerships between scientists and indigenous developmental networks

[21] On the difficulties see E. M. Williamson, 'Synergy and Other Interactions in Phytomedicines', *Phytomedicine*, 8 (2001), 401, 403.

[22] For a comprehensive assessment of the evidence in the case of plant-based treatments for malaria see M. Willcox, G. Bodeker and P. Rasoanaivo (eds.), *Traditional Medicinal Plants and Malaria* (Boca Raton, FL: CRC Press, 2005).

[23] E. M. Williamson, 'Synergy and Other Interactions in Phytomedicines', *Phytomedicine*, 8 (2001), 401, 404.

carry risks. Chapter 10 suggested that secrecy was a natural starting point of protection for indigenous developmental networks. Partnerships between indigenous developmental networks and scientists mean that indigenous people will have to reveal something of their knowledge assets. In revealing assets to outsiders indigenous groups run the risk that these outsiders will behave opportunistically with those assets.

The resolution to this problem lies in the creation of trust, but building this trust is difficult, requiring personal commitments that stretch beyond the impersonal trust that tends to characterize our relationship with organizations and institutions. Impersonal trust operates when those doing the trusting believe that those they trust are sufficiently bound by rules and accountability mechanisms to behave appropriately.[24] The prescription that indigenous developmental networks should embrace impersonal trust is not likely to gather much warm support from indigenous people. The history of colonization has given indigenous people many reasons to distrust Australian institutions. Colonial and then Australian institutions destroyed many indigenous families through the systematic removal of indigenous children from their parents. The official reports of this policy show that the removals went on for approximately one hundred years.[25]

Nevertheless the best chance that an indigenous developmental network has for achieving the goals it has for the use of its knowledge assets lies in a relationship of trust and mutual respect with a group of scientists. Trust is seen by economists as socially efficient.[26] But this instrumental version of trust is not the kind of trust that matters to indigenous people. When indigenous people enter a research relationship with scientists over plants there will be all sorts of issues that unfold over time. These may relate to restrictions about where the plants can be collected from, how the plants are to be treated, whether they can be taken off Country, under what conditions, who can handle them and what can be done to them. Writing a contract to cover every contingency that might occur over a period of years is difficult as the theorizing around the problem of incomplete contracting shows.[27]

---

[24] For an analysis of impersonal and personal trust see P. Pettit, 'Republican Theory and Political Trust' in V. Braithwaite and M. Levi (eds.), *Trust and Governance* (New York: Russell Sage Foundation, 1998), 295.

[25] See *Bringing Them Home*, ch. 2, available at www.hreoc.gov.au/social_justice/bth_report/report/index.html. See also P. Read, *The Stolen Generations: The Removal of Aboriginal Children in New South Wales 1883 to 1969* (Sydney: New South Wales Department of Aboriginal Affairs, 1981).

[26] K. Arrow, *The Limits of Organization* (New York: Norton, 1974), 23.

[27] Sampath, *Regulating Bioprospecting*, 71.

Trust and respect can resolve problems in ways that contractual rules cannot. If one group deeply trusts a second group it also believes that the trust relationship will guide the second in making decisions about problems that affect the interests of the first. There is no need to prescribe a rule for every contingency because when the contingency arises the trust relationship will drive the search for the best possible solution. Trust completes a relationship contract cannot. But this is not just any trust. The trust that allows an indigenous group to place in the hands of a scientist an ancestral being has to be something more than the trust one has in one's bank(ster) or insurance company. The trust that allows this act to take place has to be of a deep, interpersonal kind. It is not trust between an indigenous network and a research organization, but between people. The psychological literature draws a distinction between instrumental/exchange trust and social identity trust. In the latter type of trust there is a pre-existing process in which the emergence of individual identity is linked to membership of social groups. When individual identity draws on group identity, trust emerges as a by-product: 'trusting others in the group to pursue the group's interests is little different from trusting oneself to do so'.[28] Social identity trust is a group phenomenon in which trust is extended to others because it is assumed those others will act in the interests of the group with which they identify.[29] By definition, social identity trust cannot be accessed by outsiders. The group identities of scientists will be different from indigenous group identities the construction of which includes place, language, cosmologies, totems and naming systems.[30]

When an indigenous group draws a scientist into its network it creates the opportunity for a process of personal trust building to take place. The leaders of the indigenous developmental network want this relationship to move beyond the impersonal trust of market exchange and the rules of contract. They seek a relationship grounded in 'basic principles that you can adhere to no matter what' (indigenous interviewee). In this relationship the scientist comes to care and in some respects identify with the indigenous group that makes up the developmental network. Working out the factors that lead to this kind of trust is a matter of social psychological investigation, but one can be reasonably confident that time will be a crucial factor, time in which the indigenous group will test in various ways whether the scientist can be trusted with knowledge. It will most

---

[28] V. Braithwaite, 'Communal and Exchange Trust Norms: Their Value Base and Relevance to Institutional Trust' in Braithwaite and Levi (eds.), *Trust and Governance*, 52.
[29] See *ibid.*, 46.   [30] See Keen, *Aboriginal Economy*, ch. 5.

likely be a staged process of trust building in which the scientist progressively steps into a community as opposed to simply being a member of a network. I do not claim that membership of an indigenous group in the fullest sense is a prerequisite for a phenomenon akin to social identity trust to occur. Rather enough connections have to be created between the scientist and the indigenous group so that the scientist begins thinking particularistically and diffusely about the group.

Borrowing the language of Parsonian action theory, the scientist as a social actor moves away from orientations of universalism and specificity towards particularism and diffuseness.[31] The relationship between the scientist and the indigenous network ceases to be just a standard research business relationship tightly focused on the one pharmacological task (universalism and specificity). Behind the indigenous network the scientist discovers and comes to know and feel affection for a fragile human community with goals and ambitions for its children and Country (particularism replaces universalism). A process of empathetic connection with the community and its goals shapes the scientist's decisions about the directions in which to take the research. The written words of the research contract are supplemented by a broad-ranging concern for how research decisions affect the many aspects of community life (diffuseness replaces specificity). For example, more research effort might be put into examining the types of oil in the plant because a business based on extracting oils from plants is something within the capacity of the community.[32]

Under conditions of trust, the indigenous developmental network searches for an appropriate research agenda that can help it to fulfil its broader cultural goals. Their search is no longer dominated by a global pharmaceutical agenda based on the improbable success of finding a magic molecule, an agenda that relegates indigenous people to the status of knowledge tipsters, that does not draw on their expertise in an ongoing way and does not create jobs for them. It is by planning together as a high-trust network that indigenous people and scientists can find the research paths that will lead to Schumacher's goal of sustainable development based on appropriate or intermediate technologies (see chapter 9).

There are advantages for both the scientist and the indigenous developmental network once the scientist becomes the trusted insider. For the indigenous group the risk of opportunistic behaviour lessens because the scientist begins to think about the project as a group project (in Parsonian

---

[31] The discussion that follows is based on Parsons' analysis of pattern variables in T. Parsons, *The Social System* (London: Routledge & Kegan Paul, 1951).
[32] See Claudie, Semple, Smith and Simpson, 'Ancient but New', 44.

terms, collectivity-orientation replaces self-orientation). Consultation ceases to be a ritual act required by an organization's protocol and more a natural process of persons who respect each other, conferring about important decisions to be taken. For the scientist there are, of course, the inherent benefits of being trusted and of being connected to a new group.

But social identity trust may also bring instrumental benefits for scientists. Once an indigenous group begins to trust a scientist, its members may reveal more about the plant, its connections to them and Country. Not every piece of information will make sense, but just as the strokes of a brush on a canvas eventually cohere into a painting, so pieces of information revealed over time come together to reveal a system of plant knowledge. The community's insistence on working with the whole plant might eventually lead to more information about the plant being revealed and a change in the method of analysis. As we saw above, bio-assay methods have limitations when synergistic causality is at work. As the scientist's connection with the indigenous group's cosmology deepens there is always the possibility that it will spark de-routinization and bold conjecture.

11.5.   Where are the really poisonous snakes?

How many scientists will be prepared to build a long-term relationship of the kind I have described with an indigenous group? The scientist who is investigating the possibility of snake venom proteins to inhibit the spread of cancer cells arrives at a remote indigenous community and sees some old and overweight women sitting in the dust under a tree. And that is all he sees. All he wants is to find some venomous snakes to obtain the samples he needs to take back to the lab. There isn't the time to sit in the dust and talk with the women. He just wants to know where he can find the snakes, or maybe he thinks he knows that already and just wants permission to access the land. In the hurry-hurry world of grants and publication who has time to sit in the dust and talk?

The answer to my question is not that many people. During the course of the fieldwork we encountered different attitudes amongst scientists towards working with indigenous people, something hardly surprising. Some saw the indigenous control of land as a problem since it complicated getting access to land where the best specimens of a particular species might be found. For those in a hurry to push their career cart to its ultimate destination, taking the time to work with indigenous people is seen as too big a cost. Trust is found in time and those in a rush will generally pass it by. Other scientists found the on-Country encounters with indigenous people interesting. They enjoyed being showed a

Country in and out but did not find the experience scientifically useful. Yet others were prepared to invest in a process of respectful and long-term engagement with an indigenous group, but with realistic expectations about the chances of this partnership yielding discoveries that would bring benefits to both scientists and indigenous people. The odds of finding the plant that will open the way to a powerful new antibiotic, the cure for Alzheimer's disease or for cancer are slim on any objective probability assessment. And finally there were a few scientists who thought that indigenous knowledge systems contained important truths about the world. These scientists had moved from protocol-based engagement to trust-based collaboration with indigenous groups.

The observational capacities of indigenous people were seen as important by the departments of environment we interviewed. They saw huge value in indigenous people's knowledge and observations concerning various threatened species, as well as in the co-management of state parks: 'Where there is a suspicion about something that is happening on Country all of a sudden you have a few hundred extra sets of eyes and they don't miss a trick' (interview, 2010). These kinds of relationships between environmental departments and indigenous groups are grounded in practical realities of having to co-manage parks and populations of flora and fauna that are under stress. Environmental departments gain useful information for purposes such as bio-surveys and indigenous people gain useful information about things such as pollution threats to their Country. These relationships are also potentially high demand as 'staff become part of the extended indigenous family and part of the social fracas' (interview, 2010). The deeper processes of conjecture and refutation that I am suggesting are possible are more likely to spring from high-trust indigenous developmental networks than they are from co-management agreements, even though the latter are obviously important.

For the time being the creation of trust between indigenous communities and individual scientists is an ad hoc process depending on the leaders within an indigenous community seeing the need to create such trusted relationships and individual scientists being prepared to go through the testing times of such a relationship-building process. Not every scientist will be disposed to work with indigenous people and not every indigenous community will have the leadership that understands the importance of partnerships with scientists. The growth of high-trust networks to utilize indigenous knowledge will depend on a serendipitous alignment of leadership and relations of personal trust amongst individuals. It requires indigenous leadership with a clear developmental vision and scientists prepared to take a chance.

On the assumption that only a small number of scientists will be interested in becoming a part of such high-trust networks, the growth in the number of networks will be slow.

11.6.   Distrusting the state

Trusted networks represent the best organizational form of protection for the appropriate development of indigenous knowledge assets. They are also a feasible local form of organization. An indigenous group living in a remote location cannot wait for the day when states finally resolve issues arising out of the inter-relationships between indigenous knowledge and the many treaties that now affect this knowledge (see chapter 4). States may never do so or if they do it is likely to be along lines that prioritize the interests of states. Building a trusted network is a difficult but reachable goal for at least some indigenous groups. Secrecy is a powerful, natural and low-cost starting point when it comes to these networks devising strategies of protection for their assets. The other intellectual property rights that might be used by an indigenous developmental network are very much a matter of local circumstances.

Scientific membership of an indigenous developmental network is crucial. Once indigenous knowledge assets and materials enter a state's scientific and commercialization networks the chances are that it will be these networks that set the agenda around the future of these assets and materials. Indigenous people may have a contractual entitlement to a share of the commercial benefits. What they will rarely have is a voice in the network when it comes to the direction of the research and particular commercialization path. The indigenous leader David Claudie has pointed to the potential of plant-based products to foster development in indigenous homelands.[33] But this can only become the vision that drives the use of indigenous knowledge assets if there is a developmental network being led by indigenous people.

I want to conclude this final chapter by suggesting that the most rational option for indigenous developmental networks is to continue to distrust the property order of the Australian state, even if this order will in some circumstances offer a means to developmental goals.

My characterization of the relationship between indigenous people and the state is an oppositional one. The state maintains a system of property rights that permits freeriding on indigenous knowledge assets and so indigenous people have to resort to creating a networked watchman to

---

[33] *Ibid.*, 29.

guard those assets, relying first and foremost on secrecy. This is far from a picture in which indigenous people trust the state to behave appropriately with their knowledge assets. This oppositional characterization is a reasonable assumption to make. Valerie Braithwaite has demonstrated empirically, using panel data gathered on the performance of the Australian Tax Authority, that there is a pathway from institutional integrity to trust, i.e. the presence of institutional integrity increases trust amongst citizens in the institution.[34] Institutional integrity 'for a public institution means having soundness of purpose, reasonable and fair processes, competence in implementation, willingness to listen and, at all times, responsiveness and respect for others'.[35]

If we think of her conceptualization of institutional integrity as a set of tests, it is reasonably clear that the history of colonization in Australia would support the conclusion that for indigenous people the institution of colonial property lacked integrity. The colonists for the most part behaved as extractive marauders in landscapes that had been shaped by the systems of innovation of indigenous people. There has been progress in terms of the enactment of some land rights for indigenous people, but I do not believe we can jump from this progress to the conclusion that indigenous people see Australia's property institutions as having integrity and being worthy of trust.

Property rights, it is worth reminding ourselves, constitute *dominium* over others. Property rights over resources, whether those resources are tangible or intangible, allow their owners to plan towards their chosen ends. The *dominium* of property enables meaningful individual or group choices that underpin genuine autonomy. The institution of property has consistently remained a lodestar of economic, political, moral and social theory precisely because its *dominium* effects pattern so much of social and economic life. When the British Leviathan swept away indigenous peoples' property rights systems, it swept away control over the resources that supported the maintenance of their indigenous cosmologies. Indigenous people were cast back into a state that Hobbes would have recognized and described as a condition of war. It was from this Hobbesian disorder that they began the long march to recover their institutions by first recovering what they could of their property.

An attack on the property rules of one group by another aimed at extinguishing those rules is ultimately an attack on the autonomy and security of a group at the deepest level. Assuming the attacked group

---

[34] V. Braithwaite, *Defiance in Taxation and Governance: Resisting and Dismissing Authority in a Democracy* (Cheltenham: Edward Elgar, 2009), ch. 9.
[35] *Ibid.*, 191.

survives and is able to negotiate back some rights, it does not follow that the attacked group now sees the invader's property institution as a high integrity one. The effect of the attack may also be to create a low integrity institutional trap from which it is very difficult for both parties to escape. The attacked group may never come to any other view than that the invader's property institutions lack legitimacy. (Tellingly, indigenous people refer to Australia Day, which commemorates the arrival of the First Fleet, as Invasion Day.) This does not preclude the possibility of exchange trust occurring at a transactional level – if I give X, I will get Y. Exchange trust can operate even if the property institution itself is seen as low on integrity. Exchange trust in a sense is a necessary complement to using the invader's property rules for one's own gain.

The various state government departments that we interviewed understood exchange trust and how difficult even this form of trust was to obtain from indigenous groups. It required 'offering first before asking', trying to ensure that the 'same faces' dealt with indigenous groups and that one was responsive to issues that were raised by indigenous groups even if those issues were not within one's official brief.

But the presence of exchange trust does not necessarily change the core judgement by indigenous people that the invader's property institutions lack integrity because they lack legitimacy. This lack of legitimacy should be readily understandable to property theorists within the liberal tradition. Indigenous groups had collectively laboured on their respective Countries for thousands of years, Countries that were taken from them without their consent.

Let us assume for a moment that it is correct to claim that indigenous people see Australian property institutions as being of low integrity. This, as I have already mentioned, does not prevent exchange relations from arising, but it does mean that indigenous people do not place any deep trust in these institutions. For indigenous people one consequence of this situation is that it heightens the need for secrecy and networks. Faced by low-integrity property institutions the imperative is to build high-trust networks to plan for the use of their knowledge assets.

It is also not clear that the state can easily reverse the perception of its property institutions as low in integrity. Procedural justice researchers have shown that under certain conditions procedural fairness on the part of authorities increases trust and compliance by citizens in those authorities.[36] We can see this as a first-order finding in which the political or moral legitimacy of the authorities is not being questioned. In the case of

---

[36] *Ibid.*, 209.

indigenous people my argument is that the source of the low-integrity judgement about the state's property institutions does not lie in complaints about procedural unfairness that can be remedied through improvement in consultation and listening. Instead it comes from the deep emotion of having had to survive an attack on their own property institutions, the very institutions that enabled them to survive as a group. Even if the state improves its procedures for dealing with the land rights of indigenous people this improvement in procedural fairness does not erase the memory of history. The illegitimate origins of the state's property order continue to haunt it, even as it invests in greater procedural fairness. There is no neat way in which the state can ratchet up perceptions of the integrity of its institutions when the explanation for the loss of that integrity lies in a past of actions of existential threat. In the end what matters are substantive outcomes on property (Country) because property is the base from which indigenous people can rebuild their institutions. The power of respect and procedural justice to increase trust and mollify defiance is not boundless and especially so in the case of property injustices that strike at a people's way of life.

Valerie Braithwaite's analysis supports the possibility of the low integrity property trap that I am suggesting most likely characterizes relations between the state and indigenous people. Her tax data points to a group of people (the 'dismissively defiant') for whom the integrity of the tax authority does not act as a frame of reference for deciding how they will act.[37] They remain the authority's rational adversaries. There are no procedural levers that the tax office can pull to change the mindset of this group.

We should not be surprised that the settler state's destruction of indigenous people's property systems has left the state and indigenous people in a low-integrity institutional trap. Given property's existential function any other conclusion would have been surprising. Can the state escape the trap? Policy makers look for neatly packaged prescriptions that can be put onto a legislative conveyer belt and into a press release. Sometimes there are no such neat prescriptions. When the integrity problem relates to something deep in the origins of the institution, we have something much more than an institutional design problem on our hands. Design implies some sort of rule-engineering solution. But state institutions cannot slip away easily from the history of their beginnings. Memories shadow them. In Australia these memories have become part of ancestral systems. They are the memories of who gained, who lost,

---

[37] *Ibid.*, 209–10.

who died when, and how they died. They are the memories of what actually happened.

At the end of one interview with an indigenous man in which I had heard stories passed on to him by his father and uncle of water holes poisoned by white people, I asked why indigenous people ever disclosed anything of their knowledge about Country to white people. 'You can forgive, but you don't have to forget,' he replied.

References

Aaker, D. A., *Managing Brand Equity: Capitalizing on the Value of a Brand Name* (New York: Free Press, 1991).

Acemoglu, D., S. Johnson and J. A. Robinson, 'Reversal of Fortune: Geography and Institutions in the Making of the Modern World Income Distribution', *Quarterly Journal of Economics*, 117 (2002), 1235.

Adinolfi, F., M. De Rosa and F. Trabalzi, 'Dedicated and Generic Marketing Strategies: The Disconnection Between Geographical Indications and Consumer Behavior in Italy', *British Food Journal*, 113 (2011), 419.

Advisory Council on Intellectual Property, *A Review of Enforcement of Plant Breeder's Rights: Final Report* (Commonwealth of Australia, 2010), available at www.acip.gov.au.

Aiston, G., 'The Aboriginal Narcotic Pitcheri', *Oceania*, 7 (1936/37), 372.

Akerlof, G. A., 'The Market for "Lemons": Quality Uncertainty and the Market Mechanism', *Quarterly Journal of Economics*, 84 (1970), 488.

Altman, J., 'Benefit Sharing is No Solution to Development: Experiences from Mining on Aboriginal Land in Australia' in R. Wynberg, D. Schroeder, R. Chennells (eds.), *Indigenous Peoples, Consent and Benefit-Sharing: Lessons from the San-Hoodin Case* (Dordrecht: Springer, 2009), 285.

'Development Options on Aboriginal Land: Sustainable Indigenous Hybrid Economies in the Twenty-First Century' in L. Taylor, G. K. Ward, G. Henderson, R. Davis and L. A. Wallis (eds.), *The Power of Knowledge, The Resonance of Tradition* (Canberra: Aboriginal Studies Press, 2005), 34.

Altman, J., K. Jordan, S. Kerins, G. Buchanan, N. Biddle, E. J. Ens and K. May, 'Indigenous Interests in Land & Water' in *Northern Australia Land and Water Science Review* (2009).

Anaya, S. J., *Indigenous Peoples in International Law*, 2nd edn. (Oxford University Press, 2004).

Anderson, C. (ed.), *Politics of the Secret*, Oceania Monograph 45 (Sydney: University of Sydney, 1995).

Anderson, K., 'Building an Internationally Competitive Australian Olive Industry: Lessons from the Wine Industry', Discussion Paper No. 0225 (Centre for International Economic Studies, Adelaide University, 2002).

Antons, C., 'Intellectual Property Rights in Indigenous Cultural Heritage: Basic Concepts and Continuing Controversies' in C. B. Graber, K. Kuprecht and J. C. Lai (eds.), *International Trade in Indigenous Cultural Heritage: Legal and Policy Issues* (Cheltenham: Edward Elgar, 2012), 144.

'The International Debate about Traditional Knowledge, Traditional Cultural Expressions and Intellectual Property' in C. Antons (ed.), *Traditional Knowledge, Traditional Cultural Expressions and Intellectual Property Law in the Asia-Pacific Region* (Alphen aan den Rijn: Kluwer Law International, 2009), 39.

A Response to the Review of the Biodiscovery Act 2004 (Qld) (Queensland: Department of Employment, Economic Development and Innovation, 2010), http://rti.cabinet.qld.gov.au/documents/2010/Aug/.

Arrow, K., *The Limits of Organization* (New York: Norton, 1974).

Attwood, B. and A. Markus, *Thinking Black: William Cooper and the Australian Aborigines' League* (Canberra: Aborigines Studies Press, 2004).

Australian Law Reform Commission, *Essentially Yours: The Protection of Human Genetic Information in Australia* (ALRC 96, volume 2, Commonwealth of Australia, 2003).

Australian National Audit Office, *Therapeutic Goods Regulation: Complementary Medicines* (Commonwealth of Australia, 2011).

Axt, J. R., M. L. Corn, M. Lee and D. M. Ackerman, *Biotechnology, Indigenous Peoples and Intellectual Property Rights* (Congressional Research Service Report for Congress, 1993).

Bach, J., 'The Political Economy of Pearlshelling', *The Economic History Review, New Series*, 14 (1961), 105.

Bailey, J., *The White Divers Of Broome* (Sydney: Pan Macmillan, 2001).

Bandarin, F., 'International Trade in Indigenous Cultural Heritage: Comments From UNESCO in Light of its International Standard-Setting Instruments in the Field of Culture' in C. B. Graber, K. Kuprecht and J. C. Lai (eds.), *International Trade in Indigenous Cultural Heritage: Legal and Policy Issues* (Cheltenham: Edward Elgar, 2012), 306.

Bechtel, W. and A. Abrahamsen, *Connectionism and the Mind: Parallel Processing, Dynamics and Evolution in Networks*, 2nd edn. (Oxford: Blackwell, 2002).

Behrendt, L., *Aboriginal Dispute Resolution* (Sydney: Federation Press, 1995).

Bennett, W. L. and T. Lagos, 'Logo Logic: The Ups and Downs of Branded Political Communication', *Annals of the American Academy of Political and Social Science*, 611 (2007), 193.

Bird, R. B. *et al.*, 'The "Fire Stick" Hypothesis: Australian Aboriginal Foraging Strategies, Biodiversity, and Anthropogenic Fire Mosaics', *Proceedings of the National Academy of Sciences*, 105 (2008), 14796.

Birkbeck, S., *Discussion Paper on the Australian Bush Plum (Terminalia Ferdinandiana) Industry: Market Opportunities and Key Objectives in the Cosmetic Sector* (Western Australia: Department of Agriculture and Food, 2009).

Blakeney, M., 'Bioprospecting and the Protection of Traditional Knowledge of Indigenous Peoples: An Australian Perspective', *European Intellectual Property Review*, 6 (1997), 298.

'The Pacific Solution: The European Union's Intellectual Property Rights Activism in Australia's and New Zealand's Sphere of Influence' in P. Drahos and S. Frankel (eds.), *Indigenous Peoples' Innovation: Intellectual Property Pathways to Development* (Canberra: ANU E Press, 2012) 165.

Blakeney, M. and T. Coulet, 'The Protection of Geographical Indications (GI): Generating Empirical Evidence at Country and Product Level to Support African ACP Country Engagement in the Doha Round Negotiations' (2011), 11, available at www.acp.int.

Blyton, G., 'Healthier Times?: Revisiting Indigenous Australian Health History', *Health and History*, 11 (2009), 116.

Bodley, J. H., *Cultural Anthropology: Tribes, States, and the Global System* (Plymouth: AltaMira Press, 2011).

Boldrin, M. and D. K. Levine, *Against Intellectual Monopoly* (New York, Cambridge University Press, 2008).

Bowery, K., 'Indigenous Culture, Knowledge and Intellectual Property: The Need for a New Category of Rights?' in K. Bowery, M. Handler and D. Nicol (eds.), *Emerging Challenges in Intellectual Property* (Melbourne: Oxford University Press, 2011), 46.

Bowman, D., 'Bushfires: a Darwinian Perspective' in G. Cary, D. Lindenmayer and S. Dovers (eds.), *Australia Burning: Fire Ecology, Policy and Management Issues* (Victoria: CSIRO Publishing, 2003), 3.

Boyd, E., M. Gutierrez and M. Chang, 'Small-Scale Forest Carbon Projects: Adapting CDM to Low-Income Communities', *Global Environmental Change*, 17 (2007), 250.

Bradley, J. H. and A. Kearney, 'Manankurra: What's in a Name? Placenames and Emotional Geographies' in H. Koch and L. Hercus (eds.), *Aboriginal Placenames: Naming and Re-Naming The Australian Landscape* (Canberra: ANU E Press, 2009), 463.

Braithwaite, J., *Regulatory Capitalism: How It Works, Ideas For Making It Work Better* (Cheltenham: Edward Elgar, 2008).
    'Responsive Regulation and Developing Economies', *World Development*, 34 (2006), 884.
    'Rules and Principles: A Theory of Legal Certainty', *Australian Journal of Legal Philosophy*, 27 (2002), 47.

Braithwaite, J. and P. Drahos, *Global Business Regulation* (Cambridge University Press, 2000).

Braithwaite, J., T. Makkai and V. Braithwaite, *Regulating Aged Care: Ritualism and the New Pyramid* (Cheltenham: Edward Elgar, 2007).

Braithwaite, V., 'Communal and Exchange Trust Norms: Their Value Base and Relevance to Institutional Trust' in V. Braithwaite and M. Levi (eds.), *Trust and Governance* (New York: Russell Sage Foundation, 1998), 46.
    Defiance in Taxation and Governance: Resisting and Dismissing Authority in a Democracy (Cheltenham: Edward Elgar, 2009).

Bramley, C., E. Bienabe and J. Kirsten, 'The Economics of Geographical Indications: Towards a Conceptual Framework for Geographical Indication Research in Developing Countries' in *The Economics of Intellectual Property: Suggestions for Further Research in Developing Countries and Countries with Economies in Transition* (Geneva: WIPO, 2009), 109.

Brennan, F., *Land Rights Queensland Style: the Struggle for Aboriginal Self-management* (University of Queensland Press, 1992).

Brennan, G. and P. Pettit, 'The Hidden Economy of Esteem', *Economics and Philosophy*, 16 (2000), 77.

Brenner, J. G., *The Emperors of Chocolate: Inside the Secret World of Hershey and Mars* (New York: Random House, 1999).

Bringing Them Home: Report of the National Inquiry into the Separation of Aboriginal and Torres Strait Islander Children from Their Families (Australian Human Rights Commission, 1997), available at www.hreoc.gov.au/social_justice/bth_report/report/index.html.

Brown, C., T. Nardin and N. Rengger (eds.), *International Relations in Political Thought: Texts from the Ancient Greeks to the First World War* (Cambridge University Press, 2002).

Brown, M. F., *Who Owns Native Culture?* (Cambridge, MA: Harvard University Press, 2003).

Brush, S. B., 'Indigenous Knowledge of Biological Resources and Intellectual Property Rights: The Role of Anthropology', *American Anthropologist*, 95 (1993), 653.

Burton, G., 'Australian ABS Law and Administration – A Model Law and Approach?' in E. C. Kamau and G. Winter (eds.), *Genetic Resources, Traditional Knowledge and the Law: Solutions for Access and Benefit-Sharing* (London: Earthscan, 2009), 271.

Butlin, N., *Our Original Aggression: Aboriginal Populations of Southeastern Australia 1788–1850* (Sydney: George Allen & Unwin, 1983).

Campbell, J., *Invisible Invaders: Smallpox and Other Diseases in Aboriginal Australia 1780–1880* (Victoria: Melbourne University Press, 2002).

Campbell, K., *Metaphysics: An Introduction* (Encino, CA: Dickenson Publishing Company, 1976).

Caring For Our Country: Report on the Review of the Caring for our Country Initiative (Canberra: Commonwealth of Australia, 2012).

Charlesworth, M., 'Introduction' in M. Charlesworth, F. Dussart and H. Morphy (eds.), *Aboriginal Religions in Australia: An Anthology of Recent Writings* (Aldershot: Ashgate, 2005), 1.

Chaudhury, R. R., U. Thatte and J. Liu, 'Clinical Trial Methodology' in G. Bodeker and G. Burford (eds.), *Traditional, Complementary and Alternative Medicine: Policy and Public Health Perspectives* (London: Imperial College Press, 2007), 389.

Chon, M., 'Marks of Rectitude', *Fordham Law Review*, 77 (2009), 2311.

Clarke, P. A., *Aboriginal People and Their Plants* (Dural, NSW: Rosenberg Publishing, 2007).

Claudie, D. J., S. J. Semple, N. M. Smith and B. S. Simpson, 'Ancient but New: Developing Locally Driven Enterprises Based on Traditional Medicines in Kuuku I'yu Northern Kaanju Homelands, Cape York, Queensland, Australia' in P. Drahos and S. Frankel (eds.), *Indigenous Peoples' Innovation: Intellectual Property Pathways to Development* (Canberra: ANU E Press, 2012), 29.

Climate, Community & Biodiversity Project Design Standards, 2nd edn. (Arlington, VA, CCBA, December, 2008).

Cooke, P. M., 'Buffalo and Tin, Baki and Jesus' in J. Russell-Smith, P. Whitehead and P. Cooke (eds.), *Culture, Ecology and Economy of Fire Management in North Australian Savannas: Rekindling the Wurrk Tradition* (Victoria: CSIRO Publishing, 2009), 69.

Coombe, R. J., with J. F. Turcotte, 'Indigenous Cultural Heritage in Development and Trade: Perspectives from the Dynamics of Cultural Heritage Law and Policy' in C. B. Graber, K. Kuprecht and J. C. Lai (eds.), *International Trade in Indigenous Cultural Heritage: Legal and Policy Issues* (Cheltenham: Edward Elgar, 2012), 272.

Cooter, R. and T. Ulen, *Law and Economics*, 3rd edn. (Reading, MA, Addison Wesley Longman, 2000).

Cotterrell, R., *The Politics of Jurisprudence: A Critical Introduction to Legal Philosophy* (London and Edinburgh: Butterworths, 1989).

Council of Scientific and Industrial Research, *Annual Report 2010–11*, New Delhi, 165, www.csir.res.in/External/heads/aboutcsir/Annual_report/AnnualReport_1011.pdf.

Coyle, T., 'The Great Indigenous Rip-off', 11 June 2003, available at www.greatreporter.com/content/great-indigenous-rip.

Crandall, R. C., *Inuit Art: A History* (North Carolina: McFarland & Company, 2000).

Cunningham, A. B., S. Garnett and J. Gorman, 'Policy Lessons From Practice: Australian Bush Products for Commercial Markets', *GeoJournal*, 74 (2009), 429.

Cunningham, A. B., S. Garnett, J. Gorman, K. Courtenay and D. Boehme, 'Eco-Enterprises and *Terminalia ferdinandiana*: "Best Laid Plans" and Australian Policy Lessons', *Economic Botany*, 63 (2009), 16.

De Chernatony, L., M. McDonald and E. Wallace, *Creating Powerful Brands*, 4th edn. (Oxford: Butterworth-Heinemann, 2011).

Denham, T., R. Fullagar and L. Head, 'Plant Exploitation on Sahul: From Colonisation to the Emergence of Regional Specialisation During the Holocene', *Quaternary International*, 202 (2009), 29.

Douglass, L. L., H. P. Possingham, J. Carwardine, C. J. Klein, S. H. Roxburgh, J. Russell-Smith and K. A. Wilson, 'The Effect of Carbon Credits on Savanna Land Management and Priorities for Biodiversity Conservation', *PLoS ONE* 6(9) (2011), e23843. doi:10.1371/journal.pone.0023843.

Drahos, P., 'A Networked Responsive Regulatory Approach to Protecting Traditional Knowledge' in D. Gervais (ed.), *Intellectual Property, Trade and Development: Strategies to Optimize Economic Development in a TRIPS Plus Era* (Oxford University Press, 2007), 385.

A Philosophy of Intellectual Property (Aldershot: Dartmouth, 1996).

Drahos, P. with J. Braithwaite, *Information Feudalism: Who Owns the Knowledge Economy?* (London: Earthscan, 2002).

Drahos, P. and S. Parker, 'Rule Following, Rule Scepticism and Indeterminacy in Law: A Conventional Account', *Ratio Juris*, 5 (1992), 109.

Dussart, F., *The Politics of Ritual in an Aboriginal Settlement* (Washington and London: Smithsonian Institution Press, 2000).

Dutfield, G., 'Legal and Economic Aspects of Traditional Knowledge' in K. E. Maskus and J. H. Reichman (eds.), *International Public Goods and Transfer of Technology Under a Globalized Intellectual Property Regime* (Cambridge University Press, 2005), 495.

Eades, D., '*I Don't Think It's an Answer to the Question*: Silencing Aboriginal Witnesses in Court', *Language in Society*, 29 (2000), 161.

Edelman, M., *The Symbolic Uses of Politics* (Urbana: University of Illinois, 1964).

Edmond, G., 'Disorder with Law: Determining the Geographical Indication for the Coonawarra Wine Region', *Adelaide Law Review*, 27 (2006), 59.

Edwards, W. H., *An Introduction to Aboriginal Societies*, 2nd edn. (Victoria: Thomson Social Science Press, 2008).

Ehrlich, E., *Fundamental Principles of the Sociology of Law* (1936), W. L. Moll, trans. (New Brunswick: Transaction, 2002).

Elkin, A. P., *Aboriginal Men of Higher Degree*, 2nd edn. (University of Queensland Press, 1977).

Ellingson, T., *The Myth of the Noble Savage* (Berkley and Los Angeles: University of California Press, 2001).

Epstein, R. A., *Simple Rules for a Complex World* (Cambridge, MA: Harvard University Press, 1995).

Evans, G. E., 'The Comparative Advantages of Geographical Indications and Community Trade Marks for the Marketing of Agricultural Products in the European Union', *International Review of Intellectual Property and Competition Law*, 41 (2010), 645.

Federal Trade Commission, '*Pay-for-delay: How drug company pay-offs cost consumers billions*', An FTC Staff Study (Washington, DC, January 2010).

Feher, M. and J. M. Schmidt, 'Property Distribution Differences between Drugs, Natural Products, and Molecules from Combinatorial Chemistry', *Journal of Chemical Information Computing Science*, 43 (2003), 218.

Fine, B., *Marx's Capital*, 2nd edn. (Houndmills: Macmillan, 1984).

Forsyth, M., 'Do You Want it Gift Wrapped?: Protecting Traditional Knowledge in the Pacific Island Countries' in P. Drahos and S. Frankel (eds.), *Indigenous Peoples' Innovation: Intellectual Property Pathways to Development* (Canberra: ANU E Press, 2012), 189.

  'Lifting the Lid on "The Community": Who Has the Right to Control Access to Traditional Knowledge and Expressions of Culture', *International Journal of Cultural Property*, 19 (2012), 1.

Foster, M., *Emerging Animal and Plant Industries – Their Value to Australia* (Canberra: Rural Industries Research and Development Corporation, 2009).

Frankel, S., 'A New Zealand Perspective on the Protection of Mātauranga Māori (Traditional Knowledge)' in C. B. Graber, K. Kuprecht and J. C. Lai (eds.), *International Trade in Indigenous Cultural Heritage: Legal and Policy Issues* (Cheltenham: Edward Elgar, 2012), 439.

  'The Mismatch of Geographical Indications and Innovative Traditional Knowledge', *Prometheus*, 29 (2011), 253.

  'Trademarks and Traditional Knowledge and Cultural Intellectual Property Rights' in G. B. Dinwoodie and M. D. Janis (eds.), *Trademark Law and Theory: A Handbook of Contemporary Research* (Cheltenham: Edward Elgar, 2008), 433.

Frankel, S. and M. Richardson, 'Cultural Property and "the Public Domain": Case Studies from New Zealand and Australia' in C. Antons (ed.), *Traditional Knowledge, Traditional Cultural Expressions and Intellectual Property Law in the Asia-Pacific Region* (Alphen aan den Rijn: Kluwer Law International, 2009), 275.

Fransen, L., 'Why Do Private Governance Organizations Not Converge? A Political-Institutional Analysis of Transnational Labor Standards Regulation', *Governance: An International Journal of Policy, Administration, and Institutions*, 24 (2011), 359.

Fromer, J. C., 'Trade Secrecy in Willy Wonka's Chocolate Factory' in R. C. Dreyfuss and K. J. Standburg (eds.), *The Law and Theory of Trade Secrecy: A Handbook of Contemporary Research* (Cheltenham: Edward Elgar, 2011), 3.

Fuller, S., *Kuhn vs. Popper: The Struggle for the Soul of Science* (New York: Columbia University Press, 2004).

Garde, M. in collaboration with B. Lofty Nadjamerrek, M. Kolkkiwarra, J. Kalarriya, J. Djandjomer, B. Birriyabirriya, R. Bilindja, M. Kubarkku and P. Bliss, 'The Language of Fire: Seasonality, Resources and Landscape Burning on the Arnhem Land Plateau' in J. Russell-Smith, P. Whitehead and P. Cooke (eds.), *Culture, Ecology and Economy of Fire Management in North Australian Savannas: Rekindling the Wurrk Tradition* (Victoria: CSIRO Publishing, 2009), 85.

Gervais, D., 'Traditional Innovation and the Ongoing Debate on the Protection of Geographical Indications' in P. Drahos and S. Frankel (eds.), *Indigenous Peoples' Innovation: Intellectual Property Pathways to Development* (Canberra: ANU E Press, 2012), 121.

Giddens, A., *Central Problems in Social Theory: Action, Structure and Contradiction in Social Analysis* (Berkeley: University of California Press, 1979).

Goldberg, C. E., 'A United States Perspective on the Protection of Indigenous Cultural Heritage' in C. B. Graber, K. Kuprecht and J. C. Lai (eds.), *International Trade in Indigenous Cultural Heritage: Legal and Policy Issues* (Cheltenham: Edward Elgar, 2012), 331.

Gollin, M. A., *Driving Innovation: Intellectual Property Strategies for a Dynamic World* (Cambridge University Press, 2008).

Goodall, H., *Invasion to Embassy: Land in Aboriginal Politics in New South Wales, 1770–1972* (New South Wales: Allen & Unwin, 1996).

Gorman, J. and S. Vemuri, 'Social Implications of Bridging the Gap Through "Caring for Country" in Remote Indigenous Communities of the Northern Territory, Australia', *The Rangeland Journal*, 34 (2012), 63.

Graburn, N. H. H. 'Inuit Art and Canadian Nationalism: Why Eskimos? Why Canada?' *Inuit Art Quarterly*, 1(3) (1986), 5, 6.

Greenhalgh, C. and M. Rogers, *Innovation, Intellectual Property, and Economic Growth* (Princeton and Oxford: Princeton University Press, 2010).

Greiner, R., I. Gordon and C. Cocklin, 'Ecosystem Services From Tropical Savannas: Economic Opportunities Through Payments for Environmental Services', *Rangeland Journal*, 31 (2009), 51.

Gupta, A. K., P. E. Tesluk and M. S. Taylor, 'Innovation At and Across Multiple Levels of Analysis', *Organization Science*, 18 (2007), 885.

Hall, P. A. and D. Soskice (eds.), *Varieties of Capitalism: The Institutional Foundations of Comparative Advantage* (Oxford University Press, 2001).

Hanley, N. and E. B. Barbier, *Pricing Nature: Cost-Benefit Analysis and Environmental Policy* (Cheltenham: Edward Elgar, 2009).

Harvey, B. and S. Nish, 'Rio Tinto and Indigenous Community Agreement Making in Australia', *Journal of Energy and Natural Resource Law*, 23 (2005), 499.

Harvey, K. J., V. S. Korczak, L. J. Marron and D. B. Newgreen, 'Commercialism, Choice and Consumer Protection: Regulation of Complementary Medicines in Australia', *Medical Journal of Australia*, 188 (2008), 21.

Haynes, C., 'Realities, Simulacra and the Appropriation of Aboriginality in Kakadu's Tourism' in I. Keen (ed.), *Indigenous Participation in Australian Economies: Historical and Anthropological Perspectives* (Canberra: ANU E Press, 2010), 165.

Hilty, R., 'Rationales for the Legal Protection of Intangible Goods and Cultural Heritage', Max Planck Institute for Intellectual Property, Competition & Tax Law Research Paper No. 09–10 (2 August 2009), available at SSRN: http://ssrn.com/abstract=1470602 or http://dx.doi.org/10.2139/ssrn.1470602.

Hiscock, P., *Archaeology of Ancient Australia* (London and New York: Routledge, 2008).

Hohfeld, W. N., 'Some Fundamental Legal Conceptions as Applied in Judicial Reasoning', *Yale Law Journal*, 23 (1913), 16.

Holmes, J., 'Diversity and Change in Australia's Rangelands: A Post-Productivist Transition with a Difference?', *Transactions of the Institute of British Geographers, New Series*, 27 (2002), 362.

Hollowell-Zimmer, J., 'Marked by the Silver Hand: Intellectual Property Protection and the Market in Alaska Native Arts and Crafts' in M. Riley (ed.), *Indigenous Intellectual Property Rights: Legal Obstacles and Innovative Solutions* (Walnut Creek, CA: AltaMira Press, 2004), 54.

Howitt, A. W., *The Native Tribes of South East Australia* (London: Macmillan and Co., 1904).

Hubicki, S. and J. Sanderson, *Recent Trends in the Patenting of Plants and Animals* (Canberra: Rural Industries Research and Development Corporation, 2009).

Hutchens, A., *Changing Big Business: The Globalisation of the Fair Trade Movement* (Cheltenham: Edward Elgar, 2009).

Indigenous Art – Securing the Future: Australia's Indigenous Visual Arts and Craft Sector, Senate, Standing Committee on Environment, Communications, Information Technology and the Arts (Commonwealth of Australia, 2007).

Indigenous Small Business Owners in Australia (Canberra: Australian Taxation Office, 2009), 5 available at www.ato.gov.au/content/downloads/BUS00220454n72991.pdf.

Industry Commission, *Minerals Processing in Australia*, vol. 1, Report no. 7 (Canberra: Australian Government Publishing Service, 1991).

The Pharmaceutical Industry, vol. 1, Report no. 51 (Melbourne: Australian Government Publishing Service, 1996).

Janis, M. D. and S. Smith, 'Technological Change and the Design of Plant Variety Protection Regimes', *Chicago-Kent Law Review*, 82 (2007), 1557.

Janke, T., *Minding Culture: Case Studies on Intellectual Property and Traditional Cultural Expressions* (Geneva: World Intellectual Property Organization, 2003).

Our Culture: Our Future – Report On Australian Indigenous Cultural And Intellectual Property Rights (Sydney: Michael Frankel & Company and Terri Janke, 1998).

Janke, T. and R. Quiggin, *Indigenous Cultural and Intellectual Property and Customary Law, Background paper* 12 (Perth: Law Reform Commission of Western Australia, 2005).

Jones, R., 'Fire-Stick Farming', *Australian Natural History*, 16 (1969), 224.

Kalberg, S., *Max Weber's Comparative-Historical Sociology Today* (Aldershot: Ashgate, 2012).

Kavelin, C. J., 'The Protection of Indigenous Medical Knowledge: Towards the Transformation of Law to Engage Indigenous Spiritual Concerns', unpublished Ph.D. thesis, Macquarie University (2007).

Keal, P., '"Just Backward Children": International Law and the Conquest of Non-European Peoples', *Australian Journal of International Affairs*, 49 (1995), 191.

Keen, I., *Aboriginal Economy and Society: Australia at the Threshold of Colonisation* (South Melbourne, Vic.: Oxford University Press, 2004).

'Ancestors, Magic and Exchange in Yolngu Doctrines: Extensions of the Person in Time and Space', *Journal of the Royal Anthropological Institute*, 12 (2006), 515.

Knowledge and Secrecy in an Aboriginal Religion (Oxford: Clarendon Press, 1994).

'The Interpretation of Aboriginal "Property" on the Australian Colonial Frontier' in I. Keen (ed.), *Indigenous Participation in Australian Economies: Historical and Anthropological Perspectives* (Canberra: ANU E Press, 2010), 41.

Keohane, R. O., *After Hegemony: Cooperation and Discord in the World Political Economy* (Princeton University Press, 1984).

Kingsbury, B., '"Indigenous Peoples" in International Law: A Constructivist Approach to the Asian Controversy', *American Journal of International Law*, 92 (1998), 414.

Knack, S. and P. Keefer, 'Does Social Capital Have An Economic Payoff? A Cross-Country Investigation', *Quarterly Journal of Economics*, 112 (1997), 1251.

Knudsen, E. I., J. J. Heckman, J. L. Cameron and J. P. Shonkoff, 'Economic, Neurobiological, and Behavioral Perspectives on Building America's Future Workforce', *Proceedings of the National Academy of Sciences*, 103 (2006), 10155.

Koch, H. and L. Hercus (eds.), *Aboriginal Placenames: Naming and Re-Naming The Australian Landscape* (Canberra: ANU E Press, 2009).

Kolig, E., 'Darrugu – Secret Objects in a Changing World' in C. Anderson (ed.), *Politics of the Secret*, Oceania Monograph 45 (University of Sydney, 1995), 27.

Kripke, S. A., *Wittgenstein on Rules and Private Language* (Oxford: Basil Blackwell, 1982).

Laird, S., C. Monagle and S. Johnston, *Queensland Biodiversity Collaboration, The Griffith University Partnership for National Product Discovery: An Access & Benefit Sharing Case Study* (Japan: United Nations University Institute of Advanced Studies, 2008).

Langton, M., '"The Fire at the Centre of Each Family": Aboriginal Traditional Fire Regimes and the Challenges for Reproducing Ancient Fire

Management in the Protected Areas of northern Australia' in *Fire, The Australian Experience, Proceedings of the 1999 Seminar* (National Academies Forum, 2000), 3.

Langton, M., O. Mazel and L. Palmer, 'The "Spirit" of the Thing: The Boundaries of Aboriginal Economic Relations at Australian Common Law', *Australian Journal of Anthropology*, 17 (2006), 307.

Le Mare, A., 'The Impact of Fair Trade on Social and Economic Development: A Review of the Literature', *Geography Compass*, 2 (2008), 1922.

Levi-Faur, D. and J. Jordana (eds.), 'The Rise of Regulatory Capitalism: The Global Diffusion of a New Order', *The Annals*, 598 (2005), 6–217.

Levi-Strauss, C., *The Savage Mind* (University of Chicago Press, 1967).

Liddy, L. G. *et al.*, *Wagiman Plants and Animals: Aboriginal Knowledge of Flora and Fauna From the Mid Daly River Area, Northern Australia* (Darwin: Department of Natural Resources, Environment and the Arts, NT Government and the Diwurruwurru-jaru Aboriginal Corporation, 2006).

Locke, J., *The Second Treatise of Government (1690)* (Indianapolis: Bobbs-Merrill Educational Publishing, 1952).

Macmillan, F., 'International Economic Law and Public International Law: Strangers in the Night', *International Trade Law and Regulation*, 10 (2004), 115.

Mandeville, T., *Understanding Novelty: Information, Technological Change, and the Patent System* (Norwood, NJ: Ablex Publishing Corporation, 1996).

Marshall, P. (ed.), *Raparapa Kularr Martuwarra; Stories from the Fitzroy Drovers* (Broome WA: Magabala Books, 1993).

Maskus, K. E. and J. H. Reichman, 'The Globalization of Private Knowledge Goods and the Privatization of Global Public Goods', in K. E. Maskus and J. H. Reichman (eds.), *International Public Goods and Transfer of Technology Under a Globalized Intellectual Property Regime* (Cambridge University Press, 2005), 3.

Mauss, M., *The Gift: Forms and Functions of Exchange in Archaic Societies*, I. Gunnison tr. (London: Cohen and West, 1970).

McConvell, P. and N. Thieberger, *State of Indigenous Languages in Australia – 2001* (Australia, Canberra, State of the Environment Second Technical Paper Series (Natural and cultural Heritage), Department of the Environment and Heritage, 2001), 16, available at www.ea.gov.au/soe/techpapers/index.html.

McDonnell, S., *Indigenous Women Entrepreneurs Within Torres Strait* (Discussion Paper No. 188, Centre for Aboriginal Economic Policy Research, ANU, 1999) available at http://caepr.anu.edu.au/sites/default/files/Publications/DP/1999_DP188.pdf.

McFarlane, P., *Brotherhood to Nationhood: George Manuel and the Making of the Modern Indian Movement* (Toronto: Between the Lines, 1993).

McKnight, D., *Going the Whiteman's Way: Kinship and Marriage Among Australian Aborigines* (Aldershot: Ashgate, 2004).

People, Countries, and the Rainbow Serpent: Systems of Classification Among the Lardil of Mornington Island (New York: Oxford University Press, 1999).

McMichael, P., *Settlers and the Agrarian Question: Foundations of Capitalism in Colonial Australia* (Cambridge University Press, 1984).

Memmott, P. and S. McDougall, *Holding Title and Managing Land in Cape York: Indigenous Land Management and Native Title* (Perth, WA: National Native Title Tribunal, 2003).

Mier, G., *Cultivation and Sustainable Wild Harvest of Bushfoods by Aboriginal Communities in Central Australia* (Canberra: Rural Industries Research and Development Corporation, 2003).

Millennium Ecosystem Assessment, *Ecosystems and Human Well-being: Synthesis* (Washington, DC: Island Press, 2005).

Mills, C., A. R. Carroll and R. J. Quinn, 'Acutangulosides A-F, Monodesmosidic Saponins from the Bark of *Barringtonia acutangula*', *Journal of Natural Products*, 68 (2005), 311.

Mitchell, T., *Journal of an Expedition into the Interior of Tropical Australia* (1848), Ch. X, available as an e-book http://gutenberg.net.au/pages/mitchell.html.

Mokyr, J., *The Gifts of Athena: Historical Origins of the Knowledge Economy* (Princeton and Oxford: Princeton University Press, 2002).

Mooney, P. R., 'The Parts of Life: Agricultural Biodiversity, Indigenous Knowledge, and the Role of the Third System', *Development Dialogue* (1–2) 1996, 7.

Morphy, H., *Ancestral Connections: Art and an Aboriginal System of Knowledge* (Chicago and London: University of Chicago Press, 1991).

'Myth, Totemism and the Creation of Clans', *Oceania*, 60 (1990), 312.

Mulvaney, J., '"Difficult to Found an Opinion": 1788 Aboriginal Population Estimates' in G. Briscoe and L. Smith (eds.), *The Aboriginal Population Revisited: 70,000 years to the Present*, Aboriginal History Monograph 10 (Canberra: Aboriginal History Inc., 2002), 1.

National Food Plan: Green Paper 2012 (Canberra: Department of Agriculture, Fisheries and Forestry, 2012).

Nationally consistent approach for access to and the utilisation of Australia's native genetic and biochemical resources, endorsed by the Natural Resource Management Ministerial Council on 11 October 2002, www.environment. gov.au.

National Native Title Tribunal, *Annual Report, 2011–2012*, available at www. nntt.gov.au/.

Nelson, R. R., 'National Innovation Systems: A Retrospective on a Study', *Industrial and Corporate Change*, 1 (1992), 347.

Nelson, V. and B. Pound, 'The Last Ten Years: A Comprehensive Review of the Literature on the Impact of Fair Trade' (2009) available at www.fairtrade. net/fileadmin/user_upload/content/2009/about_us/ 2010_03_NRI_Full_Literature_Review.pdf.

Nettlebeck, A. and R. Foster, *In the Name of the Law: William Willshire and the Policing of the Australian Frontier* (South Australia: Wakefield Press, 2007).

Newman, D. J. and G. M. Cragg, 'Natural Products as Sources of New Drugs Over the Last 25 Years', *Journal of Natural Products*, 70 (2007), 461.

Nicol, D. and J. Nielsen, 'Patents and Medical Biotechnology: An Empirical Analysis of Issues Facing The Australian Industry' (Centre for Law and Genetics, Occasional Paper No. 6, 2003), 208–9. Available at www.ipria. org/publications/reports/BiotechReportFinal.pdf.

Nonet, P. and P. Selznick, *Law and Society in Transition: Toward Responsive Law* (New York: Harper & Row, 1978).

North Australian Indigenous Experts Forum on Sustainable Economic Development, 'Towards resilient communities through reliable prosperity', First Forum Report, Mary River Park, Northern Territory, 19–21 June 2012 available at www.nailsma.org.au/hub/resources/publication/towards-resilient-communities-through-reliable-prosperity-first-indigenous.

North, D. C., *Institutions, Institutional Change and Economic Performance* (Cambridge University Press, 1990).

North, D. C. and R. T. Thomas, *The Rise of the Western World* (London: Cambridge University Press, 1973).

Note by Secretariat, 'The Relationship Between the TRIPS Agreement And The Convention on Biological Diversity', IP/C/W/368/Rev.1, 8 February 2006.

Oguamanam, C., *International Law and Indigenous Knowledge: Intellectual Property, Plant Biodiversity, and Traditional Medicine* (Toronto, Buffalo, London: University of Toronto Press, 2006).

Orestano, F., 'Dickens on the Indians' in C. F. Feest (ed.), *Indians and Europe: An Interdisciplinary Collection of Essays* (Aachen: Edition Herodot and Rader Verlag, 1987), 277.

Padel, F. and S. Das, *Out of This Earth: East India Adivasis and the Aluminium Cartel* (New Delhi: Orient Black Swan, 2010).

Paisley, F., 'Australian Aboriginal Activism in Interwar Britain and Europe: Anthony Martin Fernando', *History Compass*, 7 (2009), 701.

Palmer, K., 'Religious Knowledge and the Politics of Continuity and Change' in C. Anderson (ed.), *Politics of the Secret*, Oceania Monograph 45 (Sydney: University of Sydney, 1995), 15.

Panda, M., 'Did Orissa Benefit from the Reforms?' in R. K. Panda (ed.), *Reviving Orissa Economy: Opportunities and Areas of Action* (New Delhi: S. B. Nangia, A. P. H. Publications Corporation, 2004), 167.

Parsons, T., *The Social System* (London: Routledge & Kegan Paul, 1951).

Paterson, A., 'Early Pastoral Landscapes and Cultural Contact in Central Australia', *Historical Archaeology*, 39 (2005), 28.

Persoon, G. A., '"Being Indigenous" in Indonesia and the Philippines' in C. Antons (ed.), *Traditional Knowledge, Traditional Cultural Expressions and Intellectual Property Law in the Asia-Pacific Region* (Alphen aan den Rijn: Kluwer Law International, 2009), 195.

Pettit, P., 'Republican Theory and Political Trust' in V. Braithwaite and M. Levi (eds.), *Trust and Governance* (New York: Russell Sage Foundation, 1998), 295.

   Republicanism: A Theory of Freedom and Government (Oxford: Clarendon Press, 1997).

   'The Reality of Rule-Following', *Mind*, 99 (1990), 433.

Polanyi, M., *Personal Knowledge: Towards a Post-Critical Philosophy* (London: Routledge & Kegan Paul, 1958).

Pollack, D. P., 'A Quantitative Assessment of Indigenous Landholdings in 2000', Discussion Paper 221/2001, Centre for Aboriginal Economic Policy Research, available at http://caepr.anu.edu.au/sites/default/files/Publications/DP/2001_DP221.pdf.

Popper, K. R., *The World Of Parmenides: Essays on the Presocratic Enlightenment* (London and New York: Routledge, 1998).

Prime Minister's Science Engineering and Innovation Council, *Biodiscovery* (2005) available at www.innovation.gov.au/Science/PMSEIC/Documents/Biodiscovery.pdf.

Principe, P. P., 'Valuing the Biodiversity of Medicinal Plants' in O. Akerele, V. Heywood and H. Synge (eds.), *The Conservation of Medicinal Plants* (Cambridge University Press, 1991), 79.

Productivity Commission, *Public Support for Science and Innovation* (Canberra: Commonwealth of Australia, 2007).

Pupchek, L. S., 'True North: Inuit Art and the Canadian Imagination', *American Review of Canadian Studies*, 31 (2001), 191.

Pyne, S. J., 'Firestick History', *Journal of American History*, 76 (1990), 1132.

Queensland Biotechnology Code of Ethics: Update of the Code of Ethical practice for Biotechnology in Queensland (2006), www.science.qld.gov.au/dsdweb/v4/apps/web/content.cfm?id=16795.

Queensland Department of State Development and Innovation in conjunction with PricewaterhouseCoopers, *Queensland Pharmaceutical Industry Profile: Springboard for Opportunities* (2004).

Quinn, R. J., P. A. Leone, G. Guymeyer and J. N. A. Hooper, 'Australian Biodiversity Via its Plants and Marine Organisms. A High-throughput Screening Approach to Drug Discovery', *Pure Applied Chemistry*, 74 (2002), 519.

Rausser, G. C. and A. A. Small, 'Valuing Research Leads: Bioprospecting and the Conservation of Genetic Resources', *Journal of Political Economy*, 108 (2000), 173.

Read, P., *The Stolen Generations: The Removal of Aboriginal Children in New South Wales 1883 to 1969* (Sydney: New South Wales Department of Aboriginal Affairs, 1981).

Regan, D. and G. Tunny, 'Venture Capital in Australia' (unpublished, 2008), 1, 6, available at http://cprs.treasury.gov.au/documents/1352/PDF/combined.pdf#page=5.

Reid, W. V., F. Berkes, T. J. Wilbanks and D. Capistrano, 'Introduction' in W. V. Reid, F. Berkes, T. Wilbanks and D. Capistrano (eds.), *Bridging Scales and Knowledge Systems: Concepts and Applications in Ecosystem Assessment* (Washington DC: Island Press, 2006), 1.

Rennell, L., 'The Kimberley Division of Western Australia', *The Geographical Journal*, 119 (1953), 306.

Report of the Committee set up to examine the representation alleging non-observance by Ecuador of the Indigenous and Tribal Peoples Convention, 1989 (No. 169), made under article 24 of the ILO Constitution by the Confederación Ecuatoriana de Organizaciones Sindicales Libres (CEOSL) (2001) available at www.ilo.org/dyn/normlex/en/f?p=1000:50012:0::NO::P50012_COMPLAINT_PROCEDURE_ID,P50012_LANG_CODE:2507223,en.

Report of the Four Member Committee for Investigation into the Proposals Submitted by the Orissa Mining Company for Bauxite Mining in Niyamgiri, submitted to the Ministry of Environment and Forests, Government of India

(New Delhi, 16 August 2010), 34, available at http://moef.nic.in/downloads/public-information/Saxena_Vedanta.pdf.

Reynolds, H. (ed.), *Aborigines and Settlers: the Australian Experience 1788–1939* (New South Wales and Victoria: Cassell Australia, 1972).

The Other Side of the Frontier (North Queensland: James Cook University, 1981).

Richards, J., 'The Native Police of Queensland', *History Compass*, 6 (2008), 1024.

Ricketson, S., *The Law of Intellectual Property* (Sydney: Law Book Company, 1984).

Rimmer, M., 'Australian Icons: Authenticity Marks And Identity Politics', *Indigenous Law Journal*, 3 (2004), 139.

Risch, M., 'Trade Secret Law and Information Development Incentives' in R. C. Dreyfuss and K. J. Standburg (eds.), *The Law and Theory of Trade Secrecy: A Handbook of Contemporary Research* (Cheltenham: Edward Elgar, 2011), 152.

Ritchie, D., 'Things Fall Apart: The End of an Era of Systematic Indigenous Fire Management' in J. Russell-Smith, P. Whitehead and P. Cooke (eds.), *Culture, Ecology and Economy of Fire Management in North Australian Savannas: Rekindling the Wurrk Tradition* (Victoria: CSIRO Publishing, 2009), 23.

Ritte, Jr., W. and L. Malia Kanehe, 'Kuleana No Haloa (Responsibility for Taro): Protecting the Sacred Ancestor From Ownership and Genetic Modification' in A. Te Pareake Mead and S. Ratuva (eds.), *Pacific Genes & Life Patents: Pacific Indigenous Experiences & Analysis of the Commodification & Ownership of Life* (Wellington: Call of the Earth Llamado de la Tierra and the United Nations University Institute of Advanced Studies, 2007), 130.

Roberts, S. H., *The Squatting Age in Australia 1835–1847* (Carlton, Victoria: Melbourne University Press, 1975).

Robinson, D. F., *Confronting Biopiracy: Challenges, Cases and International Debates* (London: Earthscan, 2010).

Rose, D. B., 'Consciousness and Responsibility in an Australian Aboriginal Religion' in W. H. Edwards (ed.), *Traditional Aboriginal Society: A Reader* (Melbourne: Macmillan, 1987), 257.

Rostkowski, J., 'The Redman's Appeal For Justice: Deskaheh and the League of Nations' in C. F. Feest (ed.), *Indians and Europe: An Interdisciplinary Collection Of Essays* (Aachen: Edition Herodot and Rader Verlag, 1987), 435.

Russell-Smith, J. *et al.*, 'Contemporary Fire Regimes of Northern Australia, 1997–2001: Change Since Aboriginal Occupancy, Challenges for Sustainable Management', *International Journal of Wildland Fire*, 12 (2003), 283.

Russell-Smith, J., T. Start and J. Woinarski, *Effects of Fire in the Landscape* available at www.savanna.org.au/land_manager/downloads/sav-burning-fire-plants.pdf.

Russell-Smith, J., P. J. Whitehead, P. M. Cooke and C. P. Yates, 'Challenges and Opportunities for Fire Management in Fire-prone Northern Australia' in J. Russell-Smith, P. J. Whitehead and P. M. Cooke (eds.), *Culture, Ecology and Economy of Fire Management in North Australian Savannas: Rekindling the Wurrk Tradition* (Victoria: CSIRO Publishing, 2009), 1.

Sahlins, M., *Stone Age Economics* (New York: Aldine de Gruyter, 1972).

Sampath, P. G., *Regulating Bioprospecting: Institutions for Drug Research, Access, and Benefit-Sharing* (Tokyo: United Nations University Press, 2005).

Sanders, D., 'The Formation of the World Council of Indigenous Peoples', April 1980, available at http://www.nzdl.org.

Schneiberg, M. and T. Bartley, 'Organizations, Regulation, and Economic Behaviour: Regulatory Dynamics and Forms from the Nineteenth to the Twenty-First Century', *Annual Review of Law and Social Science*, 4 (2008), 31.

Schuck, P., 'Legal Complexity: Some Causes, Consequences, and Cures', *Duke Law Journal*, 42 (1992), 1.

Schumacher, E. F., *Small is Beautiful: Economics as if People Mattered* (New York: Harper and Row, 1973).

Scott, J. and F. Lenzerini, 'International Indigenous and Human Rights Law in the Context of Trade in Indigenous Cultural Heritage' in C. B. Graber, K. Kuprecht and J. C. Lai (eds.), *International Trade in Indigenous Cultural Heritage: Legal and Policy Issues* (Cheltenham: Edward Elgar, 2012), 61.

Sheleff, L., *The Future of Tradition: Customary Law, Common Law and Legal Pluralism* (London, Portland, OR: Frank Cass, 1999).

Simpson, R. D., R. A. Sedjo and J. W. Reid, 'Valuing Biodiversity for Use in Pharmaceutical Research', *Journal of Political Economy*, 104 (1996), 163.

Smith, J., 'The Search for Sustainable Markets: The Promise and Failure of Fair Trade', *Culture & Agriculture*, 29 (2007), 89.

Smith, L. R., *The Aboriginal Population of Australia* (Canberra: Australian National University Press, 1980).

Spencer, M. and J. Hardie, *Indigenous Fair Trade in Australia* (Canberra, Australia: Rural Industries Research and Development Corporation, 2011).

Spjut, R. W., *Economic Botany Laboratory, United States Department of Agriculture, Foreign Travel Report: Western Australia and Tasmania, 20 August–8 November 1981*, unpublished, available at www.worldbotanical.com/who-we-are.htm#usda.

Stanner, W. E. H., 'On Aboriginal Religion', *Oceania Monograph*, XXXI (1961), 81.

'Religion, Totemism and Symbolism' in W. E. H. Stanner, *White Man Got No Dreaming* (Canberra: Australian National University Press, 1979), 106.

Steering Committee for the Review of Government Service Provision, *Overcoming Indigenous Disadvantage: Key Indicators 2011* (Canberra: Productivity Commission, 2011).

Steffen, W., J. Rockstrom and R. Costanza, 'How Defining Planetary Boundaries Can Transform Our Approach to Growth' available at www.energybulletin.net/stories/2011-05-25/how-defining-planetary-boundaries-can-transform-our-approach-growth.

Stoianoff, N. P., 'The Recognition of Traditional Knowledge under Australian Biodiscovery Regimes: Why Bother with Intellectual Property Rights?' in C. Antons (ed.), *Traditional Knowledge, Traditional Cultural Expressions and Intellectual Property Law in the Asia-Pacific Region* (Alphen aan den Rijn: Kluwer Law International, 2009), 293.

Sutton, P., *Native Title in Australia in Ethnographic Perspective* (Cambridge University Press, 2003).
'The Robustness of Aboriginal Land Tenure Systems: Underlying and Proximate Customary Titles', *Oceania*, 67 (1996), 7.
Swain, T., *A Place For Strangers: Towards a History of Australian Aboriginal Being* (Cambridge University Press, 1993).
Swanson, T. and S. Johnson, *Global Environmental Problems and International Environmental Agreements* (Cheltenham: Edward Elgar, 1999).
Symanski, R., 'Environmental Mismanagement in Australia's Far North', *The Geographical Review*, 86 (1996), 573.
Tench, W., *A Narrative of the Expedition to Botany Bay (1789)* available as an E-text at http://setis.library.usyd.edu.au/ozlit/pdf/p00039.pdf.
The Economics of Ecosystems and Biodiversity: Mainstreaming the Economics of Nature: A synthesis of the approach, conclusions and recommendations of TEEB (2010) available at www.teebweb.org/Portals/25/TEEB%20Synthesis/ TEEB_SynthReport_09_2010_online.pdf.
'The Igloo Tag', *Inuit Art Quarterly*, 5 (1990–91), 57.
'The Support System for Inuit Artists', *Inuit Art Quarterly*, 19 (2004), 86.
Tully, J., 'Consent, Hegemony and Dissent in Treaty Negotiations' in J. Webber and C. M. Macleod (eds.), *Between Consenting Peoples: Political Community and the Meaning of Consent* (Vancouver: UBC Press, 2010), 233.
UN Human Rights Council, *Report of the Special Rapporteur on the rights of indigenous peoples, James Anaya. The Situation of Maori people in New Zealand*, A/HRC/18/35Add.4, 31 May 2011 available at www.ohchr.org/Documents/ Issues/IPeoples/SR/A-HRC-18-35-Add4_en.pdf.
Report of the Special Rapporteur on the situation of human rights and fundamental freedoms of indigenous people, Rodolfo Stavenhagen, Mission to Canada, E/CN.4/2005/88/Add.3, 2 December 2004, available at http://daccess-dds-ny. un.org/doc/UNDOC/GEN/G05/100/26/PDF/G0510026.pdf?OpenElement.
Report of the Special Rapporteur on the situation of human rights and fundamental freedoms of indigenous people, Rodolfo Stavenhagen. General considerations on the situation of human rights and fundamental freedoms of indigenous peoples in Asia, A/HRC/6/15/Add.3, 1 November 2007, 4, available at http://daccess-dds-ny. un.org/doc/UNDOC/GEN/G07/148/22/PDF/G0714822.pdf? OpenElement.
United Nations Development Group, *Guidelines On Indigenous Peoples' Issues* (New York and Geneva: United Nations, 2009).
Van Caenegem, W., 'Registered Geographical Indications: Between Intellectual Property and Rural Policy – Part II', *Journal of World Intellectual Property*, 6 (2003), 861.
Van Overwalle, G., 'Patent Protection For Plants: A Comparison of American and European Approaches', *Idea*, 39 (1999), 143.
Vogel, J. H., 'Sovereignty as a Trojan Horse: How the Convention on Biological Diversity Morphs Biopiracy into Biofraud' in B. A. Hocking (ed.), *Unfinished Constitutional Business? Rethinking Indigenous Self-determination* (Canberra: Aboriginal Studies Press, 2005), 228.
Voumard, J., *Inquiry Chair, Access to Biological Resources in Commonwealth Areas* (2000), available at www.environment.gov.au/biodiversity/publications/ inquiry/.

Waitangi Tribunal, *Ko Aotearoa tēnei: A Report into Claims Concerning New Zealand Law and Policy Affecting Māori Culture and Identity*, vol. 1 (Wellington: Legislation Direct, 2011).

Watson, J., 'We Know This Country' in P. Marshall (ed.), *Raparapa Kularr Martuwarra; Stories from the Fitzroy Drovers* (Broome WA: Magabala Books, 1993), 207.

Watson, P., *This Precious Foliage: a Study of the Aboriginal Psycho-active Drug Pituri*, Oceania Monograph 26 (University of Sydney, 1983).

Weber, M., *Economy and Society: An Outline of Interpretive Sociology*, vol. 3 (G. Roth and C. Wittich eds., New York: Bedminster Press, 1968).

Weir, J. K., R. Stone and M. Mulardy Jr., 'Water Planning and Native Title: A Karajarri and Government Engagement in the West Kimberley' in J. K. Weir (ed.), *Country, Native Title and Ecology* (Canberra: ANU E Press, 2012), 81.

Whitehead, P. J., J. Gorman, A. D. Griffiths, G. Wightman, H. Massarella and J. Altman, *Feasibility of Small Scale Commercial Native Plant Harvests by Indigenous Communities* (Canberra: Rural Industries Research and Development Corporation, 2006).

Willcox, M., G. Bodeker and P. Rasoanaivo (eds.), *Traditional Medicinal Plants and Malaria* (Florida: CRC Press, 2005).

Williamson, E. M., 'Synergy and Other Interactions in Phytomedicines', *Phytomedicine*, 8 (2001), 401.

Wilson, B. and J. O'Brien, '"To Infuse an Universal Terror": a Reappraisal of the Coniston killings', *Aboriginal History*, 27 (2003), 59.

Windsor, G., 'The Recognition of Aboriginal Placenames in New South Wales' in H. Koch and L. Hercus (eds.), *Aboriginal Placenames: Naming and Re-Naming The Australian Landscape* (Canberra: ANU E Press, 2009), 71.

WIPO Intellectual Property Handbook, 2nd edn. (Geneva: WIPO, 2004).

WIPO, *Intellectual Property Needs And Expectations Of Traditional Knowledge Holders: WIPO Report on Fact-Finding Missions on Intellectual Property and Traditional Knowledge (1998–1999)* (Geneva: WIPO, 2001).

Wynberg, R. and R. Chennells, 'Green Diamonds of the South: An Overview of the San-Hoodia Case' in R. Wynberg, D. Schroeder and R. Chennells (eds.), *Indigenous Peoples, Consent and Benefit-Sharing: Lessons from the San-Hoodia Case* (Dordrecht: Springer, 2009), 89.

Yibarbuk, D. *et al.*, 'Fire Ecology and Aboriginal Land Management in Central Arnhem Land, Northern Australia: A Tradition of Ecosystem Management', *Journal of Biogeography*, 28 (2001), 325.

Yoon, C. and B. Shiv (eds.), 'Brand Insights from Psychological and Neurophysiological Perspectives', *special issue of Journal of Consumer Psychology*, 22 (2012).

Young, E., 'Rhetoric to Reality in Sustainability: Meeting the Challenges in Indigenous Cattle Station Communities' in L. Taylor, G. K. Ward, G. Henderson, R. Davis and L. A. Wallis (eds.), *The Power of Knowledge, The Resonance of Tradition* (Canberra: Aboriginal Studies Press, 2005), 116.

Zander, K. K. and A. Straton, 'An Economic Assessment of the Value of Tropical River Ecosystem Services: Heterogeneous Preferences Among Aboriginal and Non-Aboriginal Australians', *Ecological Economics*, 69 (2010), 2417.

Zografos, D., *Intellectual Property and Traditional Cultural Expressions* (Cheltenham: Edward Elgar, 2010).

Index

Cambridge Intellectual Property and Information Law

Titles in the series (formerly known as *Cambridge Studies in Intellectual Property Rights*)

Lionel Bently, Jennifer Davis and Jane C. Ginsburg
Copyright and Piracy: An Interdisciplinary Critique
978 0 521 19343 6

Megan Richardson and Julian Thomas
Framing Intellectual Property: Legal Constructions of Creativity and Appropriation 1840–1940
978 0 521 76756 9

Dev Gangjee
Relocating the Law of Geographical Indications
978 0 521 19202 6

Andrew Kenyon, Megan Richardson and Ng-Loy Wee-Loon
The Law of Reputation and Brands in the Asia Pacific Region
978 1 107 01772 6

Annabelle Lever
New Frontiers in the Philosophy of Intellectual Property
978 1 107 00931 8

Sigrid Sterckx and Julian Cockbain
Exclusions from Patentability: How the European Patent Office is Eroding Boundaries
978 1 107 00694 2

Sebastian Haunss
Conflicts in the Knowledge Society: The Contentious Politics of Intellectual Property
978 1 107 03642 0

Helena R. Howe and Jonathan Griffiths
Concepts of Property in Intellectual Property Law
978 1 107 04182 0

Rochelle Cooper Dreyfuss and Jane C. Ginsburg
Intellectual Property at the Edge: The Contested Contours of IP
978 1 107 03400 6

Normann Witzleb, David Lindsay, Moira Paterson and Sharon Rodrick
Emerging Challenges in Privacy Law: Comparative Perspectives
978 1 107 04167 7

Paul Bernal
Internet Privacy Rights: Rights to Protect Autonomy
978 1 107 04273 5

Peter Drahos
Intellectual Property, Indigenous People and their Knowledge
978 1 107 05533 9

CPSIA information can be obtained
at www.ICGtesting.com
Printed in the USA
LVHW081800100420
652980LV00008B/106

9 781107 686946